Cognitive-Behavior Modification

An Integrative Approach

THE PLENUM BEHAVIOR THERAPY SERIES
Series Editor: Nathan H. Azrin

THE TOKEN ECONOMY: A Review and Evaluation
By Alan E. Kazdin

COGNITIVE-BEHAVIOR MODIFICATION: An Integrative Approach
By Donald H. Meichenbaum

BEHAVIORAL TREATMENT OF ALCOHOL PROBLEMS
Individualized Therapy and Controlled Drinking
By Mark B. Sobell and Linda C. Sobell

Cognitive-Behavior Modification

An Integrative Approach

By Donald Meichenbaum

University of Waterloo, Waterloo, Ontario, Canada

PLENUM PRESS · NEW YORK AND LONDON

Library of Congress Cataloging in Publication Data

Meichenbaum, Donald.
  Cognitive-behavior modification.

  (Plenum behavior therapy series)
  Bibliography: p.
  Includes index.
  1. Behavior modification. 2. Cognition. I. Title.
BF637.B4M43   616.8'914   77-5847
ISBN 0-306-31013-9

First Printing—June 1977
Second Printing—May 1979

©1977 Plenum Press, New York
A Division of Plenum Publishing Corporation
227 West 17th Street, New York, N.Y. 10011

Printed in the United States of America

Preface

This book is an account of a personal journey through a research program. A number of people have helped guide my way. To them I am deeply grateful. Special thanks are offered to my students, whose constant stimulation and provocation were incentives to write this book. Moreover, in the belief that they would never show the initiative to put together a festschrift for me (i.e., a book dedicated to someone for his contributions), I decided to do it myself. Several people cared enough to offer editorial criticisms, namely, Myles Genest, Barney Gilmore, Roy Cameron, Sherryl Goodman, and Dennis Turk. The reader benefits from their perspicacity.

Finally, to my parents, who taught me to talk to myself, and to my family, without whose constant input this book would have been completed much sooner, but would have been much less fun, I dedicate this book.

D.M.

Contents

Prologue

For the last ten years I have been attempting to bridge the gap between the clinical concerns of cognitive-semantic therapists (e.g., George Kelley, Jerome Frank, Albert Ellis, Aaron Beck, and Jerome L. Singer) and the technology of behavior therapy. The present book is a description of that attempt and of the current state of the bridge. It is a progress report of research designed to explicate the role of cognitive factors in behavior modification.

In writing this book I have made no attempt to survey all the literature in the field. Instead, I have tried to provide both an integrative, empirical account of the status of cognitive-behavior modification and a theoretical explanation of the mechanisms involved in behavioral change. One could organize a field such as cognitive-behavior modification simply by presenting one's own work. This might produce a scientific tome of sorts, but not a generally useful text. Or one could comprehensively describe the entire literature in an area. This might provide both a text and, as Earl Hunt describes it, a "nonaddictive sedative." This book tries to steer a middle course. I will attempt to review many studies within a cognitive-behavioral framework, indicating how my research and that of my students and colleagues has followed from and contributed to the field of cognitive-behavior modification.

A major concern of this book is how best to conceptualize cognitive events and to understand their role in

behavior change. Inner speech and images—how shall we
conceptualize them?[1] What constructs best explain what
goes on in your head? Attributions, appraisals, interpretations, self-reinforcements, beliefs, defense mechanisms,
and many other constructs, all have been offered to explain
private conscious events or what I will refer to as "internal
dialogue." Some investigators have suggested that the nature and content of inner dialogue is relatively unimportant
in explaining and predicting behavior, whereas others have
emphasized that we are unaware of the "important" aspects of inner dialogue. Is such inner speech a developmental epiphenomenon or is it intrinsically important in
guiding behavior?[2]

That cognitions play a central role in behavior has
been noted by A. N. Sokolov. In the introduction to *Inner
Speech and Thought,* Sokolov talks about inner speech:

> In psychology, the term "inner speech" usually signifies
> soundless, mental speech, arising at the instant we think
> about something, plan or solve problems in our mind, recall
> books read or conversations heard, read and write silently. In
> all such instances, we think and remember with the aid of
> words which we articulate to ourselves. Inner speech is noth-
> ing but speech to oneself, or concealed verbalization, which
> is instrumental in the logical processing of sensory data, in
> their realization and comprehension within a definite system
> of concepts and judgments. The elements of inner speech are
> found in all our conscious perceptions, actions, and emo-
> tional experiences, where they manifest themselves as verbal
> sets, instructions to oneself, or as verbal interpretation of sen-
> sations and perceptions. This renders inner speech a rather
> important and universal mechanism in human consciousness
> and psychic activity. (1972, p. 1)

[1] I am reminded of the observation by Mark Twain that no one has a right to use
the indefinite "we," except the King of England, the Pope, and a man with a
tapeworm. (The reader should read the masculine pronouns throughout this
book as both masculine and feminine.)

[2] "Epiphenomenon" refers to a phenomenon that is secondary, rather than integral, to an organism's functioning. In other words, it is a phenomenon one
studies as a doctoral dissertation topic but is unlikely ever to touch again.

Similarly, Carlos Castaneda in his inimitable manner has also highlighted the role of inner speech. Don Juan, his quixotic philosopher, states:

> The world is such and such or so-and-so only because we tell ourselves that that is the way it is. . . . You talk to yourself. You're not unique at that. Every one of us does that. We carry on internal talk. . . . In fact we maintain our world with our internal talk. (1972, pp. 218–219)

How should we view inner speech, how can we alter inner speech and images, and what are the subsequent effects on thought, feelings, and behavior? I will attempt to answer these questions by describing the personal research journey that I have made over the last ten years. Along the way I will share the cognitions that preceded, accompanied, and followed the research and attempts at theory construction. As will become evident, such a description exemplifies the cognitive-behavior modification approach—an analysis of the thinking processes involved in performing a task, rather than merely the assessment of the product or outcome of the performance.

In 1925, John B. Watson said, "What psychologists have hitherto called thought is in short nothing but talking to oneself." In this book I am *not*, as Watson did, equating inner speech with thought. Rather, inner speech is one aspect of the thinking process, albeit a very important one, as the Sokolov quote indicates. The importance of this distinction will become evident in the chapters that follow.

The Journey, Some Beginnings

It is difficult to determine exactly where a journey begins. This is particularly true of a journey of research ideas and clinical practice. As I try to impose order on the origins of my research program, two salient events stand out. The first is an incident that occurred in 1963, when I was a first-year clinical graduate student at the University of Illinois, in Champaign (a hotbed for the development of behavior therapy procedures). I traveled to Philadelphia to attend the meeting of the American Psychological Association. At one of the sessions at the convention three psychotherapists (a Gestalt therapist, a psychoanalyst, and a semantic therapist) were offering demonstrations of their respective therapeutic techniques with volunteer "patients" from the audience of several hundred. The audience later had an opportunity to ask questions following the demonstrations. As a naïve student of the art of psychotherapy, having recently completed Jerome Frank's book, *Persuasion and Healing*, I asked if perhaps it were the case that the important component in the various therapy demonstrations were the common conceptualization that evolved between the client and therapist— throwing into my question some jargon such as "assumptive world," patient-therapist expectancy, and so forth.

The psychoanalyst and Gestalt therapist attempted to answer the question—or at least, they tried to educate me about my so-called naïvete. But it was the semantic therapist who was most forceful and direct in his answer: "Please rise young man." I dutifully stood at the back of the room filled with several hundred people. "That is complete bullshit!" He went on to explain that the nature of the irrational beliefs, etc., gave rise to psychopathology and these irrational beliefs had to be challenged, attacked, etc.

The semantic therapist was (could you guess?) Albert Ellis and this was my first, but not last, contact with Dr. Ellis. Perhaps, some day he would be in the audience and I would ask him to rise. . . .

The directness and certainty of Ellis' remarks stimulated me to quite a bit of thought, research, and clinical practice. It was to be several years before I assessed Ellis' claim. We will return to Dr. Ellis and his form of rational-emotive therapy a bit later.

However, my eventual research program arose more directly from a serendipitous finding in my doctoral dissertation (Meichenbaum, 1969). The study involved a laboratory operant training program in which a group of hospitalized schizophrenic patients was trained to emit "healthy talk" (i.e., relevant, coherent verbalizations) in an interview setting. The effects of operant training generalized over time to a follow-up interview administered by a patient confederate and to other verbal tasks (e.g., proverbs test, word association test) administered under neutral conditions. Interestingly, a number of the schizophrenic patients who had been trained to emit "healthy talk" spontaneously repeated aloud the experimental instruction "give healthy talk; be coherent and relevant" while being tested on the generalization measures.

The spontaneous self-instruction seemed to mediate generalization by aiding the subjects in attending to the demands of the task, thus preventing any internally generated distracting stimuli from interfering with their language behavior. An intriguing question thus arose: can schizophrenics (and perhaps other clinical populations) be explicity trained to talk to themselves in such a self-guiding fashion and spontaneously to produce internally generated self-statements? This question led to the research program reported in this book.

However, before describing the research program and the treatment procedures that followed, a caveat offered by Neal Miller is worth repeating: "We should be bold in what we try and cautious in what we claim." The techniques that will be described are *not* offered as "proven" procedures, but rather, as descriptions of promising tools, which have resulted in quite encouraging initial results.

I will share treatment failures as well as successes. Books that offer only success after success always seem somewhat suspect. "Is it only I who have clinical failures?" In short, I have no packages to sell, no instant cures, no panaceas. Instead, I offer a progress report by hopefully a sensitive, somewhat eclectic research-clinician. I invite you to share the journey. Obviously, I hope that what you say to yourself at the end of the journey will be altered.

In the chapters that follow I will be describing a good deal of my research. Much of this work would not have been possible without the support provided to me by the Canada Council, Ontario Mental Health Foundation and Ministry of Education, Ontario.

1

Self-Instructional Training

> *Skinner warned us against the diversionary effects of fasci-
> nation with the inner life. I agree that the possibility is om-
> nipresent. Mentalistic ideas are so seductive that one is in
> danger of being led by them down the garden path of intro-
> spection and mysticism forever. For that reason, perhaps
> only a tough-minded behaviorist can afford to entertain the
> seductress.*
>
> —ALLAN PAIVIO (1975)

Now that you are forewarned by Paivio, let me convey in
this chapter how one cognitive-behavior therapist has tried
to tame the seductress.

My two-year-old son David has a yen for apples which
my wife and I readily satisfy. The only problem is that he
dislikes apple skin and he is given to spitting it on the floor.
In fact, when I come home from the office I feel like the
woodsman in Hansel and Gretel following the path of . . .
apple skins.

"See, David, apple skin, dirty. I throw the skin into the
garbage can and not on the floor." At this point David usually applauds my performance.

Our solution to the apple skin problem seemed quite
straightforward: (a) give him apples without skin, (b) teach

17

him to swallow the skins, or (c) set up some management program involving modeling and reinforcement.

Eschewing (a) as impractical, we were experiencing considerable difficulties in implementing (b) and (c). Then an interesting event occurred. One day my wife took David to the beauty parlor with her. In order to keep him occupied she had brought an apple for him. She found that it was more likely to keep *her* occupied as David began to spit the skins on the floor. Marianne said, "David, no, dirty. See, the skins go in the ashtray" (my wife is more influenced by my cognitive modeling than is my son). What happened next is the reason for this anecdote.

David spit the apple skin on the floor, looked at it, and then, while picking it up and depositing it in the ashtray, said to himself "Bappy . . . door . . . all done." This sequence was repeated, except that the phrase, "Bappy . . . door," was verbalized while he was merely looking at the apple skin on the floor and "all done" followed the behavioral act. Over several trials the verbalizations dropped out of the repertoire and the appropriate behavior was maintained and even generalized to other settings and other foods (e.g., grape seeds).

You should know that "bappy" is David's word for garbage and he uses "door" as equivalent to the concept open, as in opening doors, bottles, envelopes, pockets, and so on. I'm even thinking of using it in the process of toilet training.

This incident calls attention to the complex developmental relationship among language, thought, and behavior. David's behavior also nicely illustrates the developmental progression that the Soviet investigators Vygotsky (1962) and Luria (1961) have offered to explain the socialization of children. On the basis of his work with children, Luria proposed three stages by which the initiation and inhibition of voluntary motor behaviors come under verbal control (1961, 1969). During the first stage, the speech of others, usually adults, controls and directs a child's behavior. In the second stage the child's own overt speech becomes an effective regulator of his behavior. Finally, the child's covert, or inner, speech assumes a self-governing role. (See Meichenbaum, 1975a; Meichenbaum and Goodman, 1976; and Wozniak, 1972, for more detailed presentations of the Soviet position.)

Kohlberg, Yaeger, and Hjertholm noted the self-guiding function of private speech when they recorded the overt verbalization of a three-and-one-half-year-old child during *solitary* play with a set of Tinker Toys:

> The wheels go here, the wheels go here. Oh, we need to start it all over again. We have to close it up. See, it closes up. We're starting it all over again. Do you know why we wanted to do that? Because I needed it to go a different way. Isn't it pretty clever, don't you think? But we have to cover up the motor just like a real car. (1968, p. 695)

An example using an adult problem will further illustrate the relationship between language and behavior. Imagine learning a new motor skill such as driving a car. Initially, and especially when driving a stick shift car, the driver actively goes through a mental checklist, sometimes aloud, which includes verbal rehearsal, self-guidance, and perhaps appropriate self-reinforcement. Only with repetition and the development of proficiency do the cognitions become condensed, abrupt, incomplete, and vanish as the behavioral sequence becomes automatic. Henry Murray noted some years ago, "when one learns to drive an automobile, one is, at first, aware of every accessory intention and subsequent motor movement, but later, when proficiency has been attained, the details of the activity are seldom in consciousness" (1938, p. 51).

In other words, early in the mastery of a voluntary act speech serves a useful supportive and guiding function. With practice, the verbalizations disappear. A number of theorists with widely different orientations have implicated a similar progression in the development of skills. For example, Kimble and Perlmutter (1970) speak of the sequence of the "automatization of voluntary acts" and Tompkins (1970) describes the "miniaturization" process which accompanies the acquisition of a skill. The Soviet neuropsychologist Gal'perin nicely described this sequence of the stages in the development of mental acts (1969). He highlighted the "abbreviation" process:

> The first form of a mental act is clearly developed as external speech to oneself. . . . as soon as external speech to oneself is sufficiently mastered . . . speech to oneself quickly passes to its highest form, that of internal speech. (p. 263)

Gal'perin hypothesized that speech fragments, which might appear strange to an observer, are nothing more than "particles" of external speech to oneself in the process of becoming internal speech. Gal'perin suggested that these fragments of private speech usually occur when the automatic flow of thought and activity are interrupted.

Gal'perin's description can be applied to the driving example. For example, you are more likely to talk to yourself (either aloud or covertly) when you see a police car or an accident, indicating that some environmental stimulus may be the occasion for you to engage in inner speech. Think of such automated acts as shaving—and you cut yourself! Or, in my own case, recently learning to ski.

"What am I doing on this hill? Now, slowly, line up the skis; good. Bend; lean back." With proficiency (and this took some time) these verbalizations dropped out of the repertoire.

In fact, I was actually learning cross-country skiing and the hill was the top of a mound on a golf course, but after a short while talking aloud—"left arm, right foot"—interfered with my performance. Once the verbalization, to use Vygotsky's term, goes "underground" it is best to leave it there. Meichenbaum and Goodman illustrated this point developmentally when they demonstrated that forcing first-grade children to talk aloud to themselves while doing a particular motor task interfered with their performance, whereas younger children (kindergartners) benefited from the opportunity to talk aloud to themselves while doing the same task (1969a).

Kendler, Kendler, and Carrick obtained similar results (1966). They found that overt labeling facilitated problem solving for kindergartners but interfered with the performance of third graders. A naturalistic study by Klein (1963) provided even further evidence of the processes Vygotsky was describing (1962). Klein recorded detectable speech in three- to seven-year-olds who were left alone in an observation room with puzzles. He found a significant age decrease in audible comprehensible speech and a significant age increase in barely audible mutterings and lip movements. With age, private speech seemed to become internalized. Although the total amount of audible comprehensible speech decreased with age, task-relevant speech actually increased. Thus, even as speech was "going underground" the remaining portion was largely task-relevant. Most importantly from a training viewpoint, children who successfully completed the puzzle produced twice as much task-relevant speech as children who did poorly on the puzzles, although the two groups did not differ in task-irrelevant private speech. Similar findings with entirely different tasks have been reported by Garrity (1975), Gratch (1966), Jensen (1971), and Rheingold and Shapiro (1976). Flavell, Beach, and Chinsky observed children in a sequential memory task and found a regular increase in task-relevant private-speech from kindergarten to fifth grade (1966). They also reported that kindergarten children who failed to demonstrate overt speech did not report using covert speech, whereas 25% of the older children who demonstrated no overt speech reported the use of covert speech. These data provided further evidence of an age-associated internalization process.

That the content of the child's self-verbalizations directly affects behavior has been reported by several investigators (Bem, 1967; Hartig & Kanfer, 1973; Kanfer, Karoly, & Newman, 1975; Kanfer & Zich, 1974; and Monahan &

O'Leary, 1971). A prototypic example of these studies is offered by Patterson and Mischel (1976). They examined the way in which self-instructional plans can affect attentional style and performance in a resistance to temptation task. Nursery school children were given one of two kinds of self-instructional plans in a resistance to temptation situation. The children were asked to perform a peg board task continuously even though they were being tempted by a distractor, "Mr. Clown Box." Children who received the temptation-inhibiting plan (viz., "I'm not going to look at Mr. Clown") maintained their attention on the task significantly more than did children who received a task-facilitating plan (viz., "I'm going to look at my work"). In fact, the task-facilitating group did not differ from a control (no plan) group and the combination group of both inhibiting and facilitating did not differ from an inhibiting group alone. Thus, directing the children's attention away from the source of temptation (i.e., temptation-inhibiting plan) was most effective in facilitating resistance, or, in more general terms, the specific content of the self-instructions is important in fostering self-control.

Perhaps the response of an eleven-year-old boy in another Mischel experiment best illustrates the sequence by which inner speech becomes automatic, abbreviated, and rapid, and comes to influence behavior:

> If I had to teach a plan to someone who grew up in the jungle—like a plan to work on a project at 10 a.m. tomorrow—I'd tell him what to say to himself to make it easier at the start for him. Like if I do this *plan* (emphasized word) on time I'll get a reward and the teacher will like me and I'll be proud. But for myself, I know all that already so I don't have to say it to myself—besides it would take too long to say and my mind doesn't have the time for all that—so I just remember that stuff about why I should do it real quick without saying it—it's like a method I know already in math; once you have the method you don't have to say every little step. (Mischel, 1975, p. 40)

The references to David's behavior, the automobile and skiing examples, the work of Soviet psychologists, and the developmental research all suggest that private speech is initially facilitative and then drops out of the repertoire with the development of task proficiency. The interesting clinical question is whether one could capitalize on this phenomena for therapeutic purposes. Could one take the developmental progression suggested by the Soviet psychologists and translate it into a therapeutic package?

Simply put, the answer is yes! The reasons for this answer are brought to light in the following section, which concerns the investigation of the nature of the hyperactive, impulsive child's problem. After this description, we will explore how the self-instructional training format has been applied to this group of children.

Hyperactive, Impulsive Children: An Illustration of a Search for a Deficit

The potential value of a self-instructional training approach is illustrated by first examining the nature of the deficit of the hyperactive, impulsive child. A major problem in schools is the high incidence of hyperactive, impulsive-behavior, problem children: 5 to 10% of school-aged children are diagnosed as hyperactive (O'Malley & Eisenberg, 1973). It has been estimated by Grinspoon and Singer that 200,000 school children in the United States daily receive some form of medication for treatment of hyperactivity (1973). There is much controversy about the merits of drug treatment with hyperactive children and the interested reader should see articles by Campbell (1977), Douglas (1975), and especially Whalen and Henker (1976). A second major treatment for these children is environmental control by such means as operant conditioning (e.g., Ayllon, Layman & Kandel, 1975; Patterson, Jones, Whittier & Wright, 1965; Rosenbaum, O'Leary & Jacob, 1975; O'Leary, Pelham, Rosenbaum & Price, in press).

The need for an additional treatment mode is particularly evident from the results of drug studies. As Douglas concluded, the use of stimulant drug treatment with

hyperactive children has resulted in therapeutic effects
that usually end almost immediately when the drug is
withdrawn (1975). Follow-up data provide little encouragement that children who receive prolonged intensive
treatment with methylphenidate (Ritalin) are doing any
better than children who have not been on the drug (e.g.,
Weiss, Kruger, Danielson & Elman, 1973). Conners suggested that when stimulants do contribute to favorable effects, they work because they help the impulsive, hyperactive child to plan and control his responding (1972).

Douglas goes so far as to state that after comparing
hyperactive children and matched control subjects on 150
variables she has been led to the conclusion that hyperactive children are:

> unable to keep their own impulses under control in order to
> cope with situations in which care, concentrated attention, or
> organized planning are required. They tend to react with the
> first idea that occurs to them or to those aspects of a situation
> which are the most obvious and compelling. This appears to
> be the case whether the task requires that they work with
> visual or auditory stimuli and it also seems to be true in the
> visual-motor   and   kinaesthetic   spheres.   These   same
> deficiencies—deficiencies which I have come to think of as
> the inability to *'stop, look, and listen'*—seem also to influ-
> ence the children's social behavior. (Emphasis added, 1972,
> p. 275)

But how shall we get children to plan, to think before they
act, to stop, look, and listen?

Luria's Model

A suggestion came from our developmental research
on impulsive children. Taking our lead from some work by
Luria (1959) and Homskaja (cited in Luria, 1959), we decided to examine how impulsive children use (or fail to
use) their language to control their nonverbal behavior.
Luria and Homskaja reported that hyperkinetic, impulsive
children lack proficiency in verbal control tasks. When

asked to control their nonverbal motor responses on a task that required them to say "push" and "don't push" in response to a signal light, and then to behave accordingly, the hyperkinetic children manifested a deficit. In short, Pavlov's second signal system seems to have less verbal control for such impulsive children.

In our laboratory we attempted to substantiate the relationship between cognitive impulsivity, as measured by Kagan's (1966) Matching Familiar Figures test (MFF), and performance on Luria's verbal control task (Meichenbaum & Goodman, 1969b). The MFF requires the child to select from a pictorial array of six common similar objects or animals, the one that is identical to a standard picture (see Fig. 1). Children who respond quickly and make many errors are identified as cognitively impulsive and those who take their time and make few errors are identified as cognitively reflective. Our results indicated that only 40% of the cognitively impulsive five-year-olds, but that 85% of the reflective children met a performance criterion of 90% correct responding on the "push"—"don't push" task. The impulsive child would often say aloud "don't push" then push in spite of the self-admonition. There was, in effect, less verbal control of nonverbal behavior by impulsive children. A similar finding was reported by Bates and Katz (1970) and several investigators have found that reflective children are better able to inhibit movement on a motor inhibition task than are impulsive children (e.g., Harrison & Nadelman, 1972; Constantini, Corsini & Davis, 1973). The verbal control differences were even more evident on a second task we administered (borrowed from Lovaas, 1964), in which the children had to modulate their own finger tapping by producing self-goads: either "faster" or "slower." The cognitively impulsive children tended to use the self-goads in metronome fashion, tapping once each time they self-instructed "faster, faster." In contrast, reflective children responded to the meaning of their self-goads by tapping several times in response to each self-instruction. Whereas

Figure 1. Sample items from the Matching Familiar Figures test for reflection-impulsivity in the school-age child.

the impulsive children seemed to respond to the motoric aspects of their private speech, the reflectives used their self-goads with greater functional precision to modify their performance, responding to the semantic aspects of their private speech.

Private Speech and Mediational Skills

These laboratory studies encouraged us to examine the use of impulsive and reflective children's private or egocentric speech (i.e., speech that is not intended for a listener) in the naturalistic setting of the nursery school (Meichenbaum, 1971a). We were interested in determining whether the child's private speech (which includes singing, chanting, emitting real and nonsense words, verbalized fantasies, and the expression of a variety of motivational and affective states) would be constituted differently with cognitively impulsive and reflective preschoolers. We therefore recorded the play behavior and private speech of sixteen four-year-old preschoolers: half were cognitively impulsive and half, reflective. The two groups were equated for age, intelligence, and socioeconomic status.

The results indicated that whereas the verbalizations of impulsive and reflective preschoolers did not differ in quantity, they did differ in quality. The cognitively impulsive children used private speech differently than their reflective counterparts. In order to appreciate these differences it is necessary to discuss briefly the findings of Kohlberg *et al.* (1968). They found that a developmental hierarchy of private speech can be organized with the lowest level self-stimulatory private speech, such as word play, animal noises, repeating words, and singing. Developmental level II is characterized by outer-directed private speech and includes remarks addressed to nonhuman objects and descriptions of the child's own activity—similar to Piaget's (1955) collective monologue category. Level III represents inward-directed or self-guiding private speech, including self-instructions. Finally, level IV represents external manifestations of inner speech in the form of inaudible mutterings.

Our results indicated that the private speech of cognitively impulsive preschoolers was largely comprised of the most immature, self-stimulatory content. In comparison, reflective preschoolers manifested significantly more outer-directed and self-regulatory speech and significantly more inaudible mutterings. Moreover, the private speech of reflective children was significantly more responsive to situational demands.[3] In situations in which specific problem-solving tasks were required, the self-directing private speech of reflectives increased from 11% to 25%, whereas the cognitively impulsive children manifested no comparable increase. The results of our observational studies suggested that cognitively reflective preschoolers use their private speech in a more mature, more instrumental, self-guiding fashion than impulsive preschoolers.

The relationship between impulsivity and private speech was partially supported by Dickie (1973), who used two different measures of impulsivity: a picture absurdities test and a game requiring the child to follow directions to drive a truck slowly and carefully along a track (à la Maccoby, Dowley, Hogan & Degerman, 1965). Dickie found that the impulsive children used more self-stimulating and outer-directed private speech but that there was no difference between impulsive and nonimpulsive children in the amount of inner-directed speech. Kleiman also found a positive relationship between preschoolers' matching accuracy and the rate of self-directed speech emitted while

---

[3] Interestingly, Bush and Dweck recently found that school-aged impulsive children were more insensitive to task demands than reflective children (1975). Reflective children exhibited long latencies on the MFF but short latencies on speeded tasks, in accordance with the demands of the situation. The difference between reflectives and impulsives was in their evaluation of task demands and their subsequent flexibility in response style. Thus, treatment should be aimed at increasing the impulsive child's attention to and utilization of situational cues rather than encouraging a stereotyped response style.

working on puzzles (1974). (See Meichenbaum and Goodman, 1976, for a more complete discussion of private speech studies.)

The relationship between private speech and behavioral style has recently been examined by Camp (1975) with young aggressive boys (77–97 months). She compared high aggressive boys, as identified by the School behavior checklist (Miller, 1972), with low aggressive boys on a number of verbal abilities tasks, including the verbal control tasks employed by us with impulsive hyperactive children. Camp found, "young aggressive boys fail to employ verbal mediational activity in many situations where it would be appropriate, and when it does occur, covert mediational activity may fail to achieve functional control over behavior." Although the aggressive boys' verbal development was adequate, they failed to use these abilities to think through and plan solutions. Camp's findings with aggressive school-aged children, and mine, with impulsive preschoolers (Meichenbaum, 1971a), are strikingly similar. Both populations tend to emit verbalizations while engaged in an activity but the majority of their verbal output is immature, self-stimulating, and often irrelevant to the task.

At this point, I am reminded of Jensen's definition of verbal mediation:

> Verbal mediation consists of talking to oneself in relevant ways when confronted with something to be learned, a problem to be solved, or a concept to be attained. In adults the process generally becomes quite automatic and implicit; only when a problem is quite difficult do we begin 'thinking out loud.' Most mediational processes take place subvocally below our level of awareness. (1966, p. 101)

Jensen's quote suggests that individuals who have not developed mediational skills or who have a high threshold for engaging in mediational activity will be handicapped in solving problems. Such a consistent deficit in problem-solving behavior has been observed in impulsive children.

The inability of impulsive and hyperactive children to take an analytic approach to problems has been evidenced on a number of cognitively demanding problem-solving tasks. Ault (1973), McKinney (1973a, 1975), and Cameron (1976), for example, using different problem-solving tasks, found that reflective children processed task information more efficiently than impulsive children and used more systematic and/or more mature strategies. Denny presented evidence suggesting that on a guessing task reflective children tend to ask more "constraint-seeking" questions (i.e., questions that seek to eliminate a number of alternatives in an array by being abstract or general) than impulsive children (1973). Moreover, impulsive children often use feedback in a nonsystematic, trial and error fashion (McKinney, 1973a) and inefficiently utilize feedback to evaluate and generate hypotheses (Neussle, 1972). Thus, one reason that reflectivity is associated with better information processing could be that reflective children are more likely than impulsive children to analyze important and relevant features of stimuli and then use feedback informatively.

In *summary*, the picture that emerges from verbal control studies in the laboratory, observational studies of private speech, and the problem-solving data is that impulsive children do not habitually and spontaneously analyze their experience in cognitively mediated terms (i.e., both verbal and imaginal) and that they do not formulate and internalize rules that might guide them in new learning situations.[4] Put slightly differently, the impulsive child's inadequate performances may be characterized in several ways: (a) he may not comprehend the nature of the problem or task and thus cannot discover what mediators to produce—what Bem (1971) called a "comprehension" deficiency; (b) he may have the correct mediators within his repertoire but fail to spontaneously and appropriately produce them—what Flavell *et al.* (1966) called a "produc-

---

[4] Other evidence to support these conclusions has been summarized by Kagan and Kogan (1970), Meichenbaum and Goodman (1975), and Cameron (1976).

tion" deficiency; (c) the mediators which the child produces may not guide his ongoing behavior—what Reese (1962) called a "mediational" deficiency. Thus, the cognitive process may be viewed from a mediational theory viewpoint as a three-stage process of comprehension, production, and mediation, and inferior performance can result from a deficiency at any one or combination of these stages.

This composite pattern of deficits led us to some potential therapeutic interventions. Could we systematically train hyperactive, impulsive children to alter their problem-solving styles, to think before they act, in short, to talk to themselves differently? Could we, in light of the specific mediational deficits observed, teach the children how to (a) comprehend the task, (b) spontaneously produce mediators and strategies, and (c) use such mediators to guide, monitor, and control their performances? This was the challenge that sparked the development of self-instructional training at Waterloo. I have described the evolution of our view of the deficits of hyperactive, impulsive children because, as I mentioned earlier, it was with this population that we first began the training. It was not long, however, before it became evident just how versatile and widely applicable was this treatment approach. Self-instructional training has been indicated as a promising approach with such other problem areas as social isolates, uncreative college students, schizophrenics, and learning-disabled children. The work with hyperactive, impulsive children is, however, exemplary of the general approach. Therefore, in this chapter I shall deal with this population.

Self-Instructional Treatment of Hyperactive, Impulsive Children: A Beginning

When Goodman and I began self-instructional training, the procedure was administered on an individual basis, as follows:

[handwritten marginalia: steps in behav. cog. mod.]

[handwritten marginalia: teaching a kid a new or behavior or skill that causes trouble]

1. An adult model performed a task while talking to himself out loud (cognitive modeling);
2. The child performed the same task under the direction of the model's instructions (overt, external guidance);
3. The child performed the task while instructing himself aloud (overt self-guidance);
4. The child whispered the instructions to himself as he went through the task (faded, overt self-guidance); and finally
5. The child performed the task while guiding his performance via private speech (covert self-instruction).

Over a number of training sessions the package of self-statements modeled by the experimenter and rehearsed by the child (initially aloud and then covertly) was enlarged by means of response chaining and successive approximation procedures. For example, in a task that required the copying of line patterns, the examiner performed the task while cognitively modeling as follows:

> Okay, what is it I have to do? You want me to copy the picture with the different lines. I have to go slowly and carefully. Okay, draw the line down, down, good; then to the right, that's it; now down some more and to the left. Good, I'm doing fine so far. Remember, go slowly. Now back up again. No, I was supposed to go down. That's okay. Just erase the line carefully. . . . Good. Even if I make an error I can go on slowly and carefully. I have to go down now. Finished. I did it! (Meichenbaum & Goodman, 1971, p. 117)

In this thinking-out-loud phase, the model displayed several performance-relevant skills: (1) problem definition ("what is it I have to do?"); (2) focusing attention and response guidance ("carefully . . . draw the line down"); (3) self-reinforcement ("Good, I'm doing fine"); and (4) self-evaluative coping skills and error-correcting options ("That's okay. . . . Even if I make an error I can go on slowly").

A variety of tasks was employed to train the child to use self-instructions to control his nonverbal behavior. The tasks varied from simple sensorimotor abilities to more complex problem-solving abilities. The sensorimotor tasks, such as copying line patterns and coloring figures within boundaries, provided first the model, then the child, with the opportunity to produce a narrative description of the behavior, both preceding and accompanying performance. Over the course of a training session the child's overt self-statements on a particular task were faded to the covert level. The difficulty of the training tasks was increased over the training sessions, using more cognitively demanding activities. Hence, there was a progression from tasks such as reproducing designs and following sequential instructions taken from the Stanford-Binet intelligence test, to completing such pictorial series as on the Primary Mental Abilities test, to solving conceptual tasks such as Raven's Matrices. The experimenter modeled appropriate self-verbalizations for each of these tasks and then had the child follow the fading procedure.

The self-instructional training procedure, relative to placebo and assessment control groups, resulted in significantly improved performance on Porteus Maze, performance IQ on the WISC, and increased cognitive reflectivity on the Matching Familiar Figures Test (MFF). The improved performance was evident in a one-month follow-up. Moreover, it was observed that 60% of the self-instructionally trained impulsive children spontaneously were talking to themselves in the posttest and follow-up sessions. (A different experimenter had conducted the assessment and training sessions.)

In a second study, it became evident that the experimenter's cognitive modeling was a necessary but not sufficient condition for engendering self-control in impulsive children (Meichenbaum & Goodman, 1971). The child's behavioral rehearsal in self-instructing was an indispensable part of the training procedures. It was necessary that the impulsive child not only be exposed to a self-instructing model but also "try out" the self-instructions

himself. A treatment condition of cognitive modeling alone
slowed down the child's performance but did not reduce
errors on the MFF test. However, cognitive modeling plus
self-instructional rehearsal resulted in both a slower and a
more accurate performance.

Our initial self-instructional studies indicated that
hyperactive, impulsive children could be taught to think
before they acted and not be given over to the dominant
motor response. They could learn to "stop, look, and
listen."

A quote from Bergin may help underscore the importance of the self-instructional training approach:

> Impulse control problems are often treated by aversive
> methods, by analysis of psychodynamics via transference, by
> modification of self-perceptions and relationships with
> others, by altering values, etc., but seldom are they dealt
> with by direct treatment of the self-regulatory defect per se.
> (1967, p. 116)

The self-instructional training approach was designed
to deal directly and explicitly with the self-regulatory
defect.

What follows is a description of the empirical studies
that contributed to and followed from this initial self-
instructional study. In the interim six years we have
learned a great deal about how to treat impulsive disorders
directly, how to teach children as well as adults to talk to
themselves in instrumental, self-guiding fashions. Let's
begin with a description of the empirical studies and then
in a later chapter examine the clinical techniques
employed.

Empirical Studies of Self-Instructional Training

An implicit assumption in most of the studies to be
reviewed is that a person's cognitions are instances of "automatic" thoughts (i.e., images and self-statements) that are
part of a "maladaptive response chain." Given this assump-

tion, the first task of therapy is to have the client become aware of the role such thoughts play in a sequence of behaviors. A number of theorists, such as Premack (1970) and Bergin (1967), have emphasized the therapeutic value of having the client interrupt the sequence of behaviors and thoughts preceding a maladaptive response, and produce incompatible self-instructions and images. The maladaptive behaviors that are habitual in nature (i.e., not premeditated) should first be returned to a "deautomatized" condition; that is, the "target" behaviors should be preceded by deliberate cognitions. Such "forced mediation" increases the likelihood of interrupting a chain of events that would otherwise lead to the maladaptive response. Illustrative of this treatment approach, which is designed to teach children to think before they act, to bring their behavior under their own verbal control, are studies by Bem (1967), Palkes, Stewart, and Kahana (1968), Palkes, Stewart, and Freedman (1972), and Schneider (1974).

Douglas describes a self-instructional training program for hyperactive children, which illustrates these principles:

> Our approach involves choosing tasks which can be solved only by careful looking, listening, or moving and for which a plan or strategy is required before action is taken. We make clear to the youngster that his ways of tackling problems of this kind are leading to difficulties and that we are going to help him learn better ways. Emphasized is the need to say aloud, before beginning, exactly what the task involves and how he is going to go about solving it. Then the therapist begins to solve the problem while modeling these kinds of behaviors and verbalizing his goals and strategies aloud.
>
> When the therapist is completing a jigsaw puzzle, for example, he talks aloud about how he is organizing the pieces according to color and how he is going to begin by trying to find some of the "straight" pieces that will form the edges of the picture. If he is working on a maze, he mentions the need to stop at choice points and plan his next step carefully. Since the children do not seem to take the trouble to "rehearse" to themselves material that is to be remembered, we also use a variety of games to teach them to do this.

In some of the tasks the child and the therapist take turns giving each other explicit instructions the other must follow. In one task, for example, each participant uses colored blocks to produce a pattern behind a screen where the other cannot see it. He must verbally record aloud each step he takes in forming the pattern, and it is then the job of the other participant to reproduce the pattern exactly. When the therapist is modeling for the child, he also deliberately makes errors and calmly notes aloud how he is going to go about correcting them.

The tasks we have used thus far include various kinds of games, problems, puzzles, home problems and projects, and academic assignments. We have also set up role-playing situations with puppets and, sometimes, with another youngster. Again, the social situations portrayed emphasize the kinds of problems typically created by these children's impulsive tendencies. We may try, for example, to get them to slow down and consider what another person's needs or intentions may be. It is important to stress that once we feel confident that the child is beginning to get his impulsive tendencies under his own verbal control, we gradually help him to "talk to himself" less and less loudly, so that eventually the verbalizations are completely silent. We also emphasize throughout the training that the skills and strategies the child is learning apply equally well at play, at home, and at school. Generalization of the strategies outside of the therapy sessions is encouraged by enlisting the child's parents and his teacher from the beginning as co-therapists. Every effort is made to help them become effective modelers and reinforcers of the behaviors being taught in the therapy sessions. (1975, pp. 206–208)

But exactly how successful are such self-instructional training programs in the long-term treatment of impulsive, hyperactive children?[5] We don't really know but let me convey the present state of the art. One can think of the

[5] In a recent personal communication, Virginia Douglas indicated that she has conducted a comparative study with hyperactive boys of the self-instructional training procedure versus a no-treatment group. The results indicated a significant improvement for the treatment group on a number of behavioral and cognitive tasks. This change was maintained at a three-month follow-up. The need to compare the self-instructional training regimen to a drug treatment group alone and to the combination of self-instructions plus medication is apparent.

studies conducted as falling along a continuum in terms of the generalization of treatment results. Some studies are designed to determine the feasibility of employing self-instructional procedures in laboratory settings, while others are concerned with extending the number of training sessions and the location of the training, with the accompanying assessment of the generalization and persistence of treatment effects.

One of the laboratory studies was performed by Palkes *et al.* (1968). They found that training hyperactive nine-year-old boys to use self-directed verbal commands improved posttest performance on the Porteus Maze compared to controls who simply practiced the training exercises. The boys were taught to verbalize a set of self-directed commands such as, "I must stop, listen, look, and think before I answer." In order to encourage and remind the children to employ self-statements, a variety of pictures was displayed (see Fig. 2).

In a second study, Palkes *et al.* found that verbalizing the self-instructions aloud was significantly more effective for hyperactive children than reading them silently (1972). The authors hypothesized that overt verbalization provided stronger controlling feedback than did silent reading.

Bender compared tutor modeling of strategies with tutor modeling plus self-verbalizations in the modification of children's impulsivity (1976). She found that the inclusion of verbal self-instruction fostered the regulation of impulsive responding more than just tutor-verbalized instructions. These effects were further enhanced when the self-instructions that the child employed included explicit strategies rather than just general instructions. There are several other studies that show the greater efficacy of overt self-verbalization over nonverbalization in a problem-solving task (Gagné & Smith, 1962; Kendler, 1960; Radford, 1966).

Recently, Finch, Wilkinson, Nelson, and Montgomery examined the relative effectiveness of verbal self-

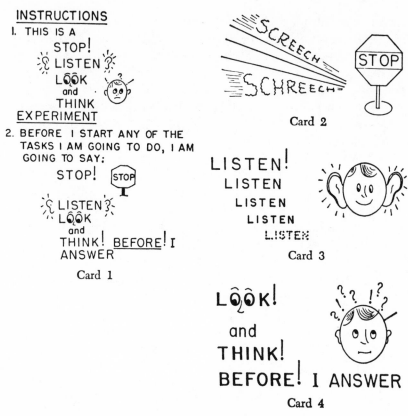

Figure 2. Training pictures (from Palkes, Stewart, and Kahana, 1968).

instructions versus delay training in altering the cognitive
style of institutionalized emotionally disturbed boys
(1975). Whereas the self-verbalization training in the
Palkes *et al.* studies was limited to two half-hour sessions,
Finch *et al.* extended treatment to six half-hour sessions
over a three-week period. Using the training format
developed by Meichenbaum and Goodman (1971), they
found that relative to the delay group and to an assessment
control group, the self-instruction group made fewer errors
on a match-to-sample task (MFF). Recall that the MFF re-

quires the subject to find, from an array of pictures, the one that matches the standard picture. Both the delay group and the self-instruction group slowed down but only the self-instruction group, who had learned specific cognitive strategies, made fewer errors.

That such cognitive strategy training can significantly alter search styles was documented by Goodman (1973). Following one session of self-instructional training Goodman monitored the eye-movements of cognitively impulsive children while taking the MFF test. He found that those impulsive children who received self-instructional training manifested a significant increase in the number of their total looks at each of the alternatives in the MFF and that they were more systematic in checking the standard picture. In short, following self-instructional training the impulsive children's performances in both the Finch *et al.* and the Goodman studies approximated those of their reflective counterparts. Thus far each of these training studies has been limited to short-term training, with no specific attempt to influence or assess long-term effectiveness.

Before we examine further training studies, it is important to appreciate that the self-verbalization paradigm that has been described represents *only one* way of altering the hyperactive, impulsive child's cognitive style and performance. A full bibliographic review of the treatment literature on impulsivity is beyond the scope of this work, the purpose of which is to highlight the clinical potential of the self-instructional approach. Some of the other means of altering impulsive styles involve changing the tasks themselves. For example, Zelniker and Oppenheimer gave impulsive children a variant of the Matching Familiar Figures test in which the children had to find from an array of six pictures the one that was *different* from the standard picture (1973). (In the standard MFF test the child's task is to find a picture that is the *same* as the standard.) The search for a *different* picture caused impulsive children to slow

down, searching all of the alternatives, which in turn generalized to the standard MFF test. Thus, by manipulating
the task we can provide the conditions under which behavioral change may occur.

There are a number of individual case studies and
comparative group studies that have highlighted the clinical potential of explicitly using children's language and
images. Perhaps the most extensive evaluation of the
pedagogical value of self-instructional training was offered
by Karnes, Teska, and Hodgins (1970). Although the study
does not directly deal with hyperactive children, it represents an important contribution. The population included
disadvantaged preschoolers, many of whom were described as impulsive.[6] To treat this impulsivity, as well as to
teach other skills, Karnes *et al.* evaluated the effectiveness
of overt verbalization training over a two-year period. Four
preschool programs for disadvantaged children were compared: a traditional nursery school, a community integrated
program, a Montessori school, and the overt-verbalization
program. Karnes *et al.* stated:

> the distinguishing feature of the self-instructional program
> was the tying of the verbalizations to sensory-motor perfor-
> mance. As the child visually and motorically assessed the
> correctness of his thinking, he was required to make appro-
> priate verbalizations at every stage of task involvement. The
> teacher began by supplying verbal models, and the repeti-
> tions involved in the game format [of the program] helped to
> establish these verbalizations. When the child was able to
> initiate such responses, the teacher helped him modify and
> expand them. (1970, p. 73)

In comparison to children in the other three programs,
the children in the self-instructional program made significant gains on such measures as the Illinois Test of
Psycholinguistic Abilities, the Stanford-Binet Intelligence
Scale, and the Frostig Developmental Test of Visual Per-

[6] Miller and Mumbauer have found a negative relationship between socioeconomic status and cognitive impulsivity (i.e., the lower the SES the higher the
impulsivity) (1967).

ception. Karnes *et al.* found that the Montessori program provided a prepared environment but it did not systematically engage the child in verbalizations around his experiences nor require verbalizations as part of the goals to be achieved. The relative absence of language activity in the highly structured Montessori program was deemed its major weakness. Thus, the preschool training program that proved most effective in improving school readiness skills with the disadvantaged children was the one that emphasized internal manipulation of experience via language, that used language in order to organize thoughts, to reflect on situations, to comprehend the meaning of events, and to structure both the environment and personal behavior in order to choose among alternatives.[7]

Spivack and Shure developed an impressive program which effectively used language to influence thought and behavior (1974). In an assessment of problem-solving abilities, Spivack and Shure found that children with behavior problems do not think of the possible consequences of their behavior nor do they conceptualize alternative options for action. To compensate for these deficiencies they provided training in two types of social reasoning over some thirty lessons. One type of reasoning involved the child's thinking of alternative solutions to simple conflict situations with peers. A related ability was the child's prediction of likely consequences should his solution be put into effect. The focus of the training, which takes the form of a variety of games, was *not what* to think, but rather, *how* to think about interpersonal problems. The initial games dealt with developing specific language and attentive skills, identifying emotions, thinking about how people have different likes and dislikes, and learning to gather information about other people. Final games posed the problem of finding several alternative solutions to interpersonal problems and

[7] Similar conclusions were offered by Blank and Solomon (1968, 1969). Meichenbaum and Turk have explored the implications of the results for such educational television programs as "Sesame Street" (1972).

evaluating cause and effect in human relationships. The
training resulted in significant increases in social reasoning
abilities and most importantly—and rather uniquely for a
training study—it showed significant and enduring positive
effects on social behaviors with peers, changes which were
maintained at a one-year follow-up in kindergarten. From a
clinical implementation viewpoint a most important aspect
of the training program is that positive results were obtained when teachers trained children and when mothers
trained their own children. In a personal communication,
Spivack described his training as follows:

> training reduces socially maladaptive behavior by enhancing
> certain mediating interpersonal cognitive skills of direct rel-
> evance to social adjustment. . . . These skills involve the
> capacity to generate alternative solutions and consequences,
> and in older individuals the ability to generate means-ends
> thought.

Camp, Blom, Herbert, and Von Doorwick (1976) nicely
combined the treatment techniques of Meichenbaum and
Goodman (1971), Spivack and Shure (1974), Palkes *et al.*
(1972), and Bornstein and Quevillon (1976—a study described below) in developing a thirteen-session training
manual, called *Think Aloud*. They employed the *Think
Aloud* approach in treating twelve aggressive second-grade
boys. The boys were seen in small groups. The program
began with a "copy-cat" game, which introduced the child
to asking himself the following four basic questions: What
is my problem? What is my plan? Am I using my plan?
How did I do? While the "copy cat" was being faded, cue
cards similar to Palkes *et al.*'s were introduced to signal the
child to self-verbalize (see Fig. 3). Over the course of training there was a shift from cognitively demanding tasks to
interpersonal tasks à la Spivack and Shure. The initial results from the Camp *et al.* study were quite promising.
Posttest comparisons, relative to control groups, yielded
significant differences on a variety of performance measures, including Porteus Maze, MFF, WISC performance

Figure 3. Training Figures (from Bash and Camp, 1975).

IQ, and reading achievement. The results generalized to the classroom. The results of the *Think Aloud* training program take on particular significance when we consider Camp's findings that aggressive boys had verbal facilities that were comparable to normal boys on various performance tasks but that the aggressive boys failed to use their abilities to think through and plan solutions to problems. Bash and Camp state:

> Even when the rules of the game call for blocking the first stimulated response, aggressive children have more difficulty performing this inhibition (e.g., playing Simon Says game). Their natural inclination is to respond rapidly, but when specifically instructed to verbalize overtly before responding, they may achieve response inhibition more readily than normals. (1975, p. 3)

The self-instructional training program, *Think Aloud*, successfully taught such self-verbalization skills.

Combining Self-Instructions and Operant Procedures

Robertson and Keeley also used a cognitive modeling procedure, in addition to explicit reinforcement, to train mediational problem-solving skills in impulsive first- and second-grade children (1974). Training was provided in the classroom, thus teaching mediational skills in the presence of extraneous stimulation from the classroom and peers. The training, which included fifteen sessions over a three-week period, employed classroom activities such as arithmetic, copying skills, etc. Individual training was conducted in a corner of the classroom while the teacher was giving individual instruction or working with small groups. As in other studies, the children were provided with self-instructional cue cards, designed to establish an attentional set, elicit relevant mediators, and foster self-reinforcement. The self-instructional training was supplemented by social and token reinforcement, with the tokens faded in the final sessions. Internalization of the self-instructions was evident in the children's increased ability to control motor behavior by coordinating verbalizations and motoric responses and by the extension of the skills to novel tasks such as scrambling sentences. Improvement was evident by a reduction of errors on both the Matching Familiar Figures Test (MFF) and the Porteus Maze, as well as by improvement on the Wide Range Achievement Test (WRAT) spelling and reading subtests. The improved performance on the MFF and Porteus Maze was more than 50% greater than that obtained in the Meichenbaum and Goodman (1971) study. Interestingly, the reduced error scores on the MFF occurred without accompanying changes in the latency score, reflecting alterations in problem-solving style. Robertson and Keely did not find that the children who received self-instructional training improved in classroom behavior and they argued that such mediational training may have to be supplemented by operant procedures in the classroom.

Several investigators have successfully combined operant and self-instructional procedures in treating hyperactive and aggressive children. For example, Bornstein and Quevillon examined the long-term effects of self-instructional and operant training techniques with three hyperactive preschool boys who were not on medication (1976). Using a multiple baseline design they demonstrated transfer from experimental tasks to classroom situations. These gains were maintained at a twenty-two-week follow-up period. Bornstein and Quevillon's case studies illustrate the variety of behaviors leading to a hyperactive diagnosis and a multifaceted treatment approach.

Scott, who was four years old, was described as "a disciplinary problem because he simply was unable to follow directions for any extended length of time." He often manifested violent outbursts of temper and rarely completed any tasks in the preschool. Rod, also four years old, was considered out of control in the classroom, as manifested by his short attention span, aggressiveness, and general overactivity. Tim, the last four-year-old treated, spent most of his time walking around the room, staring off into space and/or not attending to tasks or instructions. Bornstein and Quevillon systematically documented these behaviors by conducting classroom observations.

Using the self-instructional training of cognitive modeling, followed by overt and covert rehearsal, the children were taught to use the following self-verbalizations: (1) questions about the task (e.g., "What does the teacher want me to do?"); (2) answers to questions, in the form of cognitive rehearsal (e.g., "Oh, that's right; I'm supposed to copy that picture"); (3) self-instructions to guide the subject through the task (e.g., "O.K., first I draw a line here . . ."); and (4) self-reinforcement (e.g., "How about that? I really did that one well!").

The reward (initially M & M candies and later social praise) was used by the experimenter in two ways. Because of the difficulty in obtaining and then maintaining the children's attention during the training the experimenter reinforced the children if they followed the instruction "Watch what I do and listen to what I say." Following this phase the child received reinforcement for performing correctly while the experimenter verbalized the directions. The children actually received few candy reinforcements during the training (i.e., no more than ten candies were given to any child during any one training session). Social praise and self-reinforcement soon came to replace the material reinforcements. The second way reinforcement was employed was by the experimenter's self-reinforcing his own behavior (initially by taking M & Ms and then by praising himself) during the modeling. In short, children were trained to verbalize the nature of the task and their problem-solving strategy, and reinforcement was made contingent upon their complying with the verbalized self-statements. The treatment resulted in significant and stable changes in classroom behavior—improvement which was evident ninety days following the initial baseline assessment. These results are particularly impressive given a multiple baseline design and the inclusion of an observer expectancy control manipulation.

I have described the Bornstein and Quevillon study in some detail because it highlights the multifaceted aspects of the self-instructional package. Moreover, it underscores how behavior therapy procedures, in this case operant techniques, can be combined with cognitive self-instructional techniques, leading to a truly hyphenated cognitive-behavior modification approach. Research surely is needed to examine the relative importance of the different treatment components. The treatment package included instructions, self-instructions, cognitive modeling, prompts, reinforcement, and fading. Future studies will have to uncover the "active" agents contributing to change.

There are several further examples of studies that indicate that operant procedures can be successfully supplemented by mediational processes. For example, MacPherson, Candee, and Hohman (1974) compared three different methods of controlling disruptive lunchroom behavior of elementary school children: operant alone, operant plus punishment essays, and operant plus mediation essays. The latter group was most effective in reducing disruptive behavior. In the mediation condition the children wrote essays about "what they did wrong, what things happen when they do something wrong, what they should do, and what pleasant things happen when they behave appropriately." These results are consistent with those of Blackwood (1970, 1972).

Reasoning Rediscovered

As I read these studies and noted the manner in which mediational processes were employed, I wondered if we are merely rediscovering the potency of reasoning. Indeed, I was reminded of the "old" findings by Sears, Maccoby, and Levin (1957) and Maccoby (1968) that parents' use of reasoning with their children, in the form of explaining why what the child did was wrong and why he should act in certain ways, was related to the child's indices of internalized values, confession upon wrongdoing, and resistance to temptation. Hoffman argued that the type of reasoning used by the parent is the most important antecedent of internalized values and corresponding behavior (1970). Perhaps cognitive-behavior therapists have something to learn from these developmental studies. The interested reader should see review papers by Staub (1975a,b).

Importance of Attributional Style

The rather striking success of the studies that combined operant and self-instructional procedures could encourage an uncritical proliferation of such methods. External reinforcements need to be used with caution. In particular, hyperactive children have been found to react badly to the temptation of external material reinforcement, often with the rapid return of their performance to the prereinforcement level (Douglas, 1975; Firestone, 1974; Parry, 1973). Perhaps these findings are more understandable in the light of the importance of the children's attributions of causal agents for success and failure. This importance was indicated in a study by Bugenthal, Whalen, and Henker (1975). Hyperactive boys were individually tutored for two months in a classroom setting; half were instructed in self-controlling speech and half were given social reinforcement. There were significant interactive effects between the intervention approach and the children's attributional style. Attributions were assessed by a structured questionnaire asking the boys to assign importance to potential causal agents for success and failure. "Luck" attributors showed greater improvement on Porteus Maze and on Connors Teacher's Rating Scale following the reinforcement treatment, whereas "effort" attributors benefited more from the self-instructional training program.

The Bugenthal *et al.* study highlights the necessity of perfecting the match between a child's attributional style and the attributional assumptions implicit in the intervention approach. Moreover, the study raises the importance of the sequencing of intervention strategies. As Bugenthal *et al.* indicate, "introducing regularities or systematic extrinsic reinforcement into the environment of an individual who believes events are random or chaotic may be a productive prelude to self-management training."

The children's responses to the structured interviews indicated that the stimulant medication was a powerful source of attributional change in both children and others, such as family members. Whalen and Henker have argued that we should conduct sociocognitive analyses of drug effects (1976). They emphasized that children have a great deal to tell us (if we would only ask and then listen) about the treatments they receive, including medication. The therapeutic impact of such medication must be viewed as having more than just pharmacological effects. Thus, what the child and his parents, teachers, peers say to themselves (their attributions, expectations, etc.) about the child's behavior and treatment is likely to prove quite important in the change process. To make these points more forcefully, we can let the children speak for themselves. The following excerpts from Whalen and Henker illustrate some of the different attributional styles. First, a ten-year-old boy:

> Interviewer (I): I've been hearing a lot about that word hyperactive. What does it mean, really?
> Child (C): Well, it's a—it's a—well, you're just born with it.
> I: You're born with it.
> C: And some people can—some people get rid of it. Some people it just goes away when they're about 12 or 13.
> I: And what about the other people?
> C: They just have it.
> I: Is it just a habit that people pick up?
> C: No.
> I: Do you think people can get over it if they work on it?
> C: No.
> I: Do you think people just outgrow it sooner or later?

C: Yeah—some people.

I: And others?

C: Half of them outgrow it, and half of them just keep—just stay on it. They're still hyperactive.

Comments from an eleven-year-old boy indicate how behavioral improvement is attributed directly to the medication (and misbehavior explained by nonmedication):

C: Well, sometimes I go in the bedroom and start crying because I need it [the pill], you know. And then my mother will come in and ask me what's wrong, and I'll say, "Daddy won't let me take my pill." She'll say, "Come on down here—I'll give it to you." So, I'll go down and she'll give it to me.

I: So, sometimes you can really tell that you need it.

C: Yeah. (Pause) Sometimes I get mad at my dog and if I start getting mad at my dog, my Mother will say, "Go take your pill." I'll say, "Ah—O.K.," and I'll go downstairs and take it and then I come back upstairs and start saying "I'm sorry" to my dog.

(Later)

C: At school two boys that know karate are gonna teach me how to do it. If I don't take my pill I'll start doing it on them.

In another section of the interview, the children are asked their views about stopping the medication. One boy predicted that he would be expelled from school if he stopped taking Ritalin and a girl insisted that she would just stay home because no one would like her. The most poignant answer was given by a ten-year-old girl who said quite simply and forlornly, "I'd go nuts." Clearly, these children have come to believe that the drug is helpful, perhaps necessary, for them to function effectively. These beliefs coexist with a strong dislike of taking the drug, presumably because of the stigmatization the children endure. The public labeling and external ascriptions used by others involved with the medication program are evident in the following comments of a twelve-year-old boy:

I'll go in and take 'em and then during the afternoon she [the teacher] thinks I'm gettin' "off," you know, hyperactive, and she'll say, "Bradley, did you forget to take your little trip to the office this morning?" And I'll say, "No!".

An eleven-year-old girl indicates that peers as well as adults use (and teach) external attributions to explain the behavior of children taking medication:

One girl—like Rhonda knows about my medicine. Her grandma—because my Mom told her grandmom. Well, she spread it to a girl named Karla and now if she notices that I'm not acting calm she goes, "Did you take your hyper pills?".

The contribution of such attributional styles to the occurrence of maladaptive behavior and treatment intervention needs to be carefully examined. Some suggestion of its potential importance is offered by the work of Dweck and Reppucci who studied the contributions of children's attributions to "learned helplessness" (1973). They found that following failure, a certain group of children did not perform the response required to succeed, even though they were motivated and fully capable of doing so. The children who gave up in the face of failure tended to attribute success and failure to presence or absence of ability rather than to expenditure of effort. Dweck and Reppucci suggested attribution retraining as a potentially promising treatment intervention for such children.

In 1975 Dweck published such a training study with children who had extreme reactions to failure. Two treatment procedures were compared. One approach followed the behavior modification technique of providing contingent success experiences. This was compared to a reattribution group. Children in both groups participated in twenty-five daily sessions, during which they performed simple lab tasks. They received either successes only (contingent success group) or successes plus failures (attribution retraining group). In the attribution retraining group the experimenter accompanied each failure with a statement that the child should have "tried harder," thus conveying that inadequate performance was due to insufficient effort. Dweck found that children in the success only group continued to evidence severe deterioration in performance after failure, whereas children in the attribution retraining group maintained and improved their performance after failure. Miller, Brickman, and Bolen also demonstrated the relative usefulness of an attribution manipulation versus a persuasion and reinforcement manipulation (1975).

Hanel (1974, as cited by Heckhausen, 1975) successfully altered children's attributions more directly by employing the self-instructional format. Hanel identified a group of fourth-grade children who had a marked fear of failure and who had poor academic records. Hanel was able to teach these children to talk to themselves differently, to problem-solve, and to change their motivational style and academic performance. In group training the experimenter cognitively modeled for the children how to set standards, plan actions, calculate effort output, monitor performance, evaluate performance outcome, weigh causal attributions and administer self-reward. Then the students took turns in performing tasks while emitting similar cognitions, initially aloud and then covertly. In short, the behavioral act was broken down into its component parts and each part was translated into sets of self-statements, which could be cognitively modeled and then rehearsed.

Both the Dweck and Hanel studies need to be replicated for they suggest that a child's attributional and cognitive styles can be significantly altered. One wonders if such an approach could be applied to individuals who have an "external" locus of control orientation. If one thinks of the external's cognitive style as a reflection of a self-dialogue, then a number of interesting researchable questions are raised. Indeed, a number of investigators have discussed the potential of "attribution therapy" (e.g., Nisbett & Schachter, 1966; Ross, Rodin & Zimbardo, 1969; Storms & Nisbett, 1970; and Valins & Nisbett, 1976).

Attributions, however, represent only one aspect of a client's internal dialogue. Other authors have emphasized other aspects of the inner speech process, employing such constructs as "appraisal," "expectancy," and "self-reinforcement." Mischel said, "The nature of the game in explaining behavior has been to take a few concepts and stretch them as far as possible" (1975, p. 15). The danger is in losing perspective and attempting to explain behavior on the basis of only one set of constructs or processes, excluding others that may offer valuable different perspectives.

This danger was brought home to me several years ago when I gave a colloquium on the importance of self-instructions. That evening at a party one of the guests called me over and said, "Don, come here, I've got something to tell you." He was a wise and distinguished senior psychologist and a group of people gathered about us. He then looked to the ceiling and said:

"Lord, are you speaking to me?"

"Yes, Don, I am. I have chosen you."

"Chosen me, Oh Lord."

"Don, I want you to carry the word forth."

"Me, Oh Lord."

"The word, Don, is self-instructions."

Well, it seems we each have our "words" to carry forth. I would argue that those "words" are essentially diverse ways of conceptualizing internal dialogues.

When we attempt to alter those internal dialogues we can be very direct and explicit, and use cognitive modeling and overt and covert rehearsal (as conducted by Meichenbaum and Goodman, Hanel, etc.) or we can provide the conditions under which the cognitive changes occur on their own (e.g., Dweck) by manipulating tasks and environments so our clients naturally succeed or fail and thus are forced to reconsider their behaviors. The issue of whether we should attempt directly to modify the client or to proceed more indirectly takes on particular importance for we will see that a client's attributions about treatment and the reason for his change play an important role in the maintenance of that change. (In this regard the interested reader should see the article by Kopel and Arkowitz, 1975.)

Taking Stock

At this point it is worth taking stock or summarizing the state of the art of self-instructional training with impulsive children. The research with both impulsive and aggressive children suggested a deficiency in the children's ability to spontaneously use their language instrumentally in planning and guiding their nonverbal behavior. A natural therapeutic intervention would be directly to treat this "self-regulatory defect" by means of cognitive modeling and overt and covert rehearsal. A number of case studies, using multiple baseline and expectancy control procedures, have suggested the clinical potential of the self-instructional approach, especially in light of the reported treatment generalization and durability (usually limited to a six-month follow-up). Comparative group studies have also pointed to the clinical potential of self-instructional training but these studies have usually involved multi-faceted treatment interventions and it would be difficult at this stage to causally attribute behavioral change to the use of specific self-instructions. However, the multifaceted treatment studies did highlight the promise, as well as the potential dangers, of combining operant and self-instructional procedures. These studies also indicated the need to match the child's attributional style with particular treatment procedures (a kind of "different strokes for different folks approach"). Finally, the potential of the self-instructional approach for altering children's attributional and cognitive styles was noted. In fine, the *promise* of the self-instructional approach with impulsive disorders is there but its effectiveness is not yet fully demonstrated.

This promise has also been demonstrated with other clinical populations. The next chapter illustrates this work.

The Clinical Application of Self-Instructional Training to Other Clinical Populations: Three Illustrations

> *A cognitive strategy is an internally organized skill that selects and guides the internal processes involved in defining and solving novel problems. In other words it is a skill by means of which the learner manages his own thinking behavior. . . . Cognitive strategies have as their objects the learner's own thought processes. Undoubtedly, the efficacy of an individual's cognitive strategies exerts a crucial effect upon the quality of his own thought.*
>
> —GAGNÉ AND BRIGGS (1974)

Cognitive strategies as described by Gagné and Briggs are similar to Skinner's (1968) self-management behaviors. The self-instructional training regimen is designed to teach such cognitive strategies and self-management skills; to teach clients "how" to think. In a number of laboratories an exploration of the potential therapeutic value of self-instructional training procedures with various other clinical populations has begun. Examples of three of these populations are now offered.

55

Social Isolates

The self-instructional training procedure has been successfully employed in the treatment of children who are socially withdrawn. Three studies illustrate how behavior therapy procedures can be supplemented by cognitive therapy techniques with this population.

Gottman, Gonso, and Rasmussen treated third-grade "social isolate" children as identified by sociometric measures (1974). The children received one week of thirty-minute daily training sessions. Initially, the shy children were taught how to initiate neutral interactions using a modeling film of children interacting. Consistent with the emphasis on cognitions, the film was narrated by a voice using a Meichenbaum and Goodman (1971) coping self-statement sequence. This sequence consisted of a soliloquy of an inner debate in the following order: (1) wanting to initiate interaction; (2) worrying about negative consequences; (3) the self-debate; (4) the moment of decision to go ahead; (5) the approach; (6) the greeting; (7) asking permission to join in (or requesting help). After the film the coach said, "See if you can say to me out loud what *you* might actually think to yourself or say to yourself if *you* wanted to go over to another kid to get help or play or work with some kids." The child rehearsed the sequence out loud and then silently to himself after the coach modeled an example of the sequence.

Following the film the coach reviewed with the child the film's content and then "inoculated" him against possible rejection by other children by role-playing what one does and says to oneself in the face of possible rejection. Following the modeling and rehearsal portion of training was a phase that taught behavioral skills, such as how to ask for information and effective leave-taking. A third stage involved practice in referential communication skills, such as taking the viewpoint of others. This multifaceted cognitive-behavioral treatment led to significant behavioral changes relative to attention placebo control subjects.

Jabichuk and Smeriglio also used a cognitive-behavioral treatment approach with preschoolers who had low levels of social responsiveness (1976). Two modeling films were equated for visual and auditory information and differed only in whether the soundtrack was in self-speech (first-person form) or in narrative (third-person form). The films showed an isolated child playing alone, then approaching peers, and finally interacting with them in a variety of situations. The accompanying soundtrack (either in first or third person) described feelings of isolation, coping responses, and, finally, self-reinforcing statements for having interacted. The children who were exposed to either of the soundtrack films demonstrated significantly greater improvement on *in situ* behavioral measures than did either a group that saw the modeling film without any narration or an assessment control group. The first-person narrative was more effective than the third-person narrative. This change was maintained at a three-week follow-up. Interestingly, Jabichuk and Smeriglio reported that increases in frequency of social interactions following treatment in the self-speech group were accompanied by an increase in the frequency of children's verbalizations.

The importance of the social isolates' negative self-statements was examined by Meijers (personal communication). His approach to the problem is worth describing. As a means of developing hypotheses concerning the role of cognitions in social withdrawal, he approached a college population with a verbal description of what a ten-year-old social isolate would be like. He then asked them to indicate on a questionnaire if they were like the verbal description when they were ten years of age and he also asked them to volunteer for interviews. Almost all subjects who indicated that they were like the social isolates volunteered. Some students still saw themselves as isolates, whereas others reported having changed in the interim. The interviews proved quite fascinating. Many revealed that as socially withdrawn children they used to watch the most popular

child in the class, read books on being more outgoing and
assertive, often practiced in front of the mirror, but would
not engage in more socially outgoing behaviors because,
"It would not be me" or "I would be doing it for my mother
or teacher," etc. Although this type of retrospective study is
fraught with dangers, it did serve the purpose of generating
hypotheses concerning the nature of the deficit and highlighting the important role of the child's internal dialogue
in social withdrawal. Meijers has followed up the research
by studying ten-year-olds' reactions to social stimuli as presented by projective TAT-type slides of various scenes of
children interacting. He asked both social isolates and their
outgoing counterparts what was going on in the slides and
what the child in each picture was thinking and feeling.
Meijers has confirmed the role of negative self-statements
in the social isolate's behavior.

Creative Problem-Solving

Recently there has been increasing research on the
possible application of self-instructional training procedures with traditional academic concerns, such as creativity, problem-solving, and reading. One demonstration of
the potential of self-instructional procedures with
academic problems is a recent study that attempted to enhance creativity by explicitly modifying what college students said to themselves (Meichenbaum, 1975b).

A passage from Robert Pirsig's novel, *Zen and the Art
of Motorcycle Maintenance*, nicely illustrates the role of
self-statements in creative problem-solving. Pirsig describes the difficulty of fixing his motorcycle, among other
things:

> Stuckness. That's what I want to talk about. . . . A screw
> sticks, for example, on a side cover assembly. You check the
> manual to see if there might be any special cause for this
> screw to come off so hard, but all it says is "Remove side
> cover plate" in that wonderful terse technical style that

never tells you what you want to know. There's no earlier procedure left undone that might cause the cover screws to stick.

If you're experienced you'd probably apply a penetrating liquid and an impact driver at this point. But suppose you're inexperienced and you attach a self-locking plier wrench to the shank of your screwdriver and really twist it hard, a procedure you've had success with in the past, but which this time succeeds only in tearing the slot of the screw.

Your mind was already thinking ahead to what you would do when the cover plate was off, and so it takes a little time to realize that this irritating minor annoyance of a torn screw slot isn't just irritating and minor. You're stuck. Stopped. Terminated. It's absolutely stopped you from fixing the motorcycle.

This isn't a rare scene in science or technology. This is the commonest scene of all. Just plain *stuck*. In traditional maintenance this is the worst of all moments, so bad that you have avoided even thinking about it before you come to it. The book's no good to you now. Neither is scientific reason. You don't need any scientific experiments to find out what's wrong. It's obvious what's wrong. What you need is an hypothesis for how you're going to get that slotless screw out of there and scientific method doesn't provide any of these hypotheses. It operates only after they're around.

This is the zero moment of consciousness. Stuck. No answer. Honked. Kaput. It's a miserable experience emotionally. You're losing time. You're incompetent. You don't know what you're doing. You should be ashamed of yourself. You should take the machine to a *real* mechanic who knows how to figure these things out.

It's normal at this point for the fear-anger syndrome to take over and make you want to hammer on that side plate with a chisel, to pound it off with a sledge if necessary. You think about it, and the more you think about it the more you're inclined to take the whole machine to a high bridge and drop it off. It's just outrageous that a tiny little slot of a screw can defeat you so totally.

What you're up against is the great unknown, the void of all Western thought. You need some ideas, some hypotheses. Traditional scientific method, unfortunately, has never quite gotten around to say exactly where to pick up more of these hypotheses. Traditional scientific method has always been at

the very *best*, 20–20 hindsight. It's good for seeing where
you've been. It's good for testing the truth of what you think
you know, but it can't tell you where you *ought* to go, unless
where you ought to go is a continuation of where you were
going in the past. Creativity, originality, inventiveness, intui-
tion, imagination—"unstuckness," in other words—are completely outside its domain. (1974, pp. 279–280)

Well then, could we train low creative individuals to
recognize moments of psychological "stuckness": "Honked, kaput, no answer, stuck." And could we then use the
self-instructional training regimen to influence what subjects say to themselves at these critical moments to enhance
the creative process? Moreover, would self-instructional
training result in subjects' viewing more tasks and situations as occasions for engaging in creative thinking? For
much of creative thinking is not only the solving of a problem but also seeing that a problem exists in the first place.

I am not suggesting that moments of "stuckness" do not
occur for creative individuals. But for such people these
experiences seem to be the occasion for internal dialogues
different from those of uncreative individuals. Empirical
support for these speculations was offered by Bloom and
Broder (1950), Goor and Sommerfeld (1975), Henshaw
(1977), and Patrick (1935, 1937). Each of these investigators
asked creative and noncreative subjects to perform various
problem-solving tasks while thinking aloud. When Henshaw asked noncreative college students to describe the
thoughts and feelings they experienced while taking a battery of creativity tests they reported task-irrelevant, self-
critical thoughts (e.g., "I'm not very original or creative. I'm
better at organizing a task; don't ask me to be creative"), or
thoughts that disparaged the creativity tests, *or* if they did
produce a creative response they often devalued their own
performance by thinking, "Anyone could have produced
such an answer" (Henshaw, 1976).

Goor and Sommerfeld found that creative college students reacted differently to silences in their own produc-

tions from noncreative college students (1975). Following silences, the creative students emitted significantly more task-relevant, information-gathering thoughts. In a related study Bloom and Broder (1950) found substantial differences in cognitive strategies between good and poor problem-solvers. Patrick found that creative artists viewed the tasks differently and referred to their own experiences more readily; the uncreative artists imposed an internal standard and when they failed to meet this standard they engaged in task-irrelevant unproductive self-statements, thoughts which take on a self-fulfilling role.[8] One uncreative artist's dialogue included, "I can't draw. This is bad. I can't draw. I would like to draw a cow, well. Looks like a pig. This is funny. Looks like a rat" (Patrick, 1935, p. 63).

Given these differences in cognitive style a self-instructional training procedure was developed for training noncreative college students. (See Meichenbaum, 1975b, for details.) The first aspect of self-instructional training of creativity was to make the subject aware of the self-statements he emitted that inhibited creative performance. These negative self-statements fell into two general classes: self-attributable statements, questioning the subject's own creativity, and those statements by which he devalued the task.

Secondly, subjects were trained to produce creativity-engendering self-statements that were incompatible with the negative cognitions.

But what exactly do you train a person to say to himself in order to become more creative? Some suggestion for the content of the self-statements came from the burgeoning

[8] Recently Henshaw, in our lab, found that if you expose subjects to a model who emits negative self-statements and asked subjects to behave "as if" they were the model while doing creativity tasks, the subjects' performance markedly deteriorated (1976). There does seem to be a causal relationship between the content of one's thoughts and performance—an observation only a psychologist would need confirmed. The more interesting question "why" there is deterioration has not been answered. Whether the negative self-statements cause the subject to generate fewer strategies, to perceive the task differently, to quit sooner, or just what needs study.

literature on creativity training (see Parnes & Brunelle, 1967). Three conceptualizations of creativity seem to underlie the techniques that have been used to train creativity. These are a mental abilities approach, which emphasizes deliberate training exercises (e.g., Guilford, 1967; Torrance, 1965); an ego-analytic levels analysis of thinking, which focuses on the role of the regression of the ego and on associational techniques (e.g., Kris, 1953); and finally, an approach that emphasizes the role of general attitudinal set, including factors that characterize creative individuals (e.g., Barron, 1969). Each of these conceptualizations was translated into a set of self-statements, which could be modeled and then practiced by subjects (see Table I).

The following is an example of the type of self-statements that the experimenter modeled and subjects subsequently practiced. In this case, the task was product improvement, requiring a list of clever, interesting, and unusual ways of changing a toy monkey so children would have more fun playing with it:

> I want to think of something no one else will think of, something unique. Be freewheeling, no hangups. I don't care what anyone thinks; just suspend judgment. I'm not sure what I'll come up with; it will be a surprise. The ideas can just flow through me. Okay, what is it I have to do? Think of ways to improve a toy monkey. Toy monkey. Let me close my eyes and relax. Just picture a monkey. I see a monkey; now let my mind wander; let one idea flow into another. I'll use analogies. Let me picture myself inside the monkey. . . . Now let me do the task as if I were someone else. [After inducing this general set, the experimenter then thought aloud as he tried to come up with answers.]

Using such procedures the trainer would continue to provide both obvious and original answers to the task. Throughout, the model often used self-reinforcement by means of spontaneous affect of pleasure, surprise, eagerness, delight, and by saying such things as "good" or "this is fun." The trainer tried to capture a mood of self-

Table 1. Examples of Self-Statements Used in Creativity Training
(Meichenbaum, 1975b)

Self-Statements Arising from an Attitudinal Conceptualization of Creativity

Set inducing self-statements
  What to do:
    Be creative, be unique.
    Break away from the obvious, the commonplace.
    Think of something no one else will think of.
    Just be free wheeling.
    If you push yourself you can be creative.
    Quantity helps breed quality.
  What not to do:
    Get rid of internal blocks.
    Defer judgments.
    Don't worry what others think.
    Not a matter of right or wrong.
    Don't give the first answer you think of.
    No negative self-statements.

Self-Statements Arising from a Mental Abilities Conceptualization of Creativity

Problem analysis—what you say to yourself before you start a problem
  Size up the problem; what is it you have to do?
  You have to put the elements together differently.
  Use different analogies.
  Do the task as if you were Osborn brainstorming or Gordon doing Synectics
    training.
  Elaborate on ideas.
  Make the strange familiar and the familiar strange.

Task execution—what you say to yourself while doing a task
  You're in a rut—okay try something new.
  Take a rest now; who knows when the ideas will visit again.
  Go slow—no hurry—no need to press.
  Good, you're getting it.
  This is fun.
  That was a pretty neat answer; wait till you tell the others!

Self-Statements Arising from a Psychoanalytic Conceptualization of Creativity

  Release controls; let your mind wander.
  Free-associate; let ideas flow.
  Relax—just let it happen.
  Let your ideas play.
  Refer to your experience; just view it differently.
  Let your ego regress.
  Feel like a bystander through whom ideas are just flowing.
  Let one answer lead to another.
  Almost dreamlike, the ideas have a life of their own.

---

mobilization, of determination to do the task, and the desire to translate into answers the excitement of creative thoughts. The model also included coping with getting into a rut, feeling frustrated, and then talking himself out of it, for example:

> "Stop giving the first answer that comes to mind. One doesn't have to press . . . let the ideas just play; let things happen. The ideas seem to have a life of their own. If they don't come now, that's okay. Who knows when they will visit?"

Following such modeling the group practiced talking to themselves while performing a variety of tasks. Gradually, at each subject's own pace, the explicit use of self-statements dropped out of his repertoire.

Most importantly, subjects were not asked merely to parrot a set of self-statements but, rather, were encouraged to emit the accompanying affect and intention to comply with their self-statements. This involvement was achieved by a variety of means, including: (a) determining the subject's conceptualization of creativity and expectations concerning training; (b) explaining the rationale for self-instructional training; (c) having subjects examine their personal experiences to find instances of similar negative and positive self-statements; (d) having subjects rehearse or "try on" self-statements while performing personally selected meaningful activities (e.g., hobbies, homework).

In order to assess the beneficial effects of self-instructional training, two control groups were included in the study. The first group afforded an index of improvement on creativity tests due to factors of attention or placebo effects, exposure to creativity tests during training, and any demand characteristics inherent in our measures of improvement. This group received a type of training based on a conceptualization of creativity that did not emphasize cognitive or self-instructional factors and whose face validity was sufficient to elicit high expectations from subjects. These criteria were met by a procedure called "focusing" which Gendlin and his colleagues proposed to enhance creativity (1969). Focusing involves paying attention to one's present feelings and coming to a new formulation about them. In addition to the focusing group, which received only the pre- and post-assessments, a waiting list control group was included in the study.

The self-instructional training group, relative to Gendlin's focusing training group and to the untreated waiting list control group, manifested a significant increase in originality and flexibility on tests of divergent thinking, an increase in preference for complexity, a significant increase in human movement responses to an inkblot test, and concomitant changes in self-concept. In contrast, subjects in the focusing training group showed no objective improvement on the creativity tests, although they indicated by self-report that they felt more creative.

Moreover, the self-instructional training engendered a generalized set to view one's life style in a more creative fashion. The training seemed to direct the subjects' attention to the possibility of novel solutions that diverge from the most obvious or conventional ways of tackling a problem. The subjects reported that they had spontaneously applied the creativity training to a variety of personal and academic problems. This latter observation suggests that psychotherapy clients may benefit from such a self-instructional creativity or problem-solving regimen. Instead of the clinician's dealing with the details of the client's maladaptive behaviors, he could provide the client with self-instructional creativity training for solving personal problems. This suggestion is consistent with D'Zurilla and Goldfried's view of a problem-solving approach to psychotherapy (1971).

The self-instructional training procedure raises the interesting possibility of matching packages of self-statements to individual differences or the employment of adaptive treatments. Wallach and his colleagues, who examined the relationship between intelligence and

Wallach: categorizing into 4 clusters

creativity, suggested that subjects can be characterized as falling into one of four clusters along the dimensions of high and low intelligence and high and low creativity (Wallach & Kogan, 1965; Wallach & Wing, 1969). For each cluster of subjects a different package or sequence of self-statements could be employed. For example, Wallach and Kogan indicated that highly intelligent but rather noncreative subjects have a disinclination rather than an inability to use their imaginations. For such subjects an awareness of negative self-statements and the emission of positive attitudinal self-statements may be emphasized. In contrast, for subjects who are low on both intelligence and creativity dimensions greater emphasis on problem analysis and task execution self-statements should be considered. One could readily adapt self-instructional packages to subjects' characteristics and to the demands of the task.

A more subtle method of modeling broad thinking *styles* would be afforded by the use of modeling films. Films of multiple models of both "creative" and "noncreative" individuals could be shown to rather large groups rather than having more didactic presentations to small groups.

A number of investigators, such as Fiedler and Windheuser (1974) and Zimmerman and Rosenthal (1974), have used modeling procedures to enhance performance on creativity tests. But each of these studies, as well as the 1975b Meichenbaum study, has failed to assess the long-term effects of training and one can seriously question whether improvement on the variety of dependent measures employed in the studies truly represents "creativity." Surely these are worthy criticisms that need to be answered. Can such cognitive-behavioral modes of intervention as self-instructional training cause significant differences on real-life criteria? At best, the self-instructional training studies on creative problem-solving represent a very provocative beginning that requires careful programmatic study.

Doubt as to long range effect

Ghiselin

An issue relevant to the self-instructional approach to training creativity and other skills is evident in work by Ghiselin (1952). Ghiselin reviewed the descriptions by a number of creative people—philosophers, scientists, mathematicians, artists, writers—from Poincaré to Picasso, and concluded that "Production by a process of purely conscious calculation seems never to occur" (p. 15).[9] In other words, descriptions of the creative process by creative individuals suggest that their creative performance has little or nothing to do with intentional conscious deliberate acts of the variety included in Table I of creative-inducing self-statements.

Ghiselin's observations do not present a problem for a self-instructional training approach when we make a distinction between the naturally occurring process of creativity, or reflectivity, or whatever, and our attempt to change behavior (that is, our attempt to make noncreative individuals more creative or impulsive children more reflective). The self-instructional treatment results do *not* imply that creative individuals, or for that matter reflective children, emit a series of intentional self-statements (and images) in order to produce creative acts or manifest self-control. Rather, as Goldfried, Decenteceo, and Weinberg (1974) have indicated, it is likely that such thinking processes are automatic and seemingly involuntary, like most overlearned acts. However, if one wishes to *teach* a noncreative subject to become more creative or an impulsive child to become more reflective, then training him explicitly to talk to himself, initially overtly and eventually covertly, will enhance the change process. I am reminded of Francis Cartier, who once declared: "There is no such thing as creative thinking—there is only thinking; but thinking occurs so seldom that when it does we call it creative" (cited by

[9] Some time ago, Wallas (1926) characterized the creative process as consisting of four stages, including preparation, incubation, illumination, and verification. Preparation and verification are supposedly fully conscious, logical operations. Ghiselin's observations may be most applicable to the incubation and illumination phases of the creative process.

Parnes and Brunelle, 1967). The use of explicit self-instructional training increases the likelihood that "thinking" will occur—that the noncreative person will *consciously alter* his usual thought patterns to more closely approximate a creative style which may, in turn, eventually become as habitual and automatic to him as the noncreative patterns previously were.

Adult Schizophrenics

We left the group of schizophrenics stranded back in Illinois. Recall that it was the serendipitous finding of the spontaneous use of self-instructions by schizophrenics that initiated the research program—a program that covered such different problems as self-control, social withdrawal, and creative problem-solving. It is time to circle back and pick up the research on schizophrenics. Could the schizophrenics be *taught* to intentionally talk to themselves? What an intriguing title for an article: "Training Schizophrenics to Talk to Themselves." I felt I had to try the procedures, to collect some data, so that I could use the title.

A personal anecdote may illustrate the focus of the training approach. Recently I was giving a colloquium at Northwestern University outside Chicago, where prior to the scheduled talk I was having coffee in the lounge with a number of students. A rather attractive female student was talking to me about my work (a highly reinforcing event), when someone began to take my picture. He walked about the group snapping pictures. "What's going on here? What's he taking my picture for? That's a Japanese camera. This is Daley country" were some of the task-irrelevant ideas elicited by the incident. Upon noticing these I began to emit a number of covert task-relevant self-statements. "There must be a reason for this, some standard procedure. You're being rude. What was she saying? On target. There he goes again . . . What was she saying?"

My task-irrelevant thoughts and accompanying feelings (i.e., irrelevant to the activity of conducting a conversation) were the stimuli that elicited task-relevant, coping self-statements, which then guided my attention back to the conversation. Like the schizophrenic, we are each given over in varying degrees to task-irrelevant thoughts, images, feelings, but we censor, edit or inhibit these. Often they are the cues to produce task-relevant mediational and behavioral coping responses. The question was: Could the same paradigm be applied to schizophrenics? Could they be trained to identify instances of their own behaviors, thoughts, and feelings, and of the reactions of others that would indicate they were being task-irrelevant? Could schizophrenics also then be taught to use these signals that they were being off-target as discriminative stimuli, cues, bell-ringers, to use the inter- and intra-personal coping skills taught in therapy. As the schizophrenic developed such skills the events that triggered task-irrelevant internal dialogue would also change.

Notice that this approach would have an intrinsic form of generalization. For the client's own "symptoms," maladaptive behaviors, thoughts, feelings, would act as the reminders to use the skills developed in therapy.

The problem I am now facing is analogous to the therapy task we undertook with the schizophrenics. As I am writing this section in my office late at night, the janitor has turned on his radio, which is quite distracting, since the music often elicits task-irrelevant ideation. Attempts at getting him to lower the volume have failed. What can I do? Go home. Or can I use some self-instructions to focus attention on my writing so that the distraction wanes? The self-instructional training procedure with schizophrenics was designed to teach such self-instructional attentional skills.

The training that we undertook in a feasibility study in 1973 (described in more detail in Meichenbaum and Cameron, 1973), included eight forty-five-minute training sessions in which schizophrenics were taught to monitor

their own behavior and thinking. The schizophrenic patients were also trained to become sensitive to the interpersonal signals (viz., the facial and behavioral reactions of
others) that indicated that they were emitting "schizophrenic behaviors" (e.g., bizarre, incoherent, or irrelevant behaviors and verbalizations). Both the interpersonal observations and the self-monitoring provided cues for the patient
to emit a set of self-instructions, "to be relevant and coherent, to make myself understood." An attempt was made to
modify how the schizophrenic perceived, labeled, and interpreted such interpersonal and intrapersonal cues.

    The sequence of the self-instructional training regimen
took into account Haley's hypothesis that schizophrenic
symptoms function as covert messages aimed at grasping
control of social interactions in a devious manner (Haley,
1963). This hypothesis was supported by Shimkunas, who
found that as the demand for intense interpersonal relationships increased, the incidence of schizophrenic
symptomatology, such as bizarre verbalizations, also increased (1972). Thus, we chose to begin self-instructional
training using structured sensorimotor tasks on which the
demands for social interactions and self-disclosure were
minimal. On these initial straightforward tasks (e.g., digit
symbol, Porteus Maze) the schizophrenics were trained to
develop a set of self-controlling, self-statements. When the
schizophrenics had developed some degree of proficiency
in the use of self-statements, the task demands were slowly
increased, requiring more cognitive effort and interpersonal interaction (e.g., proverb interpretation and interviewing). In this way an effort was made to have the schizophrenic initially develop a set of self-instructional responses
with high response strength which he could apply in
the more anxiety-inducing interpersonal situations. Moreover, an attempt was made to have the schizophrenic
become aware of instances in which he was using
symptomatology to control situations. This recognition was
to be a cue to use the self-instructional controls that he had

developed on the more simply structured sensorimotor and cognitive tasks.

Each subject was individually trained to first monitor and evaluate his own performance by means of self-questioning. Then, if he judged his performance to be inferior, he learned to self-instruct in a task-relevant fashion in order to produce a more desirable response.

For example, on one of the later items of a similarities test the experimenter modeled the following verbalizations which the subject subsequently used (initially overtly, then covertly):

> I have to figure out how a bird and a flower are alike. A bird and a flower. [Pause.] A bird is small and a flower is small. I got it, the bird can eat the flower. [Pause.] No that doesn't help. That doesn't tell me how they are alike. I have to see how they are alike. Go slowly and think this one out. Don't just say the first thing that comes to mind. [Pause, while the model thinks.] I want to give the best answer I can. Let me imagine in my mind the objects . . . bird, flower . . . out in the fresh air. They both need air to live. That's it; they are both living things. Good I figured it out. If I take my time and just think about how the two objects are alike, I can do it.

Note that in this example the experimenter modeled several aspects of behavior: (a) a restatement of the task demands; (b) general instructions to perform the task slowly and to think before responding; (c) a cognitive strategy of using imagery to produce a solution; (d) self-rewarding statements; (e) an example of an inadequate response and the reason why it was inappropriate; (f) a description of how one copes and comes up with a more adequate response. This is an example of a complex, high-level set of self-statements which was slowly achieved over the course of much training. The operant conditioning principles of chaining and shaping were followed to train the schizophrenics to use such complex sets of self-statements. Initially the self-statements included only components of the desired strategy. By the experimenter's modeling and the subject's self-instructional practice addi-

Chapter 2

tional aspects of the strategy were slowly added. The experimenter would model a specific, limited set of self-statements; then the subject would practice using these; when the subject was proficient the experimenter would introduce additional components of self-statements.

In the final treatment sessions the concept of extracting information from others' reactions was introduced. The schizophrenic patient was asked to observe and report on the verbal and, especially, nonverbal reactions of staff and other patients to inappropriate behavior. The observations he made were then discussed. This led naturally to a discussion of the self-statements that the patient could employ if he noted that his behavior elicited similar reactions. The experimenter modeled and the subject practiced such self-statements as "be relevant, be coherent, make oneself understood" while taking a proverbs test and also in a semistructured interview. In addition, a set of interpersonal ploys or statements was used to maintain a task-relevant set and to improve performance. The interpersonal self-statements included phrases like "I'm not making myself understood. It's not clear, let me try again." One subject even suggested that he use the statement "I want to make this perfectly clear," an expression which was then current in President Nixon's news conferences. Initially this phase of training seemed artificial and stilted as it required the subject to repeat the question and the self-instruction, "give healthy talk, be coherent," before responding to interview questions. However, over the course of sessions these self-verbalizations were emitted covertly, so that the overt self-goads and prompts gradually dropped out of the repertoire.

In summary, the self-instructional training had progressed from having the schizophrenic subjects use their private speech in an overt fashion on simple sensorimotor tasks through stages in which they learned to monitor both their own and others' behavior in order to covertly emit task-relevant self-instructions. The components included in self-instructional training were: provision of general "set" instructions; use of imagery, monitoring, and evaluation of inappropriate responses; instructions in strategies to produce appropriate responses; and administration of self-reinforcement. These components were presented to the subject via a variety of procedures: administration of instructions (by the experimenter and the subject, overt and covert forms), modeling, provision of examples, behavioral rehearsal, operant chaining and shaping techniques, and discussion. The full clinical armamentarium was used to develop attentional controls in schizophrenics.

The schizophrenic patients who were trained included both reactive paranoid types and chronic process schizophrenics, and they covered the host of diagnostic categories. The performances of the cognitively trained schizophrenics were compared to those of yoked practice controls, who received as much exposure to the practice materials and exposure to nonspecific training aspects. The treatment of this practice control group was essentially the same as that of the operantly trained social reinforcement group that was the experimental treatment group in my doctoral dissertation (Meichenbaum, 1969). Perhaps there is no better sign of progress than that a main effect treatment condition in that study became a control group in our 1973 study.

The results of the 1973 study are presented in Fig. 4. As illustrated, cognitive training effected significant improvements on all dependent variables except digit recall in the absence of distraction. A three-week follow-up revealed that improvements in sick talk during standardized interviews, proverb abstraction, perceptual integration on Holtzman inkblots as assessed by genetic level score, and digit recall under distraction were not only maintained but actually improved relative to yoked controls.

The janitor has just arrived at my office to find me hovering over my desk talking to myself. "You still here? Go home. This work is driving you crazy. I heard you talking to

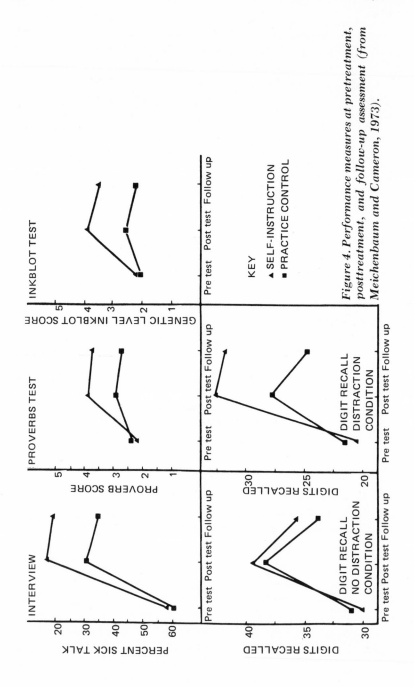

Figure 4. Performance measures at pretreatment, posttreatment, and follow-up assessment (from Meichenbaum and Cameron, 1973).

yourself." My response that he had just made it into the book did not allay his concerns. Perhaps it is time to go home. Perhaps it *is* time to go home.

Recently, Meyers, Mercatoris, and Sirota presented a case study of a 47-year-old, hospitalized chronic schizophrenic male who, by means of self-instructional training, was able to eliminate psychotic speech (1976). Fifteen sessions of training contributed to discharge from the hospital and continued improvement was evident at a six-month follow-up. A brief description of the self-instructional training regimen is worthwhile.

Following a treatment similar to Meichenbaum and Cameron's (1973), the patient was cumulatively taught to use the following self-instructions (one or two self-instructions were worked on, each session):

1. Don't repeat an answer.
2. I must pay attention to what others say. I must not talk sick talk.
3. The only sickness is talking sick. I mustn't talk sick.
4. I must speak slowly.
5. People think it's crazy to ramble on. I won't ramble on.
6. Remember to pause after I say a sentence.
7. That's the answer. Don't add anything on.
8. I must stay on the topic.
9. Relax, take a few deep breaths.

In a treatment session the therapist was asked a question by a staff member and the therapist then verbalized the target self-instruction followed by an appropriate answer. After three such demonstrations the patient was instructed to imitate the therapist's performance. This continued until the patient reached a criterion of three consecutive appropriate performances. The therapist then modeled whispering the self-instruction and verbalizing aloud the appropriate answer. The client imitated this. Finally, the therapist modeled the covert use of self-statements by pauses, nonverbal cues, and so on, which the patient in turn rehearsed. The self-instructional training resulted in a drop from 65% inappropriate psychotic speech to a low of 8% at the end of treatment. At a six-month follow-up the incidence of inappropriate verbalization was 16%—quite impressive when one learns that the patient was under stress from being off medication and from his father's recent death.

Both the Meichenbaum and Cameron study and the Meyers *et al.* case study indicate that covert self-instructions aid clients in appropriately attending to the task by performing a regulatory cueing function, by preventing internally distracting stimuli from interfering with target performance, and by mediating generalization across tasks and situations. As Meyers *et al.*'s patient stated, "The new self-instructions stopped me from talking like a crazy man," a skill which he employed in a number of situations, including a job interview.

At present, a major therapeutic innovation with schizophrenics is to provide them with training in social skills by means of structured learning techniques (e.g., Goldsmith & McFall, 1975; Goldstein, Spraflin, & Gershaw, 1976; Hersen & Bellack, 1976). The focus of such training is usually on overt stylistic aspects of interpersonal behavior, such as changes in eye contact, pausing, intonation, physical gestures, smiling, and social skills. A limitation of such training was illustrated in a study by Bellack, Hersen, and Turner (1976), who found changes of the specific overt behaviors on a role-playing test. However, improvement did not extend to the spontaneous emission of task-appropriate verbalizations in novel situations. Social skills training packages could be improved if they were supplemented with cognitive-behavioral modification techniques. One such set of cognitive techniques is self-instructional training (Meichenbaum & Cameron, 1973). Another form of cognitive training that bears careful examination follows a problem-solving training approach in which the client is taught how to identify problems, generate alternatives, test these hypotheses, assess feedback, and so forth (see Coché & Flick, 1975; Siegal & Spivack, 1976).

A beginning has been made to apply the cognitive-behavior modification technique of self-instructional training to several other academic and clinical problems, such as (1) the enhancement of children's memory recall (Asarnow, 1976) and reading comprehension (Bommarito & Meichenbaum, 1976; Wozniak & Neuchterlein, 1973); (2) the improvement of problem-solving performance in the elderly (Labouvie-Vief & Gonda, 1976; Meichenbaum, 1974b).[10] Evident in each of these self-instructional procedures is the influence of Gagné. Gagné has proposed the use of a task-analysis by beginning with a behavioral statement of an instructional objective (1966). Then he asked what were the prerequisite behaviors the individual must have within his repertoire in order to perform the desired terminal behaviors. For each of the identified behaviors the same question can be asked and a hierarchy of objectives can thereby be generated. Gagné proposed that an individual's learning of a complex behavior is contingent on his prior acquisition of a succession of simpler behaviors. Thus, instruction can be based on the cumulative learning process.

The application of self-instructions follows a similar strategy, with each step in the hierarchy translated into self-statements or cognitive strategies, which can be modeled and rehearsed. The client is taught (a) how to break the task down into manageable units, (b) how to determine the hierarchy of skills required to do the task, and (c) how to translate these skills into self-statements.

What Shall We Say to Ourselves When We Obtain Negative Results?

So far self-instructional training looks quite promising. We have some exciting reasons for continuing to assess the

[10] Two other provocative case studies using self-instructional training were offered by Tarnopol (1969, p. 217), with a learning disability child, and by Kanfer and Phillips (1970, p. 389), with brain-damaged patients.

potential of the procedures with a host of different populations. However, it is important to indicate those areas
where self-instructional training has failed to contribute to
change. Negative results should provide useful information
concerning the value and limitations of a training regimen
and the nature of the deficit; it should even shed light on
theoretical issues. In contrast, the usual pattern of treatment research, however, is the introduction of a new treatment procedure, with initial positive results and an accompanying fanfare—what Birk (1974) has called "furor
therapeutics," namely, unbridled therapeutic optimism,
with signs of a frenzy of publications, often unconstrained
by careful empirical evaluation. Such critical evaluation
usually contributes some negative results, the questioning
of the underlying treatment conceptualization, disen-
chantment; and then we are "off" onto a new training technique. Hopefully, the data on cognitive-behavior modification procedures will not follow this pattern, especially if
we try to understand what language training in the form of
self-instructional training can and *cannot* accomplish.

For example, Piagetian-oriented investigators have indicated that having a child talk to himself in certain ways
will help the child direct his attention and control perceptual activities but will not result in the development of new
cognitive operations or structures as illustrated in conservation[11] experiments (Sinclair-de-Zwart, 1969; Inhelder,
Sinclair, & Bovet, 1974). Although Piaget acknowledges
that language has an enormously facilitating effect on the
range of symbolic thinking and may be necessary for the
higher levels of logical thinking, his position is that logical
operations have deeper roots—in actions which become internalized as mental operations. The main point Piaget and
his supporters are highlighting is that a child cannot come
to understand a verbal expression until he has mastered the

---

[11] Conservation experiments require the child to maintain a constancy of interpretation in spite of changing perceptual events. The conserving child will realize
that the amount of liquid in a tall thin container does not decrease if it is poured
into a short fat container.

underlying concept. For example, Sinclair-de-Zwart (1969) presents evidence that although there are differences in the way children use words such as "some, as much as, more, and bigger than" in conservation tasks, linguistic training of the nonconservers to use comparative words does not lead to immediate improvement in performance in those conservation tasks.[12] Instead, what is required is a grasp of the logical operations involved. Negative results in Sinclair-de-Zwart's training study provide useful information. In light of the historical issues of the relationship between language and thought as documented by Sokolov (1972, Chapter 2), it is valuable to find areas of behavior that are not modifiable by means of language training.

When we obtain negative results following self-instructional training this should cause us to question the relationship between language and thought. Negative results should also cause us to examine very carefully how the cognitive-behavior modification training was conducted. We should be able to discover exactly what types of training are effective and how the nature of the skill that is being trained interacts with the training procedure. For example, consider what is involved in teaching impulsive children self-control skills versus teaching school children writing skills. Let's see how self-instructional language training is employed in each case. In the 1971 Meichenbaum and Goodman study with impulsive children, self-instructional training was found to lead to large, rapid effects. In this case the children were required to put together into a new response chain elements of responses that seemed to be already in their repertoire.

In contrast, Robin, Armel, and O'Leary found that self-instructional training did not substantially enhance children's writing skills (1975). However, in learning to write letters a number of elemental skills are required and each of these component skills must be taught before self-

[12] It should be noted that the language training that Sinclair-de-Zwart provided was more limited and did not approximate the problem-solving and coping language training that is included in self-instructional training.

instructional training will facilitate performance. Robin reports that if the child had a deficit in spatial representational skills then directional self-cues for written tasks were not effective. Instead, having the child self-instruct a "join-the-dots rule" and image the letter might be more effective (personal communication). The point to be underscored is that when self-instructional training does not work, this should be the occasion to rethink the task-analysis based on Gagné's paradigm and/or consider whether it is appropriate to this domain of behavior. We have to learn when and how the adjunctive use of self-instructional training will enhance performance. For example, in her doctoral dissertation, Burns found that general attentional self-instructions did not improve the arithmetic performance of children (Burns, 1972). She commented, "change in attending behavior would not be manifested in the arithmetic score if the child were lacking sufficient skills" (p. 62). Teaching children to respond to such self-directed verbal commands as "stop and think" will not result in incremental improvement of performance on specific tasks unless the prerequisite performance skills are already in the repertoire.

Negative treatment results also raise concerns about the issue of correspondence between what the subject says to himself and what he does. We are all too familiar with the case of the New Year's resolution that fails to control our behavior. The same phenomenon was found by Giebink, Stover, and Fahl (1968). They found that institutionalized emotionally disturbed 10- to 12-year-olds learned to verbalize the correct words (i.e., verbal solutions in frustrating problem situations) but this often failed to guide their behaviors. Smith taught normal first-grade children to focus their attention on the teacher while listening to a story (1975). Yet he reported instances in which the children emitted verbalizations such as, "I have to look at the teacher's eyes," although they were staring elsewhere. Parenthetically, Smith commented that teaching children to use self-instructions to alter attentional behavior may be easier in situations in which active instrumental behaviors are required, as in search tasks, than it is when children must verbalize while *passively* listening to someone read a story.

Both the Giebink *et al.* and the Smith studies highlight the need to make reinforcements contingent upon the correspondence between verbal and motoric responses. There is a need for a cognitive-hyphen-behavioral approach whereby reinforcements follow the appropriate correspondence between saying and doing. Focusing on only one side of the therapy equation is likely to prove less effective. How ineffective may depend upon the nature of the population, the targeted problem, and the order in which the correspondence problem is attacked (i.e., a "say-do" versus a "do-say" treatment approach or matching "word to deed" and "deed to word").

The entire issue of developing correspondence between what the child says and what he does has been examined by a number of investigators (e.g., Lovaas, 1961, 1964; Monahan & O'Leary, 1971; Risley & Hart, 1968; Karoly & Dirks, in press). Illustrative of this approach is a study by Israel and O'Leary, who examined the relative effect of a "say-do" or a "do-say" sequence in teaching correspondence (1973). They found clear evidence that teaching a child to say what he will do produced quicker correspondence than teaching the child to correctly report what he did. Such an approach is consistent with the general self-instructional training treatment approach, which encourages the child to verbalize prior to acting, thus facilitating the regulatory function of language. As Israel and O'Leary indicated, such "say-do" training capitalizes on the fact that verbal behavior is a more readily available and versatile discriminative stimulus than nonverbal behavior and thus is more likely to prompt rehearsal. Moreover, this line of investigation indicates that reinforcement of verbal behavior alone may result in only slight increases in corresponding nonverbal behavior (Lovaas, 1964; Risley & Hart, 1968). In contrast, reinforcement of a correspondence between verbal and nonverbal behavior (in that order) leads to an increased correspondence, with the consequence of the nonverbal behavior's increasing in frequency.

As we conclude the discussion of the self-instructional training studies it is appropriate to offer a brief comment on the use of language. Some investigators argue that language is essentially a weak instrument in the modification of behavior, whereas others treat language and thought as equivalent. It is necessary to remind ourselves of Furth's observation, following Piaget, that thinking can occur without language but that language can greatly enhance thinking and in turn affect behavior (1966). That is the promise of the self-instructional cognitive-behavior treatment approach.

3

Clinical Observations on Conducting Self-Instructional Training

> *The one thing psychologists can count on is that their subjects will talk, if only to themselves; and not infrequently whether relevant or irrelevant, the things people say to themselves determine the rest of the things they do.*
>
> —I. E. FARBER (1963)

Since my initial study with Goodman in 1971, self-instructional training has undergone substantial refinement. This chapter brings together the various observations from our laboratory and from others' concerning the process of conducting self-instructional training. The chapter deals primarily with children because most of the work with the procedure has been with children. However, these same observations apply to self-instructional training with adults. The treatment suggestions offered are *not* based upon careful empirical studies but rather represent a sort of cumulative "wisdom" culled from our own experiences and from the literature. I hope attention to the sorts of details presented in this chapter will enable us to avoid the "negative" results with which the last chapter concluded.

A question that is important to consider in implementing the clinical techniques described is what does the child learn from training that involves cognitive modeling with overt and covert self-instructional rehearsal? Do changes following such self-instructional training represent alterations in the child's cognitive style or merely superficial changes in specific responses that are demonstrated on a particular task? For it should be kept in mind that cognitive development cannot be equated with the mere memorization of a strategy or repetition of a mechanical integration that is demanded by the therapist.

Use of Play

A second concern for the cognitive-behavior therapist who conducts self-instructional training with a child is more practical: How does one actually engage him in self-talk? One way to conduct self-instructional training is to use the child's own medium of play, beginning treatment in the midst of ongoing activities. An illustration comes from my own clinical work. I was engaging in parallel play with a hyperactive child when he came storming through a sandbox. With appropriate effect, in order to capture the child's attention I said, "Watch it, you're just about to mess up the runway." I then went on talking to myself: "I have to land my airplane; now slowly, carefully, into the hangar. Good." I then involved the child in play and had him tell the pilot, from the imaginary control tower, to go slowly, and so on. Using play as a medium for beginning contact with the child, I was able to have the child employ a repertoire of self-guiding self-statements that could be used on a variety of tasks.

As in this example, training can begin on a set of tasks (games) in which the child is somewhat proficient and for which he does *not* have a history of failures and frustrations. The therapist employs tasks that lend themselves to a self-instructional approach and have a high "pull" for the use of cognitive strategies. For example, there are a number of games in which one has to negotiate a ball through a maze covered with plexiglass. While playing these, a therapist can model how he uses his own language to help his performance, especially when failure occurs. In fact, the therapist may fail on purpose (usually this is not necessary; failure on these tasks seems to come naturally) and then cope with the frustrations that accompany failure. The therapist tries to put into words the feelings the child may have when frustrated and then verbalizes cognitive and behavioral coping skills. For example:

> This is just impossible. I can't do this. [The therapist begins to throw the maze game down when he says,] Just wait a second. Take a slow deep breath; good. Now, what is it I have to do? Go slowly, steady. Lower this hand, etc. Let me put on my thinking cap. [The therapist then puts on his imaginary cap and continues.]

The importance of including ways of coping with failure in the treatment regimen was illustrated in research by Meichenbaum and Goodman, in which impulsive children's performance deteriorated following failure (1969b).

An interesting task that can be used to train self-instructions has been offered by Butter (1971). Butter developed a sort of tactile discrimination analogue to the MFF test. The child is asked to select from behind a screen the one object of a set that is identical to the standard object. Butter demonstrated that such a kinesthetic discrimination task can be successfully employed to alter an impulsive cognitive style. The task lends itself very nicely to cognitive modeling and self-instructional rehearsal.

Another way in which the impulsive child can learn to use language instrumentally is by verbally directing another person (e.g., the therapist) to perform a task such as Porteus Maze while the child sits on his own hands. The child has to learn to use language in an instrumental fashion in order to direct this other person to perform the task.

Bash and Camp, in their *Think Aloud* manual, sug-

Figure 5. Training Figures (from Bash and Camp, 1975).

gested that one way to have children learn to use self-instructions is by means of a "copy cat" game (1975). The game merely involves the teacher's repeating the verbalizations the children offer and then reversing roles with them. The teacher instructs the children, "Now I want you to *say* what I say and *do* what I do." "Copy cat" is then used to introduce the child to four steps in dealing with a problem: (1) identifying the problem, (2) developing a plan, (3) monitoring performance, and (4) evaluating performance and outcome. Then "copy cat" is faded and cue cards standing for each step are introduced to signal the child to verbalize for himself both the question (e.g., What is my problem?) and the answer. Over the course of the program the cognitive tasks are increased in difficulty and the child is encouraged to think of more than one plan before proceeding with a task. Then, as the child becomes adjusted to "thinking out loud" the kinds of interpersonal situations with which the program is concerned are introduced. These social tasks include identifying emotions, considering what might happen next in various situations, evaluating fairness of outcomes, and understanding the importance of cooperation. In order to generate response alternatives, a number of pictures are used (see Fig. 5). In general, one can playfully help the child employ self-statements by translating each of them into pictures with cartoonlike captions so that a picture becomes a discriminative stimulus that in turn is a cue for behavioral acts. Imagine taking the pictures in Figs. 2, 3, and 5 and having them reduced in size to that of a postage stamp. The child, before beginning a task such as Porteus Maze, could stick on the stamps at appropriate points in the task, thus making a plan and providing himself with reminders to self-instruct. The use of such stamps could then be faded.

Importance of Affect

In using such self-instructional procedures, it is important to insure that the child does not say the self-statements in a relatively mechanical, rote, or automatic fashion without the accompanying meaning and inflection. This would approximate the everyday experience of reading aloud or silently when one's mind is elsewhere; one may read a paragraph or more without recalling the content. Instead, affective modeling and practice in synthesizing and internalizing the meaning of one's self-statements are needed. This was illustrated in the application of the Camp *et al.* *Think Aloud* program with aggressive boys. Initially, the investigators reported that they failed to recognize the extent to which the aggressive boys' chatter, silliness, and inappropriate verbal activity interfered with the implementation of the program. They suggested that such silliness should be attacked directly and that the negative consequences of aggressive solutions should be emphasized.

Flexibility of Format

The rate at which the therapist proceeds with the self-instructional training procedure can be individually tailored to the needs of each child, controlling for the way the child employs the self-statements. Some children require many trials of cognitive modeling and overt self-instructional rehearsal, whereas others may proceed directly to covert rehearsal after being exposed to a model. For some children, performing the task while the therapist instructs them fosters dependency. In such cases cognitive modeling followed by covert rehearsal may suffice. In some instances it is *not* necessary to have the child self-instruct aloud. One strength of the training procedure is its flexibility.

The self-instructional approach also provides some flexibility in how quickly the therapist and the child rehearse comprehensive packages of self-statements. Usually, the self-instructional training follows the principle of successive approximations. Initially, the therapist models and has the child rehearse simple self-statements, such as,

"Stop! Think before I answer." Gradually the therapist models (and the child rehearses) more complex sets of self-statements.

Bugenthal *et al.* used hyperactive children (ages 7 to 12) as collaborators in the generation and use of self-instructions (1975). They found it difficult for a child to maintain overt speech in the self-instructional training situation since he often became embarrassed. Instead, the child's covert speech was maintained by queries on the part of the tutor as to what the child was telling himself and discussions of what he might say to himself in various classroom situations. A kind of Socratic dialogue emerged by which the child would learn to use self-instructions.

The older children's embarrassment concerning speaking aloud while doing a task is consistent with our observations that children readily comply with the instruction to "think out loud" while doing a task, whereas the instruction to "talk out loud to yourself" elicits negative connotations (viz., that is something that crazy people do). Indeed, John B. Watson suggested some time ago that the reason children's private speech drops out of the repertoire is because of the accompanying social opprobrium. No less an authority than Ann Landers has had cause to comment on this issue:

> DEAR ANN LANDERS: I am 61 years old, male, retired, under no financial pressure and in good health— physically, that is—but I'm beginning to wonder if perhaps I'm losing a few marbles.
>
> I'm ashamed to go to a doctor with this problem and I hope you can help me. This past year I've been talking to myself when no one is around. It's not a constant thing, it usually happens when I'm undecided. After verbalizing the pros and cons I ask myself, "Now what do you think you ought to do?" On occasion I even call myself by name as if there were two of us present.
>
> I have seen some squirrely characters do this in public and I'm beginning to wonder if perhaps they started alone, just as I am doing now. Is it possible that I'm becoming senile?—SOLILOQUY IN ROCHESTER

DEAR SOL: I am several years younger than you and have been talking to myself (both privately and publicly) for years. Almost everyone does this on occasion and it's nothing to become alarmed about.

If, however, you should start calling yourself by another name, like Napoleon or Alexander the Great, you'd better look into it.

Showing consistency in her therapeutic advice, Ann Landers replies to another letter as follows:

DEAR ANN LANDERS: Help! I have not only been talking to myself these last few weeks, but I've been talking right out loud. Does this mean I am going crazy? Please tell me. I need to know.

While at the neighborhood laundromat last week I was trying to forget my weightier problems by concentrating on the job at hand. I announced in a loud voice, "I'll put these in here and this goes over there."

I was all alone. The sound of my own voice gave me quite a scare. Please tell me the truth, Ann. If I'm breaking up I don't want to be the last to know. Should I seek psychiatric help? Thanks for your guidance.—WORRIED ABOUT MYSELF

DEAR WORRIED: Calm down, lady. You sound perfectly OK to me. Everyone talks to himself at some time or another. I find it very helpful, as a matter of fact, when I'm in a hurry. I tell myself, "Take it easy—slow down!" And it really works!

However, the concerns of SOL and WORRIED at one time in history may have been appropriately justified, especially when we learn of the calumnies that once accompanied talking to oneself. Mackay (1841) in his excellent book, *Extraordinary Popular Delusions*, reported that a poor woman in Scotland was executed for talking to herself aloud. The accuser stated: "None ever talked to themselves who were not witches." The devil's mark being found upon her, the woman was "convict and brynt."

Another set of clinical observations related to format was offered by Drummond (1974) who conducted self-instructional training on a group basis:

1. Self-instructional training needs to occur early in the school day, before students become distracted by fatigue or the impending dismissal from school. Early training also provides children with opportunities for trying out newly acquired skills.[13]
2. Limiting the self-instructional training group to three, rather than five, children seems more manageable.
3. One should use supplemental media, such as videotape feedback, and subjects' prerecorded self-statements (à la Kanfer & Zich, 1974) in order to provide contrasting models or videotape feedback as Bugenthal *et al.* (1975).
4. Finally, children younger than those in grades three and four would be better candidates for self-instructional training.

In order to enhance treatment generalization, Bornstein and Quevillon suggested that the self-instructional training session should be presented in a "story-like" manner (1976). The experimenter can suggest that the teacher (not the experimenter) has asked the child a question. The child can then respond by using self-instruction as though he were present in the classroom (e.g., "Mrs. X wants me to draw that picture over there. OK, how can I do that?"). In this way, since the child is told that the behavior is requested by the teacher, the role-playing of appropriate behavior is accomplished as though it were in the classroom, rather than in an experimental setting. More obvious suggestions for facilitating treatment generalization include involving in the treatment significant others, such as peers and parents, using multiple therapists in the form of classroom volunteers, and training *in vivo* whenever possible.

An ideal situation for *in vivo* and widely generalizable training can be provided by teaching parents to engage in self-instructional training with their children. The parents

---

[13] Indeed, Drummond found significant differences between early- and late-trained subjects.

can help the children to learn exactly when and where to use whatever skills they have. Implicit in this orientation is the notion that children with deficits may have some mediational skills but not think to apply them on the appropriate occasions.

Whenever we do train parents in the use of self-instructional training or, for that matter, any other treatment to be used with their children, we provide initial parental training with a child other than their own. Otherwise, when the parent begins to apply the new procedures with his own child and failures occur, the parent tends to attribute that failure to his child: "I knew it would never work. Don't you have a pill you can give him?" However, when working with an unfamiliar child the parent's attributions tend to be that perhaps he has not mastered the training techniques, didn't understand the child's response, and so on. The point is, therapy must be sensitive to the internal dialogue of the *parent* as well as that of the child.[14]

Use of Imagery

The focus of the self-instructional training thus far has been on the use of language to alter the child's thinking style on the one hand and on the other, his overt behavior. The training can be supplemented with *imagery* manipulations. Imagery has been used within laboratory settings to enhance a variety of children's cognitive abilities, including memory, problem-solving, reading comprehension (Paivio, 1971; Rohwer, 1970) as well as self-control skills as assessed by delay of gratification and resistance to temptation tasks (Mischel, 1973).

Illustrative of this latter line of investigation is a study

[14] That parents' attributions or what they say to themselves about their children's behavior may influence their reactions has been illustrated by Macfarlane (as cited by Bruner, 1975). Macfarlane, in her studies of newborn greeting behavior, found mother's imputing intent to their infants' cries, gestures, expressions, and postures. Infants were seen to be showing off, to be asking more than their share, to be "buttering-up" mother, to be "going on too much about it." Surely, any treatment program with parents will need to concern itself with the parents' internal dialogue.

by Mischel, Ebbesen, and Zeiss, who found that directing children's cognitions toward rewards by means of imagery substantially reduced their delay of gratification, whereas images that transform the meaning of rewards increased delay of gratification (1972). Children who were asked to think about tempting pretzel sticks as long thin brown logs or to think of marshmallows as white puffy clouds or as round white moons could wait for long periods of time (Mischel & Baker, 1975).

Following from the work of Mischel we decided to include imagery in our self-instructional training with impulsive children. For example, in working with young impulsive children the therapist can introduce a toy turtle and engage the child in play with it, going slowly like a turtle. As part of the interaction the child is encouraged to close his eyes and picture the turtle. When asked to do a task like Porteus Maze the therapist can model and the child can then rehearse self-instructions: "Picture the turtle. I will not go faster than that slow turtle. Slowly and carefully." In short, the child is first taught how to monitor performance, then how to set standards; and if he deviates from the standard due to impulsivity he is encouraged to spontaneously generate an imagery-based mediator of the "turtle" to control and guide his behavior.

Another technique that employed a turtle image, in a somewhat different fashion, was developed by Schneider and Robin (Schneider, 1974; and Schneider & Robin, 1975). Schneider incorporates a turtle image into a story which is read to the class. Following the story, the children imitate the turtle who withdrew into his shell when he felt he was about to lose control. While in the imaginary shell the children, like the turtle, practice relaxation and perform self-instructional and problem-solving exercises in order to exert self-control. In the Schneider study the teacher spent fifteen minutes each day for three weeks in training, which resulted in reduced aggressive behavior and fewer frustration responses. Recently, Robin, Schneider, and Dolnick have indicated how problem children's peers can be employed in the therapy regimen (1976). The problem children were taught to "do turtle" (i.e., generate the turtle image, relax, and self-instruct and generate problem-solving strategies) whenever they perceived that they were about to become aggressive with peers or if they became frustrated and angry at themselves and were about to throw a tantrum. The children were taught the relaxation exercises and how to generate alternative strategies by means of role-playing. Initially the teacher would say "do turtle" to the problem children when she noticed an incipient fight. In turn the peers used the prompt "do turtle" with each other. Using a multiple baseline approach, Robin *et al.* reported that the degree of aggressive behavior dropped by more than 40% with the range of improvement for individual children being 34% to 70%. As with the other case studies reported, caution must be observed but the procedure does raise some interesting possibilities. Although I have some reservations about the story of going into one's shell and some concern about how peers will employ the prompting of "do turtle," the technique does raise the possibility of combining cognitive and behavioral interventions. Other useful sources for training children to use imagery include Freyberg (1973), Saltz and Johnson (1974), Saltz, Dixon, and Johnson (1976), and also Smilansky's (1968) work on sociodramatic play.

The Child as Collaborator

Central to the many clinical "tips" that have been offered concerning self-instructional training is the notion that the child acts as a collaborator. Indeed, such collaboration is intrinsic in all of the cognitive-behavior modification procedures that will be described. The child who receives self-instructional training is not "passive," not merely the recipient of the thoughts and behaviors modeled by a therapist.

There are two ways in which the client (whether child or adult) acts as a collaborator. The first way is by helping to define and diagnose the clinical problem(s). The second way is by collaborating in the development and implementation of the treatment regimen.

It was suggested earlier that the children we treat have a great deal to tell us if we would only ask and then listen. Such advice may seem so straightforward and commonsensical that it need not be offered. However, in the treatment literature one rarely hears from a client, especially a child. That children have something important to tell us was illustrated by the medication interviews of Whalen and Henker, described earlier. The value of asking the child about his test performance was underscored by a dissertation by Goodman at Waterloo (Goodman, 1973). He administered the MFF test to school children and monitored their eye movements while they took the test. Goodman found that the cognitively impulsive children used their eyes quite differently while doing the MFF test than did the reflective children. The cognitively *reflective* children demonstrated significantly more eye fixations, they viewed more alternatives, devoted proportionally more looks to the standard stimulus and to the most frequently chosen alternative, and proportionally fewer looks to the other alternatives. In contrast, the *impulsive* children were less systematic in their search, infrequently searching all of the alternatives and rarely checking the standard.[15]

---

[15] These differences in search strategy between impulsive and reflective children have also been observed by Drake (1970), Nelson (1969), Siegelman (1969), Wagner (1976), and Wright (1974). However, these data partially conflict with those reported by Ault, Crawford, and Jeffrey (1972), Zelniker, Jeffrey, Ault, and Parsons (1972), especially when one looks at proportionality scores. These contradictions may, in part, be due to differences in methodology (see Goodman, 1973). Recently, Siegal, Babich, and Kirasic (1974) have demonstrated that on a forced choice visual recognition memory task, reflective children engage in a more detailed visual feature analysis of stimulus arrays than do impulsive children, a finding consistent with the Goodman search data and with recent findings by Weiner and Berzonsky (1975), who studied selective attention in an incidental learning task. Campbell has demonstrated a similar pattern for both hyperactive and impulsive boys, both of whom performed similarly on the MFF (1973).

However, an interesting thing happened after the MFF test was over, when Goodman asked the impulsive children how they went about solving the problem. Some impulsive children reported that they looked at the standard carefully and looked at each alternative, rechecked the standard, narrowed their choice down to two alternatives, and then chose. But, *in fact, they did not actually do this*! That is, there was a negative correlation between what the impulsive child did, as evidenced by his eye movements, and his post hoc strategy description. It seemed that for some cognitively impulsive children the correct or efficient search strategy was within their repertoires but they were failing to employ it spontaneously at appropriate times, evidencing what Flavell *et al.* called a "production deficiency" (1966). Cameron, using a different task requiring problem-solving also found that cognitively impulsive children could report task-relevant strategies in an interview but often failed to employ these strategies when problem-solving (1976).

The Goodman and Cameron interview data raise several interesting clinical suggestions. First, they suggest that we should ask children how they go about doing a task, both before and after taking tests, how they perceive the testing situation, and why they are being tested, etc., and in particular what suggestions they might offer to improve their performance. This latter question will permit children to act as collaborators in the development of a treatment regimen. For example, the therapist might say to a child, "What advice would you have for another boy (or girl) like yourself, to play this game (i.e., MFF test)?" In the course of the interview the therapist may state, "I noticed that you sometimes chose the wrong picture. I'm wondering what you could do to get more right?" and so forth. Out of this discussion the child and therapist are likely to evolve a strategy to go more slowly and search the alternatives more carefully; and when asked how to accomplish this, many an impulsive child will come up with self-instructional training—the idea that he ask and answer these kinds of questions for himself. The therapist can say that that sounds like good sense and ask if he could try it; and, in turn, the child can have an opportunity to employ it.

Throughout the training the therapist uses a Socratic dialogue to encourage the child to contribute to and evaluate the self-instructional approach. The trainer asks the child how he would do the task, then provides feedback and builds on that advice. The trainer then models and the child rehearses the self-statements. During the course of the Socratic dialogue, the following topics are discussed: the purpose of the task, the strategy most likely to facilitate performance, and how to execute the strategy most effectively. Initially, the trainer may provide support in generating answers to these questions; but as training progresses, the trainer fades support to the point at which the child is spontaneously generating and answering such questions on his own. Throughout, the trainer is modeling both reinforcing and coping self-statements, faltering on occasion and permitting the child to catch the errors. Central to this give-and-take exchange between therapist and client is an appreciation that the modeling or observational learning that is taking place should *not* be equated with mimicry, exact topographical matching, or superficial imitation. Instead, exposure to a model permits the acquisition of a set of discriminative responses and organized covert storage of complex and integrated behavior chains that may then be retrieved to satisfy environmental demands. Following modeling and rehearsal, the child is encouraged to generalize the strategy to other tasks and situations. The child is a true collaborator in the development and implementation of the self-instructional training.

Thus, the self-instructional technique should not be viewed as regimented or austere but, rather, individually tailored and highly responsive to each child. However, employing the child as a collaborator in diagnosis and treatment is not a simple matter. For example, even asking a child about his performance turns out to be a complex event (in part dependent upon the child's age). Blank, for example, has reported that in exploring a young child's verbalization skills in experimental tasks it is common to display the material and pose questions that require the child to justify his behavior toward the object (e.g., "Why did you pick this one?") (1975). Blank found this procedure interferes with the child's ability to verbalize, in that the presentation of the materials leads to nonverbal responses (pointing) and asking the questions of "how" and "why" often leads to irrelevant and/or uninformative replies. In contrast, more revealing verbalizations are obtained in children even as young as three years of age if the task objects are removed from view and the question is phrased in the form, "Tell me which one did you choose?" and "What did you do?" Thus, posing questions with "which" and "what" rather than "how" and "why" are likely to prove more illuminating.

A somewhat different approach to tapping children's ongoing thoughts during a task was developed by Mischel (1975). "Mr. Clown" consists of a tape recorder and a microphone disguised as a clown who says, "Hi, I have big ears and love it when children fill them with all the things they think and feel, no matter what." Mr. Clown is used to record the spontaneous verbalizations that children emit in various tasks, including delay of gratification and resistance to temptation.

In the Classroom

Although the clinical observations that have thus far been offered have been focused on the therapy setting, many of these suggestions have implications for other settings, such as the classroom. The self-instructional research that has been reviewed indicates that complex cognitive skills can be taught through the combination of observational learning or cognitive modeling and self-instructional rehearsal. In short, the self-instructional training approach permits the educator to get into the business of teaching "thinking" directly and explicitly. Thus, teaching by example rather than by exhortation permits the teacher to cognitively model various strategies and coping responses.

How the educator may employ self-instructional training techniques bears comment. Ever since the introduction of "faculty" psychology the pedagogical hope has been that the learning of logical and rigorous skills, such as Latin or geometry, would transfer to other content areas. Indeed, one can even find today in certain schools principals who have all children in the school each morning begin with fifteen minutes of arithmetic in order to wake up the mind, get the "faculties" going. Little transfer seems to follow from such training and one can seriously question the pedagogical value of such daily exercises. Although I would take issue with the manner and content of such a transfer of training approach, I do feel that "faculty" psychology was on the right track; it merely had the wrong content. Instead of expecting transfer from Latin or geometry to other areas, what would be the effect if the children were taught a general problem-solving approach to be applied across disciplines and subject areas? Polya (1945) in his book *How to Solve It?* offers a similar suggestion. Perhaps if our curriculum at all levels of education were less content-oriented and more process-oriented we might expect the transfer of training that faculty psychologists once hoped to achieve. It is proposed that a curriculum that emphasized (1) a "learning how to learn" set; (2) the acquisition of meta-rules to be applied across subject areas as well as to interpersonal problems; (3) a set of heuristic principles which could be modeled and rehearsed by children in order to learn how to generate rules could provide the basis for teaching thinking.

Illustrative of the suggested approach is the work of Stone, Hinds, and Schmidt (1975) who have recently reported an attempt to teach problem-solving skills to elementary school children. Using taped vignettes for interaction purposes and picture games they were able to teach the children to distinguish between facts, choices, and solutions. This approach is consistent with the Spivack and Shure (1974) approach described earlier and the D'Zurilla and Goldfried (1971) and Christensen (1974) problem-solving therapy approaches to be discussed in Chapter 6. Two additional comments bear mentioning concerning the use of self-instructional training in the classroom. The teacher can directly model the cognitions required in a task *or* he can provide the conditions through which the child can discover for himself what strategies to employ. These procedures could be followed by student performance and teacher feedback. Which strategy should be employed may depend on whether the component skills to be taught are already within the child's repertoire— whether disinhibition or the acquisition of new skills and behaviors is needed.

The distinction between disinhibition and acquisition was illustrated in a cognitive modeling study by Denney who found that the child's age (6, 8, and 10) and his initial competence interacted with the modeling condition (1975). Using a "twenty questions" task, Denney examined the relative efficacy of an exemplary model (who merely illustrates constraint-seeking questions) versus a cognitive model (who, prior to asking constraint-seeking questions, verbalizes her strategy for formulating such questions as well as self-statements about how to employ feedback). Cognitive modeling was more effective than exemplary modeling at all three ages; but this was most notable among the youngest children, who required the additional guidance afforded through the verbalizations of the cognitive model.

Denney's study also raised a second issue that requires systematic examination. Denney found that the addition of self-instructional rehearsal (initially aloud and then covertly) added little to the cognitive modeling alone condition. This latter finding is in contradiction to the finding by Meichenbaum and Goodman, who were working with impulsive children and teaching them match to sample behavior. They found that the modeling alone resulted in subjects' slowing down their performance but only the modeling plus self-rehearsal condition resulted in a significant decrease in errors as well as an increase in latency.[16] Besides differences in the nature of populations and tasks in the Denney and Meichenbaum and Goodman studies, one possible way to reconcile or conceptualize these differences comes from some findings by Ridberg, Parke, and Hetherington (1971). They found that combining verbal and nonverbal cues in training impulsive children worked best with low IQ subjects but that the addition of verbal cues with high IQ subjects may have interfered with their mediational processes.

In short, there may be an interaction between subject characteristics in terms of IQ or task readiness or other attributes and the usefulness of the self-rehearsal components of the self-instructional training. We may find that self-rehearsal is most important when learning a new task, as a temporary aid to performance—recall our example of learning to drive or ski. But with proficiency the need for self-rehearsal may diminish; indeed, it may even interfere with performance. From a practical training viewpoint the possibility of eliminating the self-rehearsal phase and concentrating on cognitive modeling and providing tasks that have a high "pull" for using mediational strategies may prove the most promising package. The role of the self-rehearsal component has yet to be clearly delineated.

The second consideration in applying self-instructional training to the classroom is that the teacher should not only model the cognitive strategies required in performing a

---

[16] Heider (1971) reported data consistent with the Meichenbaum and Goodman (1971) findings. She found that task strategy instructions can significantly alter impulsive children's cognitive style. Both the Heider and the Meichenbaum and Goodman studies suggest that direct instruction in information-processing and how to structure tasks may be effective modes of intervention.

task but should also include failures and frustrations and how these are dealt with.[17] The literature suggests that a "coping" model will prove more effective than a "mastery" model (viz., one who does not make errors). The empirical basis of this suggestion will be offered in the next chapter on modeling. But the point that I am making now is that teachers should be talking to themselves aloud—I'm sure teachers do this already but now it may be viewed as having some therapeutic potential.

Summary

A number of different clinical techniques can be employed to have children learn to use self-talk. The importance of using intentional mediation has been commented upon by Flavell *et al.* (1966). They propose that the genesis of internal speech in its broadest sense entails a progressive "linguification" of more and more tasks and situations. Some suggestion that impulsive children require training in internalized "linguification" comes from the conclusion offered by Dykman, Ackerman, Clements, and Peters, who state:

> We would have presumptive evidence of the importance of inner speech if it could be shown, for example, that inner-speech training decreases impulsivity, reaction time, or distractibility, or increases physiological reactivity. That is, one might train the child to talk to himself, but not aloud, possibly emphasizing inhibitory commands. (1971, p. 88)

The research we have been conducting over the last ten years with a number of different clinical populations, including impulsive children, begins to provide the evidence Dykman *et al.* sought.

The focus of the self-instructional training has been on the child's *conscious self-regulatory ability*. The self-instructional training was designed to help the impulsive

[17] Yando and Kagan have demonstrated that the teacher's cognitive style (reflective or impulsive) has an impact and is modeled by the children in their class (1968).

child to learn important skills, which are applicable in diverse problem-solving situations: (1) inhibiting impulsive responding; (2) maintaining attention to task-relevant cues and diverting attention from extraneous stimuli, whether internally or externally generated; (3) reminding the child of task goals; (4) helping to cope with frustration and failure; and (5) helping to control verbal and nonverbal behavior. By teaching the impulsive children how and when to use self-instructions (and images) in the behavioral act, by having the children develop their own self-instructions for tasks, they are taught how to comprehend the requirements of a task, rehearse problem-solving strategies, direct motor movements through self-commands, handle failures appropriately, and reward themselves. In the self-instructional treatment the child's behavior pattern is broken down into smaller manageable units to make the subject aware of the chain of events (i.e., environmental situations and behavioral and cognitive reactions) that sets off the impulsive and often explosive behavior. This process is enhanced by performing a diagnostic evaluation of the conditions under which self-control is deficient. By making the child aware of the sequence of events, he can be helped to interrupt them early in the chain and to employ coping procedures.

One of the underlying principles behind the many treatment suggestions offered is that by inhibiting an impulse at a low level of intensity or at an incipient stage and then practicing self-control or inhibition at increasingly greater levels of intensity the impulsive client will develop self-control. The goal is to teach the child to identify the impulse early and to have him attempt to control it at that stage. Thus by teaching clients (1) to recognize and label their impulses and the cues that instigate them at different levels of intensity and (2) to spontaneously employ cognitive and behavioral coping responses, they will develop self-control.

In a somewhat different context Epstein provides a

similar analysis for the control of impulses (1976). Epstein offers the following anecdote to underscore the importance of inhibiting impulses early in the behavioral chain. The client is Epstein's dog, a large German shepherd, that was used to roaming the countryside but who had decided to establish territorial rights over the whole town. Epstein describes the therapy of his dog as follows:

> Invariably when he was taken for a walk, he would get into fights with other dogs. It would happen in the following manner. While walking at heel, the dog would see another dog approaching at a great distance. Without barking or giving any other sign, he would suddenly bolt for the other dog, and pay no attention to the author's shouts of "down," "come," "heel," and much worse. Under other circumstances, the dog was very obedient, and would immediately respond to any of the above commands. Through trial and error, the author learned that if he spotted the other dog first, he could abort the run-away reaction by saying "no," firmly, as soon as he detected an incipient approach response in his dog. By following this procedure he was able to lead his dog right in front of other dogs without incident. Interestingly, his dog remained completely calm throughout such encounters. Apparently, the impulse that could not be inhibited when it was full-blown, could easily be inhibited when it was an incipient tendency. (Epstein, 1976, p. 16)[18]

The goal of self-instructional training is to teach impulsive clients spontaneously to provide themselves with such inhibitory cues at incipient stages.

---

[18] Obviously it is not being suggested that Epstein's dog repeats the instruction "No" to himself in order to generate self-control. But the child's capacity to self-instruct in this manner extends his ability for self-control.

Cognitive Factors in Behavior Therapy Techniques

> *Much of psychotherapy—even the new "behavior" therapy—*
> *is based on the assumption that reorganizing and restructur-*
> *ing a patient's verbal statements about himself and his*
> *world will result in a corresponding reorganization of*
> *the patient's behavior with respect to that world.*
>
> —RISLEY AND HART, 1968

Initial research on self-instructional training indicated that the likelihood of obtaining generalization and persistence of treatment effects was increased if we attended to the client's cognitions. If operant training procedures could be improved by explicitly including in the treatment regimen a client's thoughts and images, then perhaps other behavior therapy techniques could similarly be improved. In other words, if the Risley and Hart quote that introduces this chapter has any validity, then altering behavior therapy procedures in "reorganizing and restructuring the patient's verbal statements" should enhance their efficacy. This hypothesis was translated into a program of treatment studies in which we assessed the efficacy of "standard" behavior therapy procedures (such as desensitization, modeling, aversive conditioning) relative to behavior

therapy procedures that included self-instructional components (that is, procedures that supplemented the behavior
therapy techniques with an explicit concern for the client's
cognitions). This chapter will describe this phase of our
research program and summarize the available evidence
for the role of cognitions in behavior therapy procedures.

I can highlight the subject of this chapter by noting
that a common theme runs through these "cognitive-
behavioral" studies that we conducted. The theme is that
behavior therapy techniques, as originally conceptualized
and implemented, have overemphasized the importance of
environmental events (antecedents and consequences),
and, therefore, underemphasized and often overlooked
how a client perceives and evaluates those events. Our research on cognitive factors in behavior therapy techniques
has highlighted the fact that environmental events *per se*,
although important, are not of *primary* importance; rather
what the client says to himself about those events influences his behavior (e.g., see Mahoney, 1974; Meichenbaum, 1974a; Steiner, 1970).

However, the research on cognitive factors in behavior
therapy procedures has also indicated that what a person
says to himself, that is, how he evaluates and interprets
events, is explicitly modifiable by many of the behavior
therapy techniques that have been used to modify
maladaptive overt behaviors. We can use a number of behavior therapy techniques, such as modeling, imagery manipulations, and conditioning to alter the client's internal
dialogue as well as his overt behaviors.

In general, the results have indicated that when the
standard behavior therapy procedures were augmented
with a self-instructional package, greater treatment efficacy,
more generalization, and greater persistence of treatment
effects were obtained. Moreover, when the standard behavior therapy procedures were put under the scrutiny of experimentation, their limitations were often highlighted,
and, in some instances, the basis of their conceptualizations

was challenged. A byproduct has been the development of new, and apparently more therapeutic, procedures which will be described in Chapter 5. Since much of these empirical data have been reviewed in detail elsewhere (Meichenbaum & Cameron, 1974), this chapter will consist primarily of clinical illustrations of how to alter behavior therapy procedures to include clients' cognitions.

Beginning from Learning Theory

In order to make the following quasi-chronological summary of research clear, it may be helpful briefly to outline the conceptualization of cognition that in 1967 guided our research program, but which, for reasons that will become apparent, I no longer feel is adequate. When I began the series of studies comparing different treatments of various clinical problems, my conceptualization of covert events was very much influenced by a "learning theory" view. The writings of Dollard and Miller and Skinner were two sources encouraging a view of cognitions from a learning theory framework.

Dollard and Miller set out to translate Freudian psychoanalytic procedures into learning theory terms (1950). In doing so, they indicated that the client's higher mental processes, such as the labels he uses in a situation, can be viewed as "cue-producing responses" that may facilitate or inhibit subsequent responses. The labels the client employs or the things he says to himself are viewed as learned responses that in turn may be stimuli for succeeding responses. Within such a mediational view, the explicit use of learning techniques to teach new and more adaptive labels can be effective in altering the individual's emotional reaction (e.g., in reducing anxiety). Dollard and Miller suggested that an important consequence of changing labels and reducing anxiety is an increase in the client's problem-solving capacities. The client's newly learned "cue-producing response" leads to significant behavior change.

Skinner's operant conditioning model of self-control contends that one controls his own behavior in precisely the same way that he would control the behavior of anyone else, through manipulation of the variables of which the behavior is a function (1953). For example, for one to decrease an undesirable behavior in himself, one makes the undesirable response less probable by altering the rewards and punishments on which it depends. A behavior therapist with an operant orientation may ask: What is the immediate effect of a disruptive thought or image (e.g., a depressing or anxiety-arousing idea)? Frequently, the immediate effect is that the person labels himself depressed or anxious and hence feels he is incapable of continuing work. Often, the act of thinking such thoughts eventually leads to escape from an unpleasant situation and, thus reinforced by the termination and future avoidance of an aversive stimulus, the act is maintained. The operant behavior therapist suggests that one can significantly and directly influence the client's thinking processes by systematically manipulating their consequences.

Thus, within a learning theory framework, one can view the client's cognitions explicitly as behaviors to be modified in their own right, subject to the same "laws of learning" as are overt or nonprivate behaviors; thus, the behavioral techniques that have been used to modify overt behaviors, such as operant and aversive conditioning, modeling, and rehearsal, may be applied to covert processes. In fact, Homme has offered the concept of "coverants" (covert operants) to describe covert behavior within a learning framework (1965).

A somewhat different treatment strategy of behavior therapists is to focus treatment *not* on the client's maladaptive cognitions *per se* but on his maladaptive overt behaviors and to teach him a set of adaptive behaviors that are incompatible with those maladaptive overt behaviors. It is assumed that as the client learns new behavioral skills and receives reinforcement for these from significant others in his environment, his thinking style in turn will change. The latter treatment approach is illustrated by the aphorism, "It is easier to act your way into a new way of thinking than it is to think your way into a new way of behaving."

In 1967 three general behavior therapy strategies were available that were designed directly to alter the client's cognitions. Each of these strategies was based on a simple *contiguity* model. One could apply the viewpoints of Dollard and Miller and Skinner to therapeutic cognitive interventions by having the client pair his cognitions (1) with the onset, offset, or avoidance of an externally administered aversive consequence such as electric shock or the administration of an external reward, as in anxiety-relief conditioning; (2) with other covert events, such as another image as in covert sensitization; (3) with an overt behavior such as physical relaxation, as in systematic desensitization. By pairing these various events with the client's cognitions (i.e., his self-statements and images), the behavior therapist attempts to influence the functional significance of the client's cognitions. It was in testing these ideas that my own notions about how to view the role of cognitive factors in behavior therapy underwent change. Let's examine each of the three therapy strategies and note how the research results contributed to my changing conceptualization.

Anxiety-Relief Conditioning

A reasonable way of beginning to test the learning theory explanation for behavior change seemed to be by taking a therapy procedure that was patently based on the learning theory contiguity model and putting it under the microscope of experimentation. Such a procedure is Wolpe and Lazarus' anxiety-relief conditioning procedure, which pairs a client's cognitions with external aversive consequences. The rationale for the anxiety-relief procedures is as follows:

> If an unpleasant stimulus is endured for several seconds and
> is then made to cease almost immediately after a specified
> signal, that signal will become conditioned to the changes
> that follow cessation of the uncomfortable stimulus. (Wolpe
> & Lazarus, 1966, p. 149)

Typically, the word "calm" is the signal that is paired with
the offset of aversive stimulation (usually electric shock).
Theoretically, a stimulus such as the self-instruction
"calm" that immediately precedes the cessation of a noxious stimulus should take on "counterconditioning,"
anxiety-relief qualities, which should generalize across
situations. The client should be able to reduce his anxiety
level in virtually any situation by instructing himself to be
"calm," thus evoking the conditioned "relief" response.
Wolpe's initial procedure was to administer a strong, un-
comfortable shock to his patient until the patient said a
"relief" word, usually "calm," then immediately turn off
the shock. The whole procedure was done ten to twenty
times per session with an intertrial interval of thirty to sixty
seconds. A number of investigators (Gaupp, Stern, & Ratliff, 1971; Solyom & Miller, 1967; Thorpe, Schmidt, Brown,
& Castell, 1964) have presented data that demonstrate the
therapeutic value of such anxiety-relief techniques in alleviating phobic and obsessive behaviors.

Given these studies and the accompanying learning
theory explanation, we set out to examine the therapeutic
efficacy and rationale for the anxiety-relief procedures
(Meichenbaum & Cameron, 1972a). Could we reinforce
and punish thoughts in the same way as we could treat
overt behaviors?

The first study we conducted was quite straightforward
and designed simply to replicate the previous findings that
anxiety-relief procedures could facilitate behavior change
in phobic clients. A group of fear-avoidant phobics received
five one-hour sessions of escape and avoidance training
in which the self-instructions "calm" and "relax" termi-

nated ongoing electric shock and eventually avoided the onset of shock. This anxiety-relief group was compared to a self-instructional rehearsal group, which did not receive shock (but merely rehearsed the coping self-statements "calm" and "relax"), and with a waiting list control group, which received only the pre-, post-, and follow-up assessments. Indeed, the anxiety-relief group did evidence significantly more behavioral and affective change than the rehearsal or control groups. These results were encouraging in confirming the potential usefulness of anxiety-relief therapy.

In a second study, we attempted to modify the basic anxiety-relief treatment so as to enhance its efficacy (Meichenbaum & Cameron, 1974). Two alterations were made to the basic anxiety-relief paradigm. First, a self-instructional component was added because the clients who improved the most in the first study reported that in addition to employing the relief words, they also had covertly employed other coping verbalizations. To incorporate these self-instructions into the anxiety-relief paradigm, we had the clients who were phobic to snakes in an expanded anxiety-relief group generate and emit such coping self-statements (e.g., "Relax; I can handle the snake. One step at a time"). Shock termination was made contingent upon the production of these self-instructions rather than upon a simple cue word, such as "calm" or "relax."

The second revision was in the role of the aversive stimulation in the paradigm. In addition to its serving as the basis for the anxiety relief, the shock also assumed a punishing role. The client was asked to verbalize the fear-engendering thoughts he had previously experienced. Shock onset was contingent upon these verbalizations. The coping self-statements would in turn terminate the ongoing shock.

In summary, the sequence of the expanded anxiety-relief treatment was: (1) the therapist said the name of the phobic object (e.g., "snake"); (2) the client said the fear-engendering thoughts (e.g., "Its ugly; I won't look at it"); (3)

the therapist turned on the shock; (4) the client said the coping self-statements (e.g., "Relax; I can touch it"); (5) the therapist turned off the shock; (6) the client then relaxed.

In order to test the importance of the contingency manipulation in the anxiety-relief treatment paradigm, a separate group was included in the study: These subjects received *inverted* anxiety relief, in which the onset of the shock was made contingent upon the coping self-statements and the electric shock was terminated by the emission of what had previously been fear-engendering self-statements. Table 2 summarizes the differences between the expanded and inverted anxiety-relief treatment conditions. Note that in the inverted anxiety-relief group the expression of avoidant thoughts was paired with shock offset, whereas positive, coping self-instructions were now punished.

Well, the results proved most revealing. Findings were consistent across all behavioral and self-report measures in the posttest and follow-up assessments. As expected, the expanded anxiety-relief group was effective in reducing fears. But, to our surprise, the inverted anxiety-relief group was *equally* effective. Moreover, the two anxiety-relief groups in the second study (both regular and inverted) yielded significantly more change than did the clients who had been treated in the standard Wolpe-Lazarus anxiety-relief procedure in Study I. But hold on. How can the in-

Table 2. Sequence of the Expanded Anxiety Relief and Inverted Anxiety Relief Treatments

Expanded anxiety relief	Therapist says "snake."	Client says "It's ugly; I won't look at it."	Therapist turns on shock.	Client says "Relax; I can touch it."	Therapist turns off shock.	Client relaxes.
Inverted anxiety relief	Therapist says "snake."	Client says "Relax; I can touch it."	Therapist turns on shock.	Client says "It's ugly; I won't look at it."	Therapist turns off shock.	Client relaxes.

verted anxiety-relief group also improve? This group had been included in the study to demonstrate the importance of contingency of the shock. If the "learning theory" model of the treatment was valid then it should have done quite poorly.

While we were puzzling over these results, a number of other studies began to appear in the behavior therapy literature that also questioned the importance of the *contingency* of shock in various paradigms. For example, Carlin and Armstrong (1968) with smokers, and McConaghy and Barr (1973) with homosexuals, reported that inverted or noncontingent aversive conditioning was found to be as effective as straight aversive conditioning. Carlin and Armstrong reported that smokers treated in a noncontingent shock group showed significantly greater reduction in smoking than smokers treated according to a traditional aversive condition paradigm. McConaghy and Barr found that homosexuals who received inverted conditioning (i.e., for whom shock cessation was paired with onset of a "male" slide) improved as much as homosexuals who received standard aversive conditioning.

Whether learning theory explanations were adequate was also being questioned with other behavior therapy techniques. For example, the mechanisms underlying such techniques as flooding or implosion therapy were questioned. In flooding, phobic clients are asked to image extremely intense phobic scenes; for example, a snake phobic may be asked to image being attacked and consumed by hundreds of snakes. Marks, Boulougouris, and Marset reported a study in which they asked clients instead to image any intense emotional scene that was not related to the phobic scene, such as being attacked in a zoo by an escaped tiger (1971). They found that such anxiety-engendering thoughts that were unrelated to the phobic target behavior were equally effective in reducing fears. Such results severely questioned learning theory's "extinction" explanation of flooding.

In another behavior therapy procedure, called thought-stoppage, an obsessive client is trained to self-instruct himself by saying "stop" or to self-administer an electric shock while having obsessive thoughts. Marks reported that therapy that taught the obsessive client to use the thought-stopping procedure with nonobsessive or neutral thoughts was just as effective as therapy teaching thought stoppage with obsessive thoughts (1973).

Another behavior therapy procedure that is based on a learning theory contiguity model is Cautela's covert sensitization technique, in which the client is asked to pair two thoughts or images (1973). For example, a client who wishes to stop smoking is instructed to imagine the following:

> As soon as you start reaching for the cigarette, you get a nauseous feeling in your stomach, like you are about to vomit. You touch the package and bitter spit comes into your mouth. When you take the cigarette out of the pack, some pieces of food come into your throat. Now you feel sick and have stomach cramps. As you are about to put the cigarette in your mouth, you puke all over the cigarettes, all over your hand. The cigarette in your hand is very soggy and full of green vomit. Snots are coming from your nose. Your clothes are full of puke. . . . (Cautela, 1973, p. 23)

This "conditioning" process of contiguously pairing the two images of smoking and vomiting *supposedly* results in a significant reduction of the maladaptive behavior. I say supposedly because in a recent review of covert conditioning studies Mahoney concluded, "Notwithstanding the extensive use of covert conditioning in behavior modification, controlled empirical evaluations and refinements have lagged embarrassingly behind clinical applications" (1974). Moreover, several investigators found that a *backward* covert sensitization technique in which aversive scenes were imaged prior to symbolic rehearsal of the undesired behaviors were as effective as the standard covert sensitization (Ashem & Donner, 1968; Sachs & Ingram, 1972). That is, these studies were showing that a conditioning paradigm involving covert events was inadequate in explaining behavioral change.

Our results in the anxiety-relief study, which indicated the inadequacy of a conditioning explanation, seemed to be contributing to a trend of questioning the so-called basic "laws of learning." A conceptual shift emphasizing the role of cognitive processes seemed to be occurring (see Breger & McGaugh, 1965; Bolles, 1975; Dember, 1974; Estes, 1974; McKeachie, 1974; Mahoney, 1974).

If learning theory concepts were open to question as explanations for behavior therapy procedures, then where should one look for alternatives? One source of hypotheses was our clients. We had queried the clients who had received the anxiety-relief procedures and their answers proved quite informative, especially the clients in the inverted anxiety-relief group. They indicated that when the therapist said "snake" they would emit aloud coping self-statements in order to prepare themselves for the forthcoming electric shock. Indeed, they were learning sets of coping skills to deal with the stressor (shock). The expression of the supposedly fear-engendering self-statements that terminated the shock essentially was perceived as a communication to the therapist to turn off the shock. What seemed to be happening was that the subjects were learning a set of coping skills that could be employed *across* situations, including confronting the phobic object. Interestingly, the clients in Marks' studies also reported that they viewed the behavior therapy procedures as forms of self-regulation or coping training, which they could employ in other stressful situations (Marks *et al.*, 1971; Marks, 1973). As we will see in the next chapter, the clients' observations, as well as the other studies reviewed in this chapter, suggested to us the clinical potential of systematically teaching such coping skills, a procedure we have come to call stress-inoculation training.

Another possible source for an explanation of the results from the various behavior therapy procedures is a variety of social psychological theories, including social learning theory, dissonance theory, attribution theory, and self-perception theory. A common element to many of these approaches is an emphasis on the client's appraisal of the therapeutic process and on his perceptions and abilities to cope. Perhaps these processes were best summarized by Murray and Jacobson, who suggested that what a client learns in behavior therapy is a complex set of cognitive and behavioral skills that include (1) changes in nonadaptive beliefs, which occur by means of a succession of non-confirming experiences in the therapeutic interaction (and I would add, as a result of graded task assignments in real life); (2) changes in one's self-concept and in the belief he has about others, which occur by means of information learning; and (3) the development of new problem-solving skills and new interpersonal behavioral skills (1971). The value of Murray and Jacobson's analysis can be illustrated by examining several behavior therapy procedures in detail.

Systematic Densensitization

In systematic desensitization the fearful patient, while deeply relaxed, is asked to imagine a series of progressively more fearsome situations that fall along a continuum. According to its developer, Wolpe, the two responses of relaxation and fear are incompatible and as a result, fear is dispelled. The adequacy of this counterconditioning explanation of desensitization has been questioned by a number of people (Davison & Wilson, 1973; Locke, 1971; Weitzman, 1967; Wilkins, 1971). One source of evidence that cognitive factors play a central role in the desensitization process is offered by investigators who have conducted direct observations of Wolpe's therapy sessions. For example, Brown indicates the role cognitive factors played in Wolpe's desensitization of a young married woman who felt fear and disgust at the sight of male genitals (1967). Consistent with the desensitization treatment regimen, Wolpe instructed her to visualize a series of scenes along a fear hierarchy. Such visualized scenes as seeing "a naked little boy at a distance of 50 yards, then a nude male statue at varying distances," and so on contributed to the woman's overcoming her fear. However, Brown reported that following the imagined scenes the woman reported, "You know, I thought to myself, 'Isn't it silly, why should I let that statue bother me? . . . It's not alive, it's just a piece of stone, it shouldn't concern me!' " (p. 857). Other comments offered by the patient during the session also implicated the important role of cognitive factors in terms of a changed attitude contributing to behavior change. Similar observations of the role of cognitive factors in Wolpe's use of desensitization have been offered by Klein, Dittmann, Parloff, and Gill (1969) and Sloan, Staples, Cristol, Yorkston, and Whipple (1975).[19] However, the purpose of the present discussion is not to rehash the arguments concerning how to best explain changes following from desensitization but rather to indicate how someone with a cognitive-behavioral orientation would alter the basic desensitization format in order to more explicitly employ the client's cognitions.

Relaxation Component

After reviewing the literature on desensitization, Rachman (1967) concluded that the major contribution of relaxation to the desensitization process is a matter of *mental* rather than physical relaxation. If Rachman's conclusion is correct, then the therapist could enhance the mental relaxation processes in desensitization, through instructions

---

[19] Indeed, one of the lessons we should learn from such observational studies of desensitization is that the theory offered to explain a procedure and what a therapist does in therapy to implement or operationalize those constructs do not often correlate. I wonder how much journal space would have been saved arguing about the merits of "counterconditioning" and "reciprocal inhibition" if these observational studies had been reported sooner.

to his client such as the following:

> You can deepen the relaxation and relax away feelings of
> tension by thinking silently to yourself the words, "relax"
> and "calm," as you relax. Think or picture these words to
> yourself as you slowly exhale. This is especially helpful be-
> tween sessions when you practice relaxing or whenever you
> feel tension and anxiety.

A number of years ago, Yates described a similar process under the title "association set technique" (1946). Essentially, this involved helping the client to relax by thinking of a soothing word, such as "calm," or a pleasant image.
Clients were encouraged to rehearse concentrating on the
key word or image, such as a peaceful landscape, while
relaxed and to summon up the word or image in disturbing
situations to counteract stress. After Cautela taught clients
to say to themselves, "I am calm and relaxed," especially in
anticipation of a stressful situation, the clients reported that
"in a while the mere words calmed them down" (1966).
Kahn, Baker, and Weiss (1968) used a similar procedure in
the treatment of insomniacs and Chappell and Stevenson
(1936) successfully treated peptic ulcer patients by having
them imagine a pleasant scene whenever they experienced
anxiety.

Imaginal Component

In addition to altering the relaxation involved in desensitization, the imaginal component of the treatment can also
be improved by including self-instructions. In standard desensitization treatment, the client is instructed to imagine an
anxiety-provoking scene while relaxed. If he experiences
anxiety he signals the therapist, who then instructs the client
to terminate the image and to continue relaxing.

Rather than invoking a counterconditioning explanation for the procedure, if one views the desensitization process from a cognitive viewpoint, the clients are in fact
providing themselves with a covert model for their own
behavior when they imagine scenes from the anxiety-

provoking hierarchy. Then one should alter the desensitization treatment to make the best use of imagery. If the covert modeling notion has any merit, then we should be able to enhance treatment generalization by increasing the degree of similarity between the imagined scenes and the real-life situations. This can be accomplished by employing what I have come to call "coping" imagery, instead of the "mastery" imagery that is usually employed in standard desensitization. Recall that in the standard desensitization procedure as described by Wolpe there is never any suggestion to the client that he may falter or have to "cope" with anxiety in the criterion situation. Indeed, as soon as the client experiences any anxiety while imagining scenes, the therapist asks him to terminate the scene.

In contrast to the standard desensitization procedure, a cognitive-behavior modification approach to desensitization employs coping imagery. The coping-imagery procedure requires that while visualizing a scene from the hierarchy, the client is to see himself coping with anxiety by slow deep breaths, relaxation, and self-instructions. In other words, in the coping-imagery procedure the client visualizes both the experience of anxiety and also ways to handle and reduce this anxiety.

The coping-imagery procedure can be used in two situations. First, if the client imagines a scene from a standard hierarchy and signals the therapist that he is anxious, the therapist can have the client continue imagining the scene while seeing himself using the coping techniques to reduce the anxiety. For example, upon receiving the client's signal of anxiety, the therapist can say:

> See yourself coping with this anxiety by use of the breathing procedures that we have practiced. See yourself taking a slow deep breath, slowly filling your chest cavity. Good. Now slowly exhale. As you see yourself exhaling, note the feeling of relaxation and control you have been able to bring forth. Fine. Now stop the image and just relax.

A second means of employing coping imagery is by the therapist's including tenseness and anxiety in his presentation of an image to the client. Then, the therapist can also include the client's coping with these feelings and thoughts. For example, in the treatment of test anxiety the therapist can say:

> See yourself taking an important exam and as you are thumbing through the exam booklet, you feel some tenseness in the pit of your stomach. Your eyes begin to wander about the room, your thoughts wander. . . . (The therapist can employ specific instances of his client's experiences.) Now notice what you have been feeling and doing. These are the reminders, the cues to cope. (Therapist pauses.) Good. See yourself taking a slow deep breath, hold, hold. See yourself parting your lips and as you are breathing out you are telling yourself what to do. (The therapist can tailor the self-instructions and coping devices to his particular client. I have prepared a detailed manual of how to conduct such coping desensitization—Meichenbaum, 1973.)[20]

Several investigators have provided evidence that such coping procedures are more effective than mastery-based procedures (Debus, 1970; Kazdin, 1974a,b; Meichenbaum, 1971b, 1972; Wolpin & Raines, 1966). For instance, one outcome of including such coping procedures in treatment is that following treatment the client tends to view the experience of anxiety as positive rather than as debilitating (i.e., as a cue for employing his coping mechanisms). Whereas before treatment the symptoms of the client's presenting problem led to more anxiety and maladaptive behaviors, following treatment the client's symptoms are cues to cope, to function in spite of anxiety. In this way treatment generalization is built into the therapy package. The client's symptoms become the re-

[20] A similar approach has been offered by Yorkston, McHugh, Brady, Serber, and Sergeant, who treated patients with bronchial asthma with "verbal" desensitization (1974). Since some asthmatic patients become uneasy when they think about their asthma or its precipitants, Yorkston *et al.* presented the patients with various statements (e.g., "I'm very breathless," "It's difficult to breathe," etc.) while relaxed. In this way they desensitized the clients to their own self-statements. See their article for details.

minders to use the procedures he has learned in therapy.

Further clinical evidence of the use of coping procedures was offered by Meichenbaum (1972) and Wine (1970). In both studies, test-anxious students were given the Alpert-Haber anxiety test prior to and following a coping-oriented treatment. The Alpert-Haber scale includes two subscales, one reflecting debilitating and the other, facilitating anxiety. The clients who received coping training not only improved on behavioral measures such as grade-point average but also changed on *both* of the subscales of the Alpert-Haber anxiety questionnaire. Following the coping-based treatment, the test-anxious clients came to label their physiological arousal (i.e., sweaty palms, increased heart and respiratory rates, muscular tension) as *facilitative* rather than debilitative. Such physiological indicants became cues to use the coping techniques that the clients had imagined using in therapy. The physiological arousal that clients had previously labeled as totally debilitating anxiety and fear, the harbinger of further behavior deterioration, often leading to feelings of helplessness, was relabeled as eagerness to demonstrate competence, as a desire to get on with the task, as a sign to cope. Originally the cognitions mediated further arousal (e.g., "I'm really nervous; others will see it; I can't handle this") or task-irrelevant thoughts. After treatment the clients' cognitions had a coping orientation and moved the focus away from their arousal toward response alternatives. In itself, the shift in cognitions may mediate a shift in autonomic functioning.

The importance of the Meichenbaum and Wine findings is highlighted when we compare them to outcome results of standard desensitization treatment studies. In the 1972 Meichenbaum study, clients who received standard desensitization decreased in debilitating anxiety but did *not* change on facilitating anxiety. Limited changes were also noted by Johnson and Sechrest, who conducted desensitization of test-anxious subjects (1968). They failed to obtain changes in self-report on the Alpert-Haber anxiety test and Johnson and Sechrest indicated that the verbal behavior of reporting oneself as an anxious student is not dealt with directly by the desensitization procedures. Similar findings of the absence of self-report changes following desensitization were offered by Lang and his colleagues (Lang & Lazovik, 1963; Lang, Lazovik, & Reynolds, 1965). The cognitive coping approach to desensitization illustrates that the standard desensitization procedure can be both successfully modified and supplemented by treatment procedures designed to change the client's self-labeling or cognitive processes. A similar approach to desensitization by Goldfried is described in the next chapter, in which we will more fully explore the potential of a coping skills approach to therapy.

The proposed changes in the desensitization procedure are consistent with (a) observations that desensitization should be viewed as an active means of learning coping and self-control skills and (b) notions of the therapeutic value of the "work of worrying." The "work of worrying" is the anticipatory problem-solving and cognitive rehearsal that individuals employ in preparing for stress such as surgery (Marmor, 1958; Janis, 1958). The addition of self-instructional components to the desensitization procedure attempts to strengthen such skills.

Finally, a somewhat different variant of the desensitization procedure was offered by Feather and Rhoads in what they called "Dynamic Behavior Therapy" (1972). In this procedure, instead of having the client imagine real-life scenes while he is relaxed, the client is asked to picture the fantasy that often underlies the anxiety. The therapist elicits the client's fantasies by asking him what is the worst thing that could happen if he were confronted by the phobic situation. A speech-anxious client might offer the fantasy of getting so angry with himself and the audience that he loses control and hurts someone. It is to this fantasy that the client is then desensitized. Feather and Rhoads argue that in many instances the client is afraid of his own thoughts and much of the client's behavior is a learned avoidance of having such thoughts. The distinction between reality and fantasy and the control of fantasy are achieved by having the client imagine the fantasy scene in a controlled manner while relaxed.

Modeling

If one could enhance the therapeutic efficacy of desensitization by employing "coping" imagery as compared to "mastery" imagery, then could one also demonstrate the same effect with symbolic modeling? A second, more general possibility is raised by the contribution of cognitive-behavioral view to modeling, particularly in light of Bandura's analysis of the mechanisms involved in observational learning (1965, 1969). Bandura emphasized that the information that observers gain from models is converted to covert perceptual-cognitive images and covert mediating rehearsal responses that are retained by the observer and later used by him as symbolic cues to overt behaviors. A cognitive-behavior modification approach suggests that the explicit modeling of such mediating responses should facilitate the learning process.

A few examples will illustrate the manner in which modeling procedures may be changed to incorporate and emphasize the client's cognitions. The first example involves the use of coping modeling films for the treatment of adults who are afraid of snakes (Meichenbaum, 1971b). Although the implications that can be drawn from the treatment of such a circumscribed problem is limited, the study illustrates the clinical potential of a cognitive modeling treatment approach, which can be applied to more widespread clinical problems.

In a cognitive approach to modeling treatment, the therapist enhanced the perceived similarity between the observer and model by including models who demonstrated coping behaviors (i.e., initially modeling fearful behaviors, then coping behavior, and finally mastery behavior). The models began by commenting on their anxiety and fear and the physiological accompaniments (sweaty palms, increased heart rate and breathing rate, tenseness, etc.). But at the same time, the models attempted to cope with their fear by such means as instructing themselves (1) to remain relaxed and in control by such activity as slow, deep breaths, (2) to take one step at a time, (3) to maintain a determination to forge ahead and overcome their fear. The models were—to use the colloquial term—"psyching" themselves up to perform each task and upon completion of that task, they emitted self-rewarding self-statements and positive affective expressions for having performed the task. One model in the snake study talked to the snake:

> I'm going to make a deal with you. If you don't scare or hurt me, I won't scare or hurt you. . . . [And after concluding the final step, added] Wait until I tell my mom I was able to handle a snake barehanded for a full minute; she won't believe it. I'm so happy with myself. I was able to overcome my fear.

It is interesting to note that two subjects who observed this series of coping verbalizing self-statements, upon return to the posttreatment assessment room, stated aloud (in essence):

> You [referring to the snake] made a deal with her [referring to the model]; I will make you a deal, too. If you don't hurt me, I won't hurt you. I'm going to pick you up.

As in the case of desensitization, the evidence suggests that additional therapeutic benefits can be gained if models demonstrate coping rather than mastery behavior. The perceived similarity between models and observer is enhanced by having the model portray at first the maladaptive behaviors, thoughts, and feelings that are similar to those of the client. The models then demonstrate the sequence of coping skills that can be employed in overcoming the client's deficit.

The models evidence not only desirable behaviors but also coping cognitions, reevaluations, and ways of coping with feelings of frustration or self-doubt. In the final stage they demonstrate self-reinforcing statements.

The model's cognitions can be included in videotaped presentations in many ways. In each case, the observing client is told that the model was asked to share his thoughts or think aloud as he was performing the task. In one instance the model can talk aloud to himself while performing the task. Another possibility is having the videotaped model perform the task but have the cognitions presented off camera. At present there has been little research to indicate the best procedures for conducting such treatment.[21]

Another illustration of a cognitive modeling procedure is provided by the work of Sarason on test anxiety (1973). Sarason had models explicitly demonstrate the process by which they arrived at overt responses. He found that the opportunity to observe a model who verbalized general principles while working on an anagram task resulted in high test-anxiety subjects' solving anagrams more quickly than low test-anxiety subjects. The Sarason models, while doing an anagram task, used such verbalizations as: "I want to be sure not to let myself get stuck on just one approach to letter combinations. At times it looks like a hopeless group of letters, but I'm sure I'll hit on something."

Richardson developed a semiautomated, self-study

[21] Note that care should be taken in setting up a coping model sequence, for the research on vicarious emotional conditioning has indicated that the negative affective expression by models can serve as powerful arousal cues that interfere with subsequent performance (Bandura, 1969; Berger, 1962). Thus care should be taken in how the coping model manifests initial fearfulness and subsequent coping responses. Bandura and Barab point out that one could capitalize on the motivational benefits of the similarity between the model and client, without exacerbating fear arousal, by presenting the similarity historically (1973). The client could be told that the fearless model was a person who had previously suffered similar fears that were eliminated through treatment. This procedure approximates the therapy regimen employed in self-help groups. (See Meichenbaum, 1971b, for a description of procedural guidelines of modeling treatment of avoidance behavior.)

manual to teach cognitive coping skills to high test-anxiety students (1973). Bruch examined the variables of mastery and coping modeling in the treatment of interview anxiety in psychiatric inpatients and also found the coping condition more effective than the mastery condition (1975).

Such observational opportunities promote restructuring of the client's thought processes. The inclusion and modeling of covert responses related to performance seem to enhance the change process. More research will allow us to tailor the particular modeling technology to individual clients. It is possible, for example, that with children a mastery model may prove more effective than a coping model in helping overcome fears (see Kornhaber & Schroeder, 1975), although a recent study by Melamed and Siegel indicated that a coping modeling film was useful in reducing children's anxiety in facing hospitalization and surgery (1975). Recall the studies by Jabichuk and Smeriglio and Gottman *et al.* described in Chapter 2 as other instances in which a coping model has been successfully employed with children.

In the treatment of adults, Kazdin showed that the coping modeling procedure could be extended to imaginal or covert modeling (1974a,b). The modeling cues are presented to the client by means of instructions and the client imagines a model engaging in the various behaviors. Kazdin found that an imaginary coping model was more effective than an imagined mastery model.

Modeling provides the therapist with an opportunity to include in therapy the thoughts and feelings the client is likely to experience. The therapist can show the client several models coping with their urges and exerting self-control. This exposure serves several purposes: it teaches specific cognitive and behavioral skills, it provides models of others who have mastered their problems and demonstrates the reinforcements that they accrue, and it alerts the client to the style of thinking he may likely engage in. Thus, when he has such thoughts they will have a "déjà vu" flavor (namely, "those are the thoughts that we discussed in therapy. They are the reminders to cope").

Two further examples illustrate the way in which a cognitive coping model can be used in therapy. The first example deals with the problem of assertion training and the second, with weight control.

Assertion

In the late 1950s the major behavioral response studied in clinical doctoral dissertations was the verbalization of plural pronouns (or alternatively verbs or nouns) within an operant conditioning framework designed to study the role of awareness. In the early 1960s the major target behavior was avoidant behaviors (e.g., picking up phobic objects) in desensitization studies. It appears that assertiveness is the target behavior of the late 1960s and 1970s for doctoral dissertation study. One cannot attend a conference or visit a bookstore without being bombarded with advice designed for every conceivable population on how to become more assertive. The books play on such themes as "If you can't and you want to, but you're not sure, and maybe you would like to, so why don't you try, and this is how to" or "A guide to . . . [you fill in your problem]."

My concern with these "tomes" is that as psychologists we are behaving like the impulsive children I described earlier. We respond quickly and likely make many errors. We offer advice to change behaviors before we fully understand them. I can illustrate this point (and how to avoid the pitfall) by the work of Schwartz and Gottman (1974). In trying to understand the nature of social anxiety or low assertiveness, they conducted a *task analysis* of the behavioral deficit. They identified groups of low-assertive and high-assertive individuals and then conducted multiple assessments in order to discern the role cognitive factors might play in the behavioral deficit. They found that low-assertive individuals did not differ from their more outgoing counterparts with regard to knowledge of what was an appropriate assertive response. Moreover, when both groups were placed in a "hypothetical" behavioral role-playing situation of having a friend ask how he could handle specific assertive situations, once again the two groups did not differ in their knowledge or in the behavioral expression of assertion. Then what is the nature of the deficit? If both groups know *what* to do and *can* do it under the circumstance of a "safe" role-playing situation, then what is the nature of the initial behavioral deficit? To answer this question Schwartz and Gottman performed one more assessment. This time the assessment was in the form of role-playing in a situation that approximated a "real life" situation of the subject having imagined himself being confronted by an unreasonable request. It is in regard to this last assessment that the low-assertive, highly socially anxious subjects manifested a deficient repertoire. Why? Schwartz and Gottman did an ingenious thing. They asked the subjects. They asked them in the form of a questionnaire designed to assess the subjects' thoughts and feelings (i.e., their internal dialogues) during the respective role-playing scenes. Subjects were asked to fill out a thirty-four-item questionnaire (an Assertive Self-Statement Test, ASST), which included seventeen positive self-statements that would make it easier to refuse an unreasonable request and seventeen negative self-statements that would make it harder to refuse. For example, positive self-statements included: "I was thinking that it doesn't matter what the person thinks of me," "I was thinking that I was perfectly free to say no," "I was thinking that the request is an unreasonable one." In contrast, the negative self-statements included: "I was worried about what the other person would think about me if I refused," "I was thinking that the other person might be hurt or insulted if I refused." The subjects were asked to indicate on a scale from 1 to 5 how frequently these self-statements characterized their thoughts during the preceding assertive situations, with 1 = hardly ever and 5 = very often.

The moderate- and high-assertive subjects had significantly more positive than negative self-statements, whereas the low-assertive subjects did not differ in their positive and negative self-statements. For the high-assertive subjects there was a marked discrepancy between positive and negative self-statements and usually little doubt in their minds about the appropriateness of their actions. In contrast, the low-assertive subject could be characterized by an "internal dialogue of conflict" in which positive and negative self-statements competed against one another, interfering with interpersonal behavior.

The clinical significance of these findings was indicated in treatment studies by Glass (1974) and Shmurak (1974), who found that cognitive modeling therapy in the form of the alteration of self-statements was most effective in reducing nonassertiveness. Specifically, Glass and Shmurak compared the relative effectiveness of coaching and rehearsal versus cognitive self-statement modification in enhancing dating skills in girl-shy college males. They found that the cognitive self-statement intervention caused the greatest transfer effects to untrained, laboratory, role-playing situations and to ratings made by females whom the subjects called for dates.

The subjects in the Glass and Shmurak studies were trained to become aware of the negative self-statements that they emitted, for such recognition was the signal to produce incompatible self-statements and behaviors. The training included a coach who presented the situation and then acted as a cognitive-coping model, verbalizing what he would say to himself if her were actually in the situation. This self-talk began negatively, continued with the model's realizing that he was being negative, and then switched to positive self-talk. Finally, the coach modeled giving himself verbalized reinforcement for changing his self-talk from negative to positive.

Following is an example of the training taken from Shmurak:

1. *Situation.* Let's suppose you've been fixed up on a
   blind date. You've taken her to a movie and then
   for some coffee afterwards. Now she begins to talk
   about a political candidate, some man you've never
   heard of; she says, "What do you think of him?" You
   say to yourself:
2. *Self-talk.* An example of self-talk might be: "She's
   got me now. I'd better bullshit her or she'll put me
   down. I hate politics anyway so this chick is obviously not my type . . . Boy, that's really jumping
   to conclusions. This is only one area and it really
   doesn't show what type of person she is. Anyway,
   what's the point of making up stuff about somebody
   I never heard of? She'll see right through me if I lie.
   It's not such a big deal to admit I don't know something. There are probably lots of things I know that
   she doesn't.
3. *Self talk reinforcement.* "Yeah, that's a better way
   to think about it. She's just human, trying to discuss
   something intelligently. I don't have to get scared
   or put off by her." (1974, pp. 29–30)

The Schwartz, Gottman, Glass, and Shmurak work illustrates the fact that there is substantial value in performing a careful task analysis of the nature of the behavioral
deficit, exploring the role cognitions play in contributing to
the deficit. From such an analysis, treatment interventions
naturally follow.

The Shmurak and Glass studies also illustrate how
cognitive modeling can be employed for therapeutic purposes. It is not being suggested that all low-assertive individuals will present a similar deficit profile. The point to be
underscored is that such a task analysis should be conducted before we hastily offer therapeutic advice. The differential pattern of behavioral deficit is illustrated by
Glasgow and Arkowitz, who also studied high- versus low-
dating adults (1975). They found that the main difference
between high-dating and low-dating men appeared to be

the degree to which high-dating males initiated and approached heterosexual social situations rather than any social skill differences once they are actually engaged in heterosexual interactions. Thus, among low-dating males a social skills deficit contributed less to a performance deficit than did critical self-evaluation (negative self-statements). However, in the case of low-dating females, a social skills deficit seemed to play a larger role.

In short, any attempt to teach assertive responses should carefully analyze the nature of the deficit and, where appropriate, supplement behavioral skills training with cognitive restructuring techniques. Cognitive modeling may prove to be a useful way to achieve such restructuring.

Obesity

An illustration of how cognitive modeling can be used to supplement a behavioral treatment approach was offered by Mahoney and Mahoney (1976). As part of a comprehensive treatment program to develop self-control in overweight clients, Mahoney and Mahoney included cognitive modeling of covert assertion and thought management exercises. Using the term "cognitive ecology" they trained clients "to clean up what they say to themsleves" about their weight. The Mahoneys taught their clients to become aware of such weight-relevant self-verbalizations as "I just don't have the will power," "If I don't lose my two pounds I'll never make it." Table 3 illustrates the cognitive modeling that was incorporated into a multifaceted treatment approach, which included self-monitoring of relevant behaviors, nutritional counseling, exercise management, regulation of cues that influence eating, relaxation training, self-reward training, and family support.[22]

---

[22] Pechacek (1976), Nash (1975), and Richardson (1973) employed a similar cognitive modeling approach to teach clients to cope with the stress of not smoking, to foster exercise in overweight clients, and to treat evaluation anxiety, respectively.

Table 3. Cognitive Ecology: What You Say to Yourself
(from Mahoney and Mahoney, 1976)

Problem category	Negative monologues	Appropriate monologues
1. Pounds lost	"I'm not losing fast enough." "I've starved myself and haven't lost a thing." "I've been more consistent than Mary and she is losing faster than I am—it's not fair."	"Pounds don't count; if I continue my eating habits, the pounds will be lost." "Have patience—those pounds took a long time to get there. As long as they stay off permanently, I'll settle for any progress." "It takes a while to break down fat and absorb the extra water produced. I'm not going to worry about it."
2. Capabilities	"I just don't have the will power." "I'm just naturally fat." "Why should this work—nothing else has." "I'll probably just regain it." "What the heck—I'd rather be fat than miserable; besides I'm not that heavy."	"There's no such thing as 'will power'—just poor planning. If I make a few improvements here and there and take things one day at a time, I can be very successful." "It's going to be nice to be permanently rid of all this extra baggage—I'm starting to feel better already."
3. Excuses	"If it weren't for my job and and the kids, I could lose weight." "It's just impossible to eat right with a schedule like mine." "I'm just so nervous all the time—I have to eat to satisfy my psychological needs." "Maybe next time . . ."	"My schedule isn't any worse than anyone else's. What I need to do is be a bit more creative in how to improve my eating." "Eating doesn't satisfy psychological problems—it creates them." "Job, kids, or whatever, I'm the one in control."
4. Goals	"Well, there goes my diet. That coffee cake probably cost me two pounds, and after I promised myself—no more sweets."	"What is this—the Olympics? I don't need perfect habits, just improved ones." "Why should one sweet or an extra portion blow it for me?"

Table 3. (Continued)

Problem category	Negative monologues	Appropriate monologues
	"I always blow it on the weekends." "Fine—I start the day off with a doughnut. I may as well enjoy myself today."	I'll cut back elsewhere." "Those high standards are unrealistic." "Fantastic—I had a small piece of cake and it didn't blow the day."
5. Food thoughts	"I can't stop thinking about sweets." "I had images of cakes and pies all afternoon—it must mean that I need sugar." "When we order food at a restaurant, I continue thinking about what I have ordered until it arrives."	"Whenever I find myself thinking about food, I quickly change the topic to some other pleasant experience." "If I see a magazine ad or commercial for food and I start thinking about it, I distract my attention by doing something else (phoning a friend, getting the mail, etc.)."

By including cognitions in behavioral modeling, as the Mahoneys did, the therapist is able to encourage the client to covertly recognize his own maladaptive thoughts, feelings, and behaviors when they occur. In effect, this results in the client's becoming vigilant for the signals that tell him he should use the behavior-altering skills that he has learned in therapy.

Aversive Conditioning

Somewhat related to the anxiety-relief conditioning treatment paradigm discussed earlier is aversive conditioning, which can also be modified to include the client's self-statements. Typically, aversive conditioning involves showing the client a taboo stimulus or its representation (e.g., a slide) and when the client responds (as indicated by physiological measures of arousal) he is shocked. Shock is terminated by the reduction of autonomic arousal or by an instrumental response such as choosing another slide. In some paradigms the onset and offset of shock is made contingent upon the start and termination of an instrumental act such as drinking alcohol or smoking. The aversive conditioning can be expanded to include the client's self-statements. For example, if we were treating a child molester by means of aversive conditioning and the conditioned stimuli were slides of young children, the therapist could make the onset of shock contingent upon the meaningful expression of the set of self-statements and descriptive images, feelings, and fantasies the client experiences when confronted by a real child. Shock offset could then be made contingent upon incompatible self-statements which might involve self-instructions that he is mistaking his arousal as sexual, or that he should remove himself from the playground, or that he is not that kind of person.

Illustrative of the cognitive-behavioral approach to aversive conditioning is a study conducted by Steffy, Meichenbaum, and Best (1970). They treated a group of smokers by altering the aversive conditioning paradigm to include the clients' cognitions in the form of images and self-statements. While smoking, clients imagined themselves in "real-life" situations in which they smoked and at some point during the simultaneous acts of imagining and smoking, the client received electric shock. The client terminated the shock by putting out the cigarette while emitting some personally selected self-statements, such as not wanting a "cancer weed." The subjects in this cognitively-oriented aversive conditioning group showed significantly more reduction in smoking behavior following treatment and at a two- and six-month follow-up periods than did comparison treatment groups.

The value of including such cognitive activity as covert rehearsal behavioral treatment programs has been indicated by a number of investigators. For example,

McFall and Lillesand examined the use of behavioral rehearsal therapy in developing assertion-refusal behavior
(1971). The behavioral rehearsal therapy consisted of three
main components: overt or covert practice, symbolic verbal
modeling, and therapist coaching. They found that covert
rehearsal in the form of imagining or reflecting about possible responses was more effective than behavioral rehearsal.
The covert rehearsal procedures consistently resulted in
the largest absolute magnitude of improvement. McFall
and Lillesand indicated that one drawback of the overt
condition is the nature of the feedback the subject receives,
which may have an unexpected inhibiting effect on learning. Also to the extent that a subject's response is inadequate, it would be punitive to confront him with such
feedback. In contrast, the covert procedure protects subjects from an external evaluation, minimizes avoidance behavior and emotional reactions, and thus fosters learning.

In both the Steffy *et al.* and the McFall and Lillesand
studies, covert rehearsal in the form of imagining supplemented and enhanced the behavior therapy procedure of
aversive conditioning and assertive training, respectively.

Value of Mental Rehearsal

Richardson, in his review of the mental practice literature, indicated that in a variety of different physical tasks,
subjects improved their performance after spending varying amounts of time in "thinking about" or imagining
themselves in the act of performing (1967a,b).

Several hypotheses have been forwarded to explain
the facilitating effect of mental rehearsal, although, as Corbin has indicated, much research is needed to tease apart
the alternatives that have been offered (1972). Steffy *et al.*
suggested that the inclusion of imagining or mental rehearsal (a) leads to a better representation of the implicit
stimuli that contributed to the maladaptive behavior, (b)
involves many more different situational cues in the train-

ing, and (c) causes greater emotional involvement. Interestingly, an analysis of the role of mental rehearsal in the acquisition of motor skills and in sport psychology has implicated similar processes. Corbin indicated that mental practice may contribute to improved motor skills performance because it provides the learner initially with a gross outline of the skill, the "gestalt," or entirety of the task rather than concentrating on details (1972). With the development of task proficiency, mental practice permits selective attention to the important elemental skills or the important details of the desired act.

The importance of internalizing a very clear model of the criterion performance is indicated by the fact that the more familiar a task has become the greater the relative gain that can be expected from mental practice. Thus, an examination of the many variables that have been found to be of importance in the research area of mental practice is likely to be of importance to cognitive-behavior therapists. These variables include the degree of task familiarity, accuracy of anticipated outcomes, clarity and control of imagery, degree of proficiency on the task, length of time provided for imagery, and the alternation of mental and physical practice.

A number of investigators are beginning to explore the usefulness of cognitive training (imagery, self-verbalizations) in the training of athletes. Ski racers, gymnasts, and golfers have been subjected to cognitive-behavior modification procedures. For example, Anderson and Carter have used cognitive practice with golfers and self-monitoring and social feedback in a physical fitness class (1976). Suinn (1972) used mental rehearsal training with skiers and Mahoney (personal communication) has explored cognitive strategies of gymnasts. The study of changes in cognitive strategies in athletes as well as others, such as chess players (DeGroot, 1965), raises some fascinating possibilities. Given that most athletic events entail learned behaviors and complex skill chains, they provide an interesting opportunity to discover what happens to cognitions with the acquisition of skills.

Before concluding my comments on the role of cognitive factors in behavior therapy procedures, I would like to share one other set of reactions that my presentation has elicited in the past. The focus of the cognitive training described so far in this book has been on teaching various classes of clients (hyperactive children, phobics, anxious patients, schizophrenics) to *talk* to themselves, to use *intentional* images, or to provide the experimental and therapeutic conditions under which an internal dialogue may change. Ostensibly in opposition to this approach is an orientation that teaches clients, athletes, and others to *stop* their internal dialogues, to eliminate self-verbalizations. The quote of Castenada that I offered in the prologue, concerning internal talk, underscores this point. Don Juan admonishes us to stop the internal talk. A similar edict has recently been offered in various forms to athletes (e.g., Gallwey, 1974, to tennis players; Lund, 1975, to skiers). Upon closer examination this popular approach is also basically concerned with cognitions. However, in contrast to the deliberate, conscious speech and images that we have considered, an attempt is made to foster an environment for the occurrence only of images with the activity. The images are supposed to occur with little effort and without conscious direction, and all internal dialogue or self-verbalizations are to stop. For example, a training approach that highlights the importance of mental imagery or visualization rehearsal in the acquisition of athletic skills was offered by Gallwey in *The Inner Game of Tennis* (1974). Gallwey described how one can enhance the teaching process by having the novice tennis buff carefully observe the instructor perform certain strokes with the student not thinking about what the instructor is doing in any analytic sense. He should simply try to grasp a visual image of the stroke. Following this, the student is to repeat the image in his mind several times and then "just let his body imitate."

Gallwey's approach differed from the more traditional functional approach, which involved the acquisition of various
subskills. Instead, in Gallwey's approach there is a demonstration of the entire maneuver, followed by previsualiza-
tion (the learner's seeing himself in his mind's eye successfully performing and approximating the maneuver).
Gallwey advises throughout that the student should employ visual imagery and engage in a "benign period of verbal neglect" as he more closely approximates the demonstration. Note that such an approach is consistent with the
cognitive-behavior modification approach of covert modeling which was described. Moreover, the focus of Gallwey's
advice is on what one should do in terms of one's attention
while performing a behavioral act, such as hitting the ball.
What one says to oneself before engaging in the tennis
match or following it is usually not commented upon.

The description of the imagery procedures is usually
couched in terms deriving from a Zen philosophy, including "being one with the act" or "not thinking"—where
thinking refers to self-verbalizations. But wait a second.
How did we get to tennis and Zen in a chapter on cognitive
factors in behavior therapy? The point is that there are a
variety of different ways to employ cognitions—both verbal
and imaginal—in the acquisition of skills, whether these
skills involve overcoming a clinical problem or learning a
motor skill such as in sports. As I will discuss in subsequent
chapters, we need to study the different ways that cognitions can be conceptualized and employed in explaining
behavior change. We may come to find that certain types of
imagery procedures or certain types of self-instructional
approaches are more useful than others. The important
point is that we need to recognize that such cognitive processes play a central role in therapies, including behavior
therapies.

Bolles, in summarizing the historical trends of cognitive viewpoints, indicates that psychology has always been
more or less cognitive in outlook (1975). Except for a recent
turn to mechanistic philosophy, the general concern has

been with the nature and role of cognition. Bolles (1975), Dember (1974), and Mahoney (1974) have each noted a turnaround from the brief flirtation with a mechanistic approach to behavior, back to a cognitive orientation.

To further underscore the role of cognitive factors, let us permit various behavior therapists to speak for themselves. A number of investigators have made comments that converge to suggest that the alteration of the client's self-statement may represent a common mediator of the behavioral change brought about by many of these behavior therapy techniques. For example, Lang suggested that systematic desensitization is:

> designed to shape the response, 'I am not afraid' (or a potentially competing response such as, 'I am relaxed') in the presence of a graded set of discriminative stimuli. When well learned, the response could have the status of a 'set' or self-instruction, which can then determine other mediated behavior. (1969, p. 187)

Similarly, Geer and Turtletaub hypothesized that self-statements (such as, "If the other client can do it, so can I") may mediate the behavior change derived from a modeling procedure (1967). Marks *et al.* reported that following flooding, some clients spontaneously reported talking themselves out of feelings; others reported that they found it helpful to remind themselves that reality was never as bad as the horrors of fantasy; still others indicated that they had used self-challenging self-statements (e.g., "I'll show him" [the therapist] to bolster their endurance during and after flooding) (1971). Davison (1968) and Valins and Ray (1967) provided further instances of self-instruction's being identified as a potential mediating mechanism of behavioral change. Thus, there is a suggestion that each of these therapy procedures operates by means of modifying the client's self-statements. If the hypothesis that the client's self-instructions mediate behavior change is valid, one would expect that explicit self-instructional training would enhance treatment effectiveness. The studies reviewed in this chapter have confirmed this hypothesis.

Stress-Inoculation Training

If your stomach disputes you lie down and pacify it with cool thoughts.

—SATCHEL PAIGE

By now, it should be apparent that something is happening to behavior therapy. Its "learning theory" basis is being challenged and is being replaced, in part by a cognitive orientation. The conceptual basis of "learning theory" that provided the framework and heuristic background for a variety of behavior therapy procedures is being oppugned on both theoretical grounds (e.g., Bandura, 1974; Breger & McGaugh, 1965; McKeachie, 1974) and empirical grounds (e.g., Brewer, 1974; Mahoney, 1974; Meichenbaum, 1974a). Such time-honored concepts as the automaticity of reinforcement and the continuity assumption between overt and covert events are being seriously questioned. As Bandura stated in his presidential address to the American Psychological Association:

> So-called conditioned reactions are largely self-activated on the basis of learned expectations rather than automatically evoked. The critical factor, therefore, is not that events occur together in time, but that people learn to predict them and to summon up appropriate reactions. (1974, p. 860)

Questioning the adequacy of "learning theory" and introducing cognitive processes have caused changes in how we view behavior therapy procedures. Behavior therapy is shifting from an emphasis on discrete, situation-specific responses and problem-specific procedures to a concern with coping skills that can be applied across response modalities, situations, and problems. For example, instead of viewing systematic desensitization as a therapy procedure designed to countercondition separately each of the client's fears, one can view it as an instance in which a client learns a set of coping skills that can be applied across a number of fearful situations. Illustrative of this approach is Goldfried's self-control approach to desensitization, in which he teaches his clients a broad set of self-relaxation skills that can be employed while imagining a number of scenes from different hierarchies (1971). Thus, while the client is relaxed he will be asked to image scenes from various hierarchies and imagine himself coping with each of these fear-inducing scenes by such means as self-instructing and stimulus-labeling strategies. Contrast such a skills-oriented treatment approach with the "learning theory" stimulus-response, identical-elements-based description of desensitization offered by Wolpe:

> Unless different hierarchies have *unmistakable common features* desensitization to one hierarchy does not in the least diminish the reactivity to another (untreated) hierarchy. (1961, p. 201, emphasis added)

Within the Wolpeian desensitization framework, the degree of treatment generalization is a function of the stimulus gradient or the number of identical elements that occur across situations or hierarchies. Within a self-control-skills framework, the degree of treatment generalization is a function of the common set of coping responses that are emitted across situations, including, as we will see, self-instructional responses. In other words, the degree of consistency of behavior across situations (or treatment generalization) is a function of the likelihood that the same set of covert mediators will be elicited. Thus, training clients to emit a set of coping responses, including self-instructional, imaginal, and behavioral, across stress-inducing situations will likely enhance generalization. Lang noted that "the absence of programs for shaping cognitive sets and attitudes may contribute to the not infrequent failure of transfer of treatment effects" (1968, p. 94).

Coping Skills Techniques

It was mainly in attempting to enhance treatment generalization that a number of investigators developed threrapy procedures concerned with skills training. The investigations of Goldfried and his colleagues illustrate one such approach to training coping skills (Goldfried, 1971, 1973; Goldfried et al., 1974; Goldfried & Trier, 1974). For example, in the coping skills version of desensitization, Goldfried emphasizes four components: (1) describing the therapeutic rationale in terms of skills training, (2) the use of relaxation as a generalized coping strategy, (3) use of multiple theme hierarchies, and (4) training in "relaxing away" scene-induced anxiety and the accompanying use of stimulus labeling and self-instructional training (1971). Empirical support for the efficacy of a skills-oriented approach to desensitization has been offered by Goldfried and Davison (1976), Meichenbaum (1972), and Spiegler et al. (1976). Recently, Goldfried et al. (1974) developed a coping skills approach, labeled "systematic rational restructuring," which incorporates rational-emotive therapy (Ellis, 1962) within a behavioral framework. Goldfried et al. argued that the way an individual labels or evaluates a situation determines his subsequent emotional reactions. Thus an individual can acquire a more effective coping repertoire by learning to modify his cognitive "set" in dealing with anxiety-provoking situations. A five-step treatment procedure is employed to teach the coping skills. These include (1) exposing the client to anxiety-provoking situations by means of imagery and/or role-playing, (2) requiring the client to evaluate his anxiety level, (3) noticing the anxiety-provoking cognitions he is experiencing in the situation, (4) rationally reevaluating these cognitions or self-statements, and, finally, (5) noting the level of anxiety following the rational reevaluation.

A skills-training approach similar to Goldfried *et al.* has been offered by Langer, Janis, and Wolper who successfully trained surgery patients to use coping devices such as cognitive reappraisal of anxiety-provoking events, calming self-talk, and cognitive control through selective attention (1975). The surgery patients were told that people are somewhat anxious before an operation but that people can often control their emotions if they know how to. It was explained that it is rarely events themselves that cause stress but rather the views people take of them and the attention they give to these views. Consistent with these introductory remarks, patients were given several examples from everyday life of alternative ways of viewing negative events, including undergoing surgery. Patients were asked to rehearse realistic, positive aspects of the surgical experience. Such training of reappraisal skills, combined with preparatory information concerning postsurgery discomforts and operative care, resulted in significant reduction of postsurgical distress, as indicated by nurses' observations, requests for sedatives, and length of hospital stay.

Another approach to coping-skills training, called anxiety management training, was developed by Suinn and Richardson (Richardson, 1973; Suinn, 1972; Suinn & Richardson, 1971). As in the Goldfried approach, anxiety management training emphasizes relaxation training as an active coping skill. The training involves the application of such skills to anxiety-engendering imaginal scenes, which may be unrelated to the client's particular problem. Instead of being desensitized to a particular set of stimulus events the client is trained to emit coping responses to a variety of anxiety-engendering events.

Such coping-skills training approaches have been successfully applied in a number of different problem areas. These include speech anxiety (Meichenbaum, Gilmore, & Fedoravicius, 1971), test anxiety (Sarason, 1973), phobias (Meichenabum & Cameron, 1972b; Tori & Worrell, 1973), anger (Novaco, 1975a), social incompetence (Christensen, 1974; Glass, 1974; Kazdin, 1973; Shmurak, 1974), alcoholism (Sanchez-Craig, 1975, 1976), social withdrawal in children (Gottman *et al.*, 1974), and laboratory and clinical pain (Turk, 1975, 1976; Langer *et al.*, 1975; Levendusky & Pankratz, 1975).

Certain common treatment components underlie these many different coping-skills programs. The components include: (1) teaching the client the role of cognitions in contributing to the presenting problem, through both didactic presentation (often in the form of Socratic dialogue) and guided self-discovery; (2) training in the discrimination and systematic observation of self-statements and images, and in self-monitoring of maladaptive behaviors; (3) training in the fundamentals of problem-solving (e.g., problem definition, anticipation of consequences, evaluating feedback); (4) modeling of the self-statements and images associated with both overt and cognitive skills; (5) modeling, rehearsal, and encouragement of positive self-evaluation and of coping and attentional focusing skills; (6) the use of various behavior therapy procedures, such as relaxation training, coping imagery training, and behavioral rehearsal; (7) *in vivo* behavioral assignments that become increasingly demanding.

Thus, a complex multifaceted training procedure is employed to teach coping skills. When we consider the nature of the coping response to stress it becomes evident that a varied treatment program is indeed required. A number of investigators have commented on the complexity of the coping process (Murphy, 1962; Janis, 1965; Meichenbaum, Turk, & Burstein, 1975). For example, Janis suggested that a successful program to increase tolerance for an impending stressful situation requires (1) preparatory communication regarding the situation to be experienced and the probable results; (2) reassuring statements, which indicate how the potentially aversive consequences will be kept under control or mitigated; (3) recommendations of what can be done to protect the individual or reduce the damaging impact of the potential changes; and (4) the belief or expectation that these recommendations will be effective in reducing the threat. Put even more simply is Haggard's admonition:

> A person is able to act realistically and effectively in a stressful situation only if he knows the nature and seriousness of the threat, knows what to do, and is able to do it. (1949)

After reviewing the stress literature in 1975, Meichenbaum *et al.* suggested the following guidelines for training coping skills:

1. Coping devices are complex and need to be flexibile. Coping devices that are successful in one situation may be quite unsuccessful in another situation, or even in the same situation at another time. Thus, any coping-skills training approach should be flexible enough to incorporate a variety of cognitive and behavioral strategies that can be differentially employed.
2. Consistent with a call for flexibility is the need for any training technique to be sensitive to individual differences, cultural differences, and situational differences.
3. Skills training should encourage the utilization of available information and the incorporation of potentially threatening events into cognitive plans. To be effective, information should stimulate mental

rehearsal or the "work of worrying" which may "short-circuit" the experience of stress or reduce its aftereffects (Marmor, 1958; Janis, 1958; Lazarus & Alfert, 1964).

4. Actual exposure during training to less threatening stressful events has a beneficial effect. *stress inoculation*

With regard to this last point, Epstein cogently highlighted the importance of "self-pacing" in the development of coping skills (1967). Epstein argued that adaptive defenses differ from maladaptive defenses in that the former allow mastery to proceed by dealing with threatening material in small doses, while defending against excessive exposure that would be overwhelming. Adaptive defenses or coping skills allow paced mastery to occur, which provides "inoculation" against greater intensities of threat. In contrast, maladaptive defenses or inadequate coping skills operate more in an all-or-none fashion, completely shutting out the awareness of threat or exposing the individual to the threat in its full intensity. Epstein provides a convincing case that naturally occurring paced inoculations can be used to explain such diverse phenomena as experimental neuroses in subhuman animals, traumatic neuroses, recovery from grief in humans, and proactive mastery of stress in combat flying and in parachuting. Any skills-training procedure should pay particular attention to the value of what Epstein calls "paced defensiveness" or what we call the "systematic acquisition of coping skills." Treatment should result in the development of Epstein's "modulated control system," which evolves from learning to cope with small, manageable units of stress.

A similar conclusion was reached by Orne:

> One way of enabling an individual to become resistant to a stress is to allow him to have appropriate prior experience with the stimulus involved. The biological notion of immunization provides such a model. If an individual is given the opportunity to deal with a stimulus that is mildly stressful and he is able to do so successfully (mastering it in a

psychological sense) he will tend to be able to tolerate a
similar stimulus of somewhat greater intensity in the future.
. . . It would seem that one can markedly affect an individual's tolerance of stress by manipulating his beliefs about his
performance in the situation . . . and his feeling that he can
control his own behavior. (1965, pp. 315–316)

The stress-inoculation procedure that is described
below is the behavioral analogue of such an immunization
model. It incorporates the suggestions offered by the
studies that have been summarized.

Procedures of Stress Inoculation

Operationally, the stress-inoculation training involves
three phases. The first phase, educational in content, is designed to provide the client with a conceptual framework
for understanding the nature of his stressful reactions. The
exact content of the conceptualization offered varies with
the presenting problem. This will be illustrated when we
examine how stress-inoculation training has been applied
to such varied problems as phobic reactions, anger-control
problems, and pain tolerance. From the conceptual
framework, a number of behavioral and cognitive coping
skills are offered for the client to rehearse, in the second
phase of training. In the third phase, the client is given an
opportunity to practice his coping skills during exposure to
a variety of stressors.

I: Educational Phase

The first phase of stress-inoculation training is designed to provide the client with a conceptual framework in
lay terms, for understanding the nature of his response to
stressful events. The most important aspect of this phase is
that the conceptual framework should be plausible to the
client and its acceptance should naturally lead to the practice of specific, cognitive, and behavioral coping techniques.

Thus, the logic of the training regimen becomes more comprehensible to a client in light of the conceptualization offered.

It should be underscored that the scientific validity of a particular conceptualization is less crucial than its face validity or air of plausibility for the client. In the studies reported here, the various conceptualizations that were offered include Schachter's theory of emotion (1966) and Melzack and Wall's theory of pain (1965). Each of these theories has been duly criticized on both empirical and theoretical grounds (e.g., Averill & Opton, 1968; Chaves & Barber, 1973; Iggo, 1972; Plutchik & Ax, 1967; Trigg, 1970). The validity of these criticisms does not detract from the usefulness of the theories in helping clients construe stress reactions and in the acquisition of new coping skills. Naturally, any conceptualization must be offered with clinical sensitivity. The purpose of providing a framework is not to convince the client—perhaps against his will—that any particular explanation of his problem is valid but rather to encourage him to view his problem from a particular perspective and thus accept and collaborate in the therapy that will follow.

Indeed, I will argue in more detail in Chapter 8 that therapists, and behavior therapists in particular, have failed to pay sufficient attention to the initial conceptualization phase of therapy. What transpires between client and therapist prior to the implementation of specific treatment procedures plays an important role in understanding the change process. Whereas such interactions have been viewed as nonspecific therapy factors or have been included as aspects that go "beyond" behavior therapy, in the stress inoculation treatment the initial conceptualization phase receives much attention.

Let us now examine how a conceptualization of the client's presenting problem was employed in the initial stress-inoculation training study on multiphobic clients (see Meichenbaum & Cameron, 1972b). The study in-

volved volunteer adult subjects who had identified themselves as avoiding both harmless snakes and rats. Their age
range was from seventeen to forty-five and much care was
taken in identifying subjects who were clinically phobic, as
compared to the "typical" college sophomore population.
In virtually all cases the phobias restricted the clients' activities: the clients avoided many activities, such as camp-
ing, picnicking, attending certain movies which involved
the most remote possibility of contact with the phobic objects. The reason multiphobic subjects were included in
the study will become apparent in a moment.

Initially, all subjects underwent a behavioral assessment, which involved a graduated set of approaches to the
phobic objects. The therapist then met with the clients individually for six one-hour sessions over a four-week
period. In the initial session the therapist listened atten-
tively as the client described the extent and duration of the
phobic responses. Discussion topics included how the
client felt and what he thought about when confronted by
the phobic objects, and how he was currently coping with
stressors in general and his phobic fears in particular. In
order to help tap the nature of the client's thoughts and
feelings concerning the phobic objects, the client was
asked to close his eyes and "run a movie" of his reactions in
the pretreatment assessment situation—reporting the
thoughts and feelings that preceded, accompanied, and followed that approach task. The clients often reported such
thoughts as the following: "I can't do this, I'll lose control.
What if the snake gets out. What will they think of me. I
must be going crazy," and so on. They also described intense feelings of arousal and tenseness.

Following this assessment the therapist went on to describe the client's anxiety in terms of a Schachterian model
of emotional arousal. That is, the therapist indicated that
the client's fear reaction involved two major elements,
namely, (a) his heightened arousal (e.g., increased heart
rate, sweaty palms, rapid breathing, bodily tension, or
whatever symptoms the client had described), and (b) the

set of anxiety-engendering avoidant thoughts that the client had conveyed (e.g., disgust evoked by the phobic object, a sense of helplessness, panic thoughts of being overwhelmed by anxiety, a desire to flee, social embarrassment, fears of going crazy). After laying this conceptual groundwork for therapy in a nondidactic manner, the therapist noted in lay terms that one's self-statements while experiencing arousal are prime determinants of emotional avoidant behavior. The therapist then indicated that treatment would be directed toward: (1) helping the client control his physiological arousal and (2) changing the self-statements that habitually occupied his mind under stressful conditions.

The educational phase concluded with a discussion encouraging the client to view his phobic or stress reactions as a series of phases rather than as one massive phobic reaction. Four phases were suggested: preparing for a stressor, confronting or handling a stressor, possibly being overwhelmed by a stressor, and, finally, reinforcing oneself for having coped. The inclusion of the phase of being overwhelmed derived from the clients' concerns that even though they had received coping training, they might still be overcome by fear. Thus, practicing ways of coping with this reaction helped to alleviate and "defuse" the client's dread of losing control, of being immobilized.

In this way, the client was led to view his problem as a reaction to stress consisting of two components (i.e., arousal and the accompanying self-statements) which progressed through four stages. This was in contrast to his previous view of an all-or-nothing acute phobic attack. The client could then become sensitive to the prodromal cues signaling anxiety and could learn to short-circuit the impending threat, or use paced self-mastery techniques.

II: Rehearsal Phase

The second phase of the stress-inoculation training was designed to provide the client with a variety of coping techniques to employ at each of the various stages of the coping process. The coping techniques involved both direct actions and cognitive coping modes.

Direct action included collecting information about the phobic objects, arranging for escape routes, and learning physical relaxation exercises that would provide the basis for reducing physiological arousal. It was also pointed out that if the client used these relaxation exercises in an anxiety-provoking situation, his concentration on doing something positive about his discomfort (i.e., relaxing) would in itself tend to eliminate the negative self-statements. The relaxation exercises involved systematically tensing and relaxing various muscle groups, as outlined by Paul (1966). Emphasis was placed on the importance of control of breathing. This emphasis was suggested by Deane (1964, 1965), Westcott and Huttenlocher (1961), and Wood and Obrist (1964), who demonstrated that the amplitude and frequency of respiration has an effect on heart rate and the accompanying experience of anxiety.

Cognitive coping was introduced with the suggestion that both maladaptive and adaptive responses are mediated by sets of statements that the client says to himself. Such constructs as appraisal, expectancy, attribution, and self-perception were translated into specific self-statements which the client could rehearse at each of the four stages of the fear reaction. The modification of the client's internal dialogue was accomplished by having him become aware of, and monitor, the negative, anxiety-engendering, self-defeating self-statements he emitted in phobic situations. Noticing the occurrence of such cognitions was to be the occasion for producing incompatible, coping self-statements. It bears repeating that treatment generalization was built into this therapy package. The client's maladaptive behaviors, thoughts, and feelings became the signals, the cues for him to employ the coping techniques he learned and practiced in therapy.

The client was encouraged to offer examples of self-

statements that he could emit during each phase of a stressful event. In a collaborative fashion a package of self-
statements emerged, similar to those listed in Table 4. The
self-statements encouraged the client to (a) assess the reality of the situation; (b) control negative thoughts and images; (c) acknowledge, use, and relabel the arousal he was

---

**Table 4. Examples of Coping Self-Statements Rehearsed in
Stress-Inoculation Training (from Meichenbaum, 1974a)**

Preparing for a stressor
 What is it you have to do?
 You can develop a plan to deal with it.
 Just think about what you can do about it. That's better than getting anxious.
 No negative self-statements: just think rationally.
 Don't worry: worry won't help anything.
 Maybe what you think is anxiety is eagerness to confront the stressor.

Confronting and handling a stressor
 Just "psych" yourself up—you can meet this challenge.
 You can convince yourself to do it. You can reason your fear away.
 One step at a time: you can handle the situation.
 Don't think about fear; just think about what you have to do. Stay relevant.
 This anxiety is what the doctor said you would feel. It's a reminder to use your
  coping exercises.
 This tenseness can be an ally; a cue to cope.
 Relax; you're in control. Take a slow deep breath.
 Ah, good.

Coping with the feeling of being overwhelmed
 When fear comes, just pause.
 Keep the focus on the present; what is it you have to do?
 Label your fear from 0 to 10 and watch it change.
 You should expect your fear to rise.
 Don't try to eliminate fear totally; just keep it manageable.

Reinforcing self-statements
 It worked; you did it.
 Wait until you tell your therapist (or group) about this.
 It wasn't as bad as you expected.
 You made more out of your fear than it was worth.
 Your damn ideas—that's the problem. When you control them, you control your
  fear.
 It's getting better each time you use the procedures.
 You can be pleased with the progress you're making.
 You did it!

experiencing; (d) "psych" himself to confront the phobic situation; (e) cope with the intense fear he might experience; (f) reflect on his performance and reinforce himself for having tried. It is interesting to note that over the course of training, clients gravitated to specific combinations of self-statements, suggesting the possibility of tailoring self-instructions to a number of individual-difference dimensions.

III: Application Training

Once the client had become proficient in employing such behavioral and cognitive coping skills, the therapist suggested that the client should test out and practice his coping skills by actually employing them under stressful conditions other than the phobic situation. At this point the therapist could expose the client to a variety of ego-threatening and pain-threatening laboratory stressors in a graded fashion of exposure (e.g., unpredictable electric shocks [Meichenbaum & Cameron, 1972a; Klepac, 1975], cold pressor test [Turk, 1976], imaginary stress [Suinn, 1975], stress-inducing films [Lazarus, Averill, & Opton, 1970], failure and embarrassment situations).

In short, the therapist could convey, following the skills training phase, that things seemed to be going well and that it would prove helpful for the client to further rehearse coping skills under stress-inducing circumstances. For example, when electric shock was used for inducing anxiety, the client was told:

> Sometime in the next two or three minutes, maybe in a few seconds, maybe after three minutes, maybe somewhere in between, you will receive a shock. Just exactly how intense and exactly when you receive the shock depends on a random predetermined schedule. Try to cope with the anxiety and tenseness elicited by the situation by means of the coping techniques you have learned.

The client, who had had the nature of electric shock explained to him prior to training, was exposed to ten one-second shocks, which ranged in intensity from .5mA to 3 mA. There was an interval of one minute between shock trials. A number of investigators have demonstrated that such unpredictable shock (in terms of intensity and timing) represents a very stressful, anxiety-inducing situation. Indeed, Thornton and Jacobs used unpredictable shock to induce a state of "learned helplessness" in human subjects (1971).

The purpose of employing the shock manipulation was to provide the client with a stressful situation in which he could experiment with the variety of different coping techniques (relaxation and self-statements) that he had been taught during phase II of the stress-inoculation training. The therapist modeled how to use the various coping skills to deal with the stressor. This modeling was followed by the client's rehearsing the coping strategies, self-instructing initially aloud, and then covertly. This format followed the self-instructional training technique described in Chapter 2. Thus the application training phase permitted the rehearsal and implementation of the coping skills that were acquired during the first two phases of training. Note that clients could pick out particular coping tools in cafeteria-style, individually tailoring their coping responses.

In *summary*, stress-inoculation training involved discussing the nature of emotion and stress reactions, rehearsing coping skills, and testing these skills under actual stressful conditions. A variety of therapeutic techniques was woven into the training. These included didactic training, discussion, modeling, self-instructional and behavioral rehearsal, and reinforcement. Obviously, the stress-inoculation regimen is complex and multifaceted but this was an intentional design, in order to incorporate the guidelines suggested by Janis, Epstein, Orne, and Meichenbaum. Only future research can determine which are the necessary and sufficient conditions for promoting change. Initially, we deemed it best to bring the full clinical armamentarium to bear.

In the initial study on stress-inoculation training, the relative therapeutic efficacy of the stress-inoculation training procedure in reducing multiple phobias was determined relative to (a) a systematic desensitization group, (b) a self-instructional rehearsal group, which received the coping skills (phase I and II) but did not receive application training (phase III), and (c) a waiting list assessment control group (Meichenbaum & Cameron, 1972b).

Half the multiphobic clients were inoculated or desensitized only to rats, while the other half were inoculated or desensitized only to snakes, thus providing the means to assess the degree of treatment generalization that resulted from desensitization as compared to stress inoculation. The results indicated that the stress-inoculation training was the most effective treatment in reducing avoidance behavior and in fostering treatment generalization. The desensitization treatment proved effective in reducing fear *only* to the desensitized object. When the desensitized client was confronted with the nondesensitized object, *minimal* treatment generalization was evident. In contrast, the two self-instructionally based treatment procedures (i.e., stress-inoculation and self-instructional rehearsal) yielded treatment generalization (see Meichenbaum, 1976a, and Meichenbaum & Cameron, 1972b, for details of the study).

The finding that the desensitization group showed minimal generalization (to the nondesensitized object) is consistent with the findings of Bandura, Blanchard, and Ritter (1969), Meyer and Gelder (1963), and Wolpe (1958, 1961), who indicated that desensitization seems to alleviate only those phobias that are being treated without mitigating other coexisting phobias. In contrast, the stress-inoculation training provided a useful way of altering the phobic client's cognitive set, or what he said to himself. Typical of most phobic patients, our clients reported that prior to training they felt that they could do nothing about their debilitating fears; their pretreatment condition seemed to be one of "learned helplessness." The stress-inoculation paradigm was designed specifically to modify this attitude by training coping skills. This approach is consistent with a burgeoning literature on both animals (Mowrer & Viek, 1948; Richter, 1959; Seligman, Maier, & Solomon, 1969) and humans (Glass & Singer, 1972; Hokanson, DeGood, Forrest, & Brittain, 1971) that having some instrumental response at one's disposal and being able to perceive the relationship between one's actions and the termination of an aversive stimulus breaks this pattern of helplessness and hopelessness. R. Lazarus (1966) and Rotter (1966) have also hypothesized (from somewhat different vantage points) that the availability of coping responses will reduce stress-related responding. Following stress inoculation, the multiphobic client's perception of his condition had changed from "learned helplessness" to "learned resourcefulness." It was quite common for clients in the stress-inoculation group to report spontaneously that they had successfully applied their new coping skills in other stressful situations, including final exams and dental visits. One client even taught the procedure to his pregnant wife. The change in attitude seemed to encourage clients to initiate confrontations with real-life problems.

Positive Thinking

Before describing the application of stress-inoculation training to other clinical populations, a distinction should be drawn between the way self-statements are employed in the stress-inoculation training and the general approach of schools of so-called "positive thinking." Some of the more senior readers may recall the popularity of Baudouin (1920), Coué (1922), and the Nancy School of psychiatry. A modern-day version of this approach has been offered under the general heading of "positive thinking," as described by Norman Vincent Peale and W. Clement Stone. For example, Stone, in urging the repetition of "good thoughts" to oneself says, "You will keep your thoughts off the things you should not want by keeping your thoughts on the things you should want." Interestingly, the same idea is presented in the Lamaze birth-delivery procedure in which the parturient is urged to occupy herself with thinking about relaxing specific muscles and performing somewhat complicated breathing exercises during labor contractions so that the pain is not experienced as intensely.

It is worth noting that at times the procedures outlined by the Nancy School came quite close to modern-day behavior therapy interventions. For example, Bonnet in *1911* advised a patient who had stage fright:

> Isolate yourself in a room where no one will come to disturb you . . . lie down on a sofa, close your eyes . . . relax your body to the utmost, for this physical inertia favors mental passivity, and renders the mind more accessible to suggestion. . . . At the outset, endeavor to stop thinking altogether. Try to think of nothing at all for a time. Then direct your thoughts toward the idea which is worrying you, and counteract it by its converse, saying to yourself: "I don't suffer from stage fright; I sing well; I am perfectly easy in mind."
>
> Repeat the process several times according to the amount of leisure at your disposal. Have a number of such sessions. . . . If you carry out this plan with assurance and conviction, success is certain. (reproduced in Baudouin, 1920, p. 154)

General formulas such as "tous les jours, à tous points de vue, je vais de mieux en mieux" ("day by day, in every way, I'm getting better and better"), were offered to patients by Coué and others. Brook argued that such a "general formula leaves every mind free to unfold and develop in the manner most natural to itself" (1922). However encouraging, the use of a formula or "psychological litany" tends often to lead merely to rote-repetition and emotionless patter, which has been found ineffective as a coping tool (Meichenbaum & Cameron, 1972b). It is, in effect, a self-instruction that fails. Several reasons for this failure have been logically and experimentally derived. In the first place, the client's self-statements may be too general or broad, not sufficiently individualized. For instance, the client may resolve that he will do something like give up smoking but not specify when and how or what incompatible responses he will substitute in its place. It is as if one were attempting to become a vegetarian without specifically substituting anything for the meat in his diet. Moreover, very general self-statements are likely to be insensitive to situational conditions and are unlikely to incorporate such contingencies of rewards and punishments that would strengthen appropriate, and weaken inappropriate, responses to the self-statements. This point was most clearly illustrated by the results of the phobic clients who had received only self-instructional rehearsal. The results indicated that self-instructional rehearsal was a necessary but not sufficient condition for the elimination of fears. Having clients merely cognitively rehearse the self-instructions, saying that they could overcome their fears, did not lead to consistent significant behavioral and affective change. In fact, when the phobic clients who had received only self-instructional rehearsal confronted the phobic object following treatment they initially reported minimal anxiety, indicating that they were calm and in control. However, when the demands to handle the phobic object increased, their self-reports of anxiety precipitously rose, with the consequence of a rearousal of their fears. The initial bravado that followed from mere self-instructional training gave way when the task demands increased. In comparison, those phobic clients who rehearsed the self-controlling self-statements and who had then had an opportunity to use them in confronting a stress (e.g., electric shock) significantly reduced their fears following treatment.

Thus, the mere rehearsal of self-instructions without opportunity for application training will likely result in those self-instructions exerting a minimal self-controlling influence. Saying the "right" things to yourself may not be a sufficient condition for change. One may have to "try out" these self-statements gradually in real situations that, like the criterion tasks, present real threats.

It is important to highlight that a rejection of the positive-thinking approach, Couéism, and the Nancy School tradition should not lead us to overreact and thus reject the systematic exploration of how cognitive control could be employed successfully in learning how to cope with stress.[23]

Application of Stress-Inoculation Training to the Control of Anger

An interesting and promising application of stress-inoculation training was offered by Novaco who used the procedure to teach personal competence in managing provocations and regulation of anger arousal to persons having chronic anger problems (1975a).

Novaco's conceptualization of the complex nature of anger indicates the necessity of employing a multifaceted treatment technique such as stress-inoculation training. Novaco conceptualized anger as an emotional response to provocation that is determined by three response modalities: cognitive, somatic-affective, and behavioral. At the cognitive level anger is a function of appraisals, attributions, expectations, self-statements, and images that occur in the context of provocations. In the somatic-affective modality, anger is primed and exacerbated by tension and agitation. Thus, accumulated physiological tension can potentiate the anger response and the resultant antagonistic interpersonal behavior can escalate the provocation se-

[23] Critiques of such positive thinking approaches have come from many quarters. Two of the best evaluations come from Dornbush (1965) and Miller (1955) who offered some negative thinking about Norman Vincent Peale's positive thinking approach. Dornbush indicated that "it is easy to look at the positive thinking notion as a childish American attempt to impose the search for happiness as a perceptual category upon the unyielding objects of man's environment" (1965, p. 130).

quence. Behaviorally, both withdrawal and antagonism can contribute to anger; the former by leaving the instigation unchanged and the latter by escalating the provocation sequence and providing further cues from which the person infers anger.

A similar analysis of anger was offered by Bandura (1973). From a social learning formulation, he identified many factors that influence the cognitive control of anger and aggression. Bandura indicated how cognitive processes could function in stimulus control, the guidance of behavior, the representation of reinforcement contingencies, and in problem-solving operations.

Novaco provided treatment for thirty-four volunteer subjects (eighteen male, sixteen female), ranging in age from seventeen to forty-two. Prior to treatment the clients' problems in controlling anger were quite intense: Several clients had physically assaulted others, one had had a fist fight in a public library, several others destroyed property or possessions (e.g., one kicked in a glass door at an ice cream parlor when refused service, another hurled a brick through a car window, and another decorated objects with blood from his fists after having intentionally smashed them into a wall).

The stress-inoculation training format began with the clients' being brought together in small groups to discuss the duration and extent of their anger problems. A situational analysis was conducted in order to have them ascertain what were the particular aspects of provocations that triggered anger and, more specifically, to explore the thoughts and feelings that clients experienced in provocation encounters. This self-exploration was facilitated by having clients vicariously relive recent anger experiences by closing their eyes and "running a movie" of the provocations, reporting their feelings and thoughts. This is the same imagery technique Meichenbaum used with anxious clients in order to make them aware of the negative anxiety-engendering thoughts and feelings that they emit

(1976a). The elicitation of such cognitive and affective self-reports were incorporated into the presentation of the therapy rationales.

Novaco suggested to his clients that the feelings of anger that they experienced were influenced by their own thoughts, that is, by the things they said to themselves: "A basic premise [of the treatment] is that anger is fomented, maintained, and influenced by the self-statements that are made in provocation situations" (p. 33). The group was then given an account of the varied functions of anger, emphasizing disruptive and defensive roles. What a client perceived as a provocation, and the content of his self-statements, influenced the anger reaction. When he was provoked, the client's negative self-statements tended to include intolerance of mistakes, beliefs about the necessity for success, unreasonable expectations of others, and the necessity for retaliation. Emphasis was placed on the facts that the client perceived a threat to his self-worth, he wanted to be in control of a situation, and he engaged in acts of antagonism, which escalated his own anger. Thus, such provocation-related self-statements as "Who the hell does he think he is; he can't do that to me," "He wants to play it that way; okay; I'll show him," "He thinks I'm a pushover; I'll get even," in combination with emotional arousal, influenced the anger reaction.

Given the rationale that one's anger reactions consist of two components, namely, emotional arousal and cognitive activity (i.e., appraisals, attributions, self-statements, and imagery), a stress-inoculation treatment regimen naturally followed. The clients were taught to use relaxation skills to enable them to reduce arousal and cognitive controls in order to control their attentional processes and thoughts, images, and feelings. The cognitive training would make clients aware of the negative, anger-instigating self-statements they emitted when provoked. In this way, they were taught to conduct a situational analysis of what triggered anger for them and to reflect on the set of cognitive and behavioral alternatives available. The similarity between this rationale for anger and the Schachter-based rationale offered to phobic patients is apparent.

As Cameron and I encouraged phobics to view a phobic confrontation as a series of stages, so did Novaco have his clients view their provocation and anger reactions as if they were composed of a sequence of stages. These consisted of (1) preparing for the provocation whenever possible, (2) the impact and confrontation, (3) coping with arousal, and (4) subsequent reflection when conflict was resolved successfully or when conflict was unresolved. See Table 5 for the self-statements employed by the clients to cope with each stage.

In summary, the Novaco adaptation of stress-inoculation training for anger included: (1) an educational phase in which clients were given a conceptualization of how to view their anger-reactions in terms of a sequence of stages that involved cognitive and arousal processes; (2) relaxation and cognitive skills training, the latter in the form of self-instructional rehearsal; and (3) an application phase, in which clients were asked to imagine various anger-engendering situations and to cognitively rehearse coping with such provocations by means of relaxation, deep-breathing, and personally generated self-statements. These three stages were conducted within five forty-five-minute sessions. Whereas session one, the educational phase, was conducted in groups, sessions two through five were conducted individually. In order to consolidate the conceptualization process and acquire the relaxation and cognitive skills, the subjects were asked in session one to conduct homework assignments of (1) listening to their anger-related self-statements; (2) performing situational analyses of anger-provoking situations; and (3) ordering these situations into an hierarchical fashion on index cards. During sessions two to five, the clients cognitively rehearsed coping with these provocations. A coping imagery procedure was employed in which clients could imagine

Table 5. Examples of Self-Statements Rehearsed in Stress Inoculation Training for Controlling Anger (from Novaco, 1975)

Preparing for provocation

This is going to upset me, but I know how to deal with it.
What is it that I have to do?
I can work out a plan to handle this.
I can manage the situation. I know how to regulate my anger.
If I find myself getting upset, I'll know what to do.
There won't be any need for an argument.
Try not to take this too seriously.
This could be a testy situation, but I believe in myself.
Time for a few deep breaths of relaxation. Feel comfortable, relaxed, and at ease.
Easy does it. Remember to keep your sense of humor.

Impact and confrontation

Stay calm. Just continue to relax.
As long as I keep my cool, I'm in control.
Just roll with the punches; don't get bent out of shape.
Think of what you want to get out of this.
You don't need to prove yourself.
There is no point in getting mad.
Don't make more out of this than you have to.
I'm not going to let him get to me.
Look for the positives. Don't assume the worst or jump to conclusions.
It's really a shame that he has to act like this.
For someone to be that irritable, he must be awfully unhappy.
If I start to get mad, I'll just be banging my head against the wall. So I might as well just relax.
There is no need to doubt myself. What he says doesn't matter.
I'm on top of this situation and it's under control.

Coping with arousal

My muscles are starting to feel tight. Time to relax and slow things down.
Getting upset won't help.
It's just not worth it to get so angry.
I'll let him make a fool of himself.
I have a right to be annoyed, but let's keep the lid on.
Time to take a deep breath.
Let's take the issue point by point.
My anger is a signal of what I need to do. Time to instruct myself.
I'm not going to get pushed around, but I'm not going haywire either.
Try to reason it out. Treat each other with respect.
Let's try a cooperative approach. Maybe we are both right.
Negatives lead to more negatives. Work constructively.
He'd probably like me to get really angry. Well I'm going to disappoint him.
I can't expect people to act the way I want them to.
Take it easy, don't get pushy.

Table 5. (Continued)

Reflecting on the provocation
a. *When conflict is unresolved*
   Forget about the aggravation. Thinking about it only makes you upset.
   These are difficult situations, and they take time to straighten out.
   Try to shake it off. Don't let it interfere with your job.
   I'll get better at this as I get more practice.
   Remember relaxation. It's a lot better than anger.
   Can you laugh about it? It's probably not so serious.
   Don't take it personally.
   Take a deep breath.
b. *When conflict is resolved or coping is successful*
   I handled that one pretty well. It worked!
   That wasn't as hard as I thought.
   It could have been a lot worse.
   I could have gotten more upset than it was worth.
   I actually got through that without getting angry.
   My pride can sure get me into trouble, but when I don't take things too
       seriously, I'm better off.
   I guess I've been getting upset for too long when it wasn't even necessary.
   I'm doing better at this all the time.

---

themselves occasionally losing control but then seeing that
this loss of control was a cue to use the coping procedures.
In this way clients became more educated about their
anger patterns, learning to discriminate about events or
areas for which anger was justified and proper and how it
could be manifested in a socially appropriate form. The
clients could thus learn to distance themselves from a particular episode and adopt the role of an outside observer. It
is important to appreciate that the goal of treatment was to
teach clients socially acceptable ways to express anger and
not to inhibit the natural expression of anger.

Novaco found that stress-inoculation training was most
effective in reducing anger as assessed by self-report and
physiological indices obtained during laboratory-based
provocations which included imaginal, role-playing, and
direct experience confrontations. A daily diary of "anger
experiences" confirmed the laboratory results. The stress-
inoculation treatment package that included both relaxa-

tion and self-instructions was superior to the component treatments of self-instructions alone or relaxation training alone, although differences between the combined and self-instruction-alone group did not reach significance on a number of measures. The self-instruction-alone group was superior to the relaxation-alone group except when measures were taken during imaginal provocations.

It is interesting to note that the subjects in Novaco's study reported that an important aspect of the stress-inoculation package was the idea of being "task-oriented" when presented with a provocation, thus defining the situation as a problem that called for a solution rather than a threat that called for attack. In this way, the client was led to focus his attention on the issues involved and avoid responding in ways that would escalate the provocation sequence. The same process of appraisal manipulation and differential attending was evident in the stress-inoculation treatment of fear and anxiety and as we will see illustrated below, in the handling of pain. With repeated practice in interrupting the habitual reaction, the client can learn to short-circuit or totally eliminate the customary accompanying emotional reaction.

Novaco's initial study is provocative as a demonstration of the therapeutic potential of the stress-inoculation training procedure with an important clinical problem. Recently, Novaco reported a case study of a thirty-eight-year-old male hospitalized patient who had a diagnosis of depressive neurosis with suicidal ruminations and beliefs of worthlessness and inadequacy (1975b). The patient, who was married, the father of six children and held a job as a credit manager, had a history of problems with anger control. Tension at work would accumulate and he would vent this at home. These confrontations at home resulted in arguments and physical abuse, with the consequence that one of the patient's sons left home. The patient received fifteen sessions of stress-inoculation training, with impressive results. Changes were evidenced from a variety of sources, including an anger diary, reports from significant others, and observational data. Following the stress inoculation training, the patient was able to control his anger in spite of provocations.

Perhaps the most exciting extension of the stress-inoculation procedures is to anger management in the training of law enforcement officers (Novaco, in press). The training includes (a) cognitive preparation regarding the functions of anger, properties of aggressive sequences, and the importance of cognitive factors; (b) skills acquisition and rehearsal whereby participants discover and review coping processes through small group exercises; and (c) application and practice of coping techniques during a graduated series of role-playing provocations. Novaco's study with policemen represents the first application of the stress-inoculation procedure on a preventive basis with a nonclinical but highly stressed population. The stress-inoculation treatment procedures can be readily applied to such varied populations as child abusers,[24] hypertensives, and assaultive juveniles.

Application of Stress-Inoculation Training to Pain Tolerance

Although the stress-inoculation treatment approach has been employed successfully with handling psychological stressors, such as interpersonal anxiety and anger, the procedure also seems applicable to the handling of physical stressors, which also have psychological aspects.

An Overview of Pain Treatment Literature

The search for an effective means to alleviate pain has been long and arduous. Thousands of nostrums and proce-

---

[24] Prior to becoming a parent, I was rather upset by the relative high incidence of child abuse. Now, as a parent of four children, I instead wonder why the incidence is not much higher. What is the nature of the coping mechanisms parents are using to control anger?

dures have been employed in the quest to relieve pain, including emetics, enemas, blister raising, bleeding, soothing potions, and palliatives. Modifications and refinements of these techniques, no less esoteric, are currently utilized to facilitate pain relief. Among the most frequently applied are: (1) pharmacological agents whose sites of action may be at the receptor, dorsal horn in spinal column, or at higher levels of the nervous systems, such as the brain stem; (2) anesthetic nerve blocks which require injection of alcohol or local anesthetic (e.g., procaine) into a nerve root; (3) and surgical procedures performed at nearly every possible site along the pathways from the peripheral receptors to the cortex (e.g., from the sectioning of peripheral nerves to thalamotomies and prefrontal lobotomies). These treatments often result in untoward effects and have a disheartening tendency for the original pain to recur subsequent to treatment (Melzack, 1973). To date, none of the most commonly employed procedures has proven to be completely satisfactory for adequate or permanent amelioration of pain.

Melzack and Casey, after reviewing the medical treatment of pain, drew the following important conclusions:

> The surgical and pharmacological attacks on pain might well profit by redirecting thinking toward the neglected and almost forgotten contribution of motivational and cognitive processes. Pain can be treated not only by trying to cut down sensory input by anesthetic blocks, surgical intervention and the like, but also by influencing the motivational-affective and cognitive factors as well. (1968, p. 435).

Individuals have used cognitive strategies for as long as man has experienced pain. For example, the Stoic philosophers believed that man could get the better of pain by force of reason, by the "rational repudiation" of pain. Descartes and Spinoza recommended that pain should be overcome through the "permeation" of reason. One of the oldest cognitive techniques employed is distraction or attention-diversion. In the *Koran*, the prophet instructs the faithful of Islam, "When anyone suffers from toothache, let him lay a finger upon the sore spot and recite the sixth sura." Perhaps a quote from the philosopher Kant best illustrates the cognitive technique:

> For a year I have been troubled by morbid inclination and very painful stimuli which from other's descriptions of such symptoms I believe to be gout, so that I had to call a doctor. One night, however, impatient at being kept awake by pain, I availed myself of the stoical means of concentration upon some different object of thought such for instance as the name of 'Cicero' with its multifarious associations, in this way I found it possible to divert my attention, so that pain was soon dulled. . . . Whenever the attacks recur and disturb my sleep, I find this remedy most useful (cited by Fulop-Miller, 1938, p. 28).

Although the image of Cicero may not serve the same function for us today, Kant highlights the potential of the cognitive strategy of attention-diversion. Many additional examples could be offered, illustrating the long history of cognitive techniques. One other example worth sharing comes from the writings of Bernheim, who discussed the relationship between hypnosis and suggestion (1964). In his classic book, he quotes observations on the Inquisition, reported in 1629, on the power of cognitions in controlling pain:

> Some rascals trusted so strongly in the secrets they possessed to make themselves insensible to pain, that they voluntarily gave themselves up as prisoners, to cleanse themselves of certain sins. Some use certain words pronounced in a low voice, and others writings which they hide on some part of their body. The first one I recognized as using some sort of charm, surprised us by his more than natural firmness, because after the first stretching of the rack, he seemed to sleep as quietly as if he had been in a good bed, without lamenting, complaining or crying, and when the stretching was repeated two or three times, he still remained as motionless as a statue. This made us suspect that he was provided with some charm, and to resolve the doubt he was stripped as naked as his hand. Yet after a careful search nothing was found on him but a little piece of paper on which were the figures of the three kings, with these words on the other side:

"Beautiful star which delivered the Magi from Herod's per-
secution, deliver me from all torment." This paper was stuffed
in his left ear. Now although the paper had been taken
away from him he still appeared insensible to the torture,
because when it was applied he muttered words between his
teeth which we could not hear, and as he persevered in his
denials, it was necessary to send him back to prison. (p. 85)

Only recently, however, have cognitive coping strategy techniques been systematically explored in laboratories. Two major types of strategies have been examined
within the laboratory, namely, imagery and nonimagery.
The imagery strategies include (1) imaginative inattention—ignoring the pain by engaging in "goal-
directed fantasy," which, if real, would be incompatible
with the experience of pain (e.g., Chaves & Barber, 1974;
Horan & Dellinger, 1974); (2) imaginative transformation
of pain—acknowledgment of the noxious sensations, but
transforming or interpreting these sensations as something
other than pain, or minimizing the sensations as trivial or
unreal (e.g., Barber & Hahn, 1962; Blitz & Dinnerstein,
1971; Spanos, Horton, & Chaves, 1975); and (3) imaginative transformation of context—the acknowledgment of the
noxious sensations but transforming the context in which
these sensations are received (e.g., Blitz & Dinnerstein,
1968; Knox, 1972; Wolff & Horland, 1967). The nonimagery
strategies include (1) somatization—the focusing on the
existence of bodily processes or sensations to the exclusion
of other sensations (e.g., Bobey & Davidson, 1970; Evans
& Paul, 1970); (2) attention-diversion via external
distraction—the focusing on objects in the physical environment to the exclusion of noxious sensations (Kanfer &
Goldfoot, 1966; Kanfer & Seider, 1973); and (3) relaxation
and controlled breathing (e.g., Bobey & Davidson, 1970;
Mulcahy & Janz, 1973; Neufeld & Davidson, 1971).
Specific examples of each of these strategies will be offered
below when we describe the stress-inoculation training
procedure that incorporated them into treatment.

The typical experimental design of these treatment studies has been to instruct an experimental group to employ *one* strategy (i.e., the one in which the experimenter is interested), while a second group employs a different strategy or functions as a control group given no specified instructions regarding the utilization of a strategy. The results of such cognitive training studies have been inconsistent and often contradictory. Most of the inconsistencies in results among studies can be attributed to such methodological factors as (1) the use of different pain stressors, (2) different kinds of instructions to subjects concerning the experimental demands, (3) different demand characteristics of the experimental assessment, including sex of subject and experimenter, (4) the nature of the experimental design (e.g., whether a preassessment is employed), (5) the role of subjects' own spontaneous use of strategies. (See Meichenbaum and Turk, 1976, for a description of these factors.)

Pain-treatment research, while tacitly acknowledging the significance of a variety of psychological factors, has emphasized isolation and manipulation of one or another specific factor. Perhaps a more appropriate research and treatment strategy is one that takes into consideration, and indeed capitalizes on, the multidimensional nature and marked individual differences of pain reactions. Such a procedure is the skills-oriented, stress-inoculation treatment approach.

Experimentally Induced Pain

In order to appreciate how stress-inoculation training can be employed, picture the following scene. You are a volunteer subject in a pain experiment. With an appropriate amount of trepidation you watch as a blood pressure cuff is inflated around your upper left arm. You are asked by the experimenter to tolerate for as long as possible the pain you will experience.

The ischemic pain you are experiencing is the closest to clinical pain that can be produced in the laboratory (Beecher, 1966). The submaximum effort tourniquet procedure induces a dull, aching, slowly mounting pain (Smith, Egbert, Markowitz, Mosteller, & Beecher, 1966). How long will you tolerate the pain? Five minutes, twenty minutes, forty minutes? What coping techniques will you employ to tolerate and endure the pain? How would you train someone to cope more adequately with such an experimentally induced stressor?

Turk successfully applied the stress-inoculation training procedure to an ischemic pain situation (1975, 1976). As in the stress-inoculation training study with phobias and control of anger, the training procedure began with an educational phase. In the 1975 Turk study Melzack and Wall's (1965) gate control theory of pain was offered in the conceptualization phase.[25]

The gate control theory of pain suggests that the pain experience consists of three different components, namely, sensory-discriminative, motivational-affective, and cognitive-evaluative. Although Melzack indicated that the three components interact in a complex fashion, the components were presented separately to the subject in order that he could better appreciate the nature of pain and the stress-inoculation training procedures (1973).

Following a discussion of how the subject felt and what he thought about during the pretraining phase, the trainer described the various coping techniques that the subject could employ to deal with each of the various aspects of the pain experience as described by Melzack and Wall's theory.

First, the subject was shown that he could control the sensory input or *sensory-discriminative* components of pain by such means as physical and mental relaxation and

[25] In Turk's (1976) study a somewhat simpler conceptualization of pain was offered in the stress-inoculation training. The conceptualization of pain was Beecher's (1959) version of pain which includes mainly two elements: the sensory input and the client's reactions to the sensory input.

by attending to slow, deep breathing. The work on natural childbirth (Dick-Read, 1959) was offered as an illustration of how one's expectations concerning pain increases anxiety, which in turn fosters muscle tension, leading to more pain and consequently more anxiety. This cycle can be interrupted by the use of relaxation procedures. At this point the subjects were given relaxation exercises (e.g., Paul, 1966; Meichenbaum, 1973).

According to Melzack the *motivational-affective* component includes the feelings the subject has while experiencing pain. Such feelings as helplessness and the absence of control exacerbate the painful experience. To counteract such feelings, the therapist discussed with the subject the strategies the subject may have employed in the pretraining situation and the therapist offered a variety of other strategies that have been shown to be of help to subjects in pain. These strategies included: (1) attention diversion—focusing attention on things other than experimentally induced pain. For example, doing mental arithmetic or attending to cues in the environment such as counting ceiling tiles, studying one's clothes, etc.; (2) somatization—focusing attention on bodily processes or bodily sensations including the experimentally induced pain. For example, watching and analyzing the changes in the arm and hand, etc.; (3) imagery manipulations—changing or transforming the experience of pain by means of imagery. The more elaborate, detailed, and involved the imagery, the greater the amount of pain tolerance. A number of different imagery manipulations were offered. These included (a) imaginative inattention in which the subject ignores the experimentally induced pain by engaging in "goal-directed fantasy," which, if real, would be incompatible with the experience of pain, for example, imagine lying on the beach; (b) imaginative transformation of pain in which the subject includes the experience of pain in the fantasy, but transforms or interprets these sensations as something other than pain or minimizes the sensation as unreal or trivial, for example, imagining the arm as only cold and not painful, thinking of the arm as being numb as if injected with novocaine; (c) imaginative transformation of context in which the subject also includes the pain in the fantasy but now transforms the context or setting in which the pain occurs, for example, imagining that one is a spy who has been shot in the arm and who is being chased by enemy agents in a car down a winding mountain road (Knox, 1972).

Thus, the subject was exposed to a variety of different coping strategies, which he could choose from in "cafeteria style." The subject was encouraged to develop a plan to deal with the pain and especially to use the coping techniques at "critical moments" when the pain seemed most unbearable and when the subject would like to give up. The availability of such strategies would help control the motivational-affective components of pain.

One way to deal with the *cognitive-evaluative* component of pain was to conceptualize the painful experience as consisting of several phases, such as preparing for the painful stressor, confronting and handling the stressor, coping with feelings at critical moments, and self-reinforcement for having coped. In collaboration with the trainer the subject generated a list of self-statements that he could emit at each phase of the stress reaction (see Table 6). The therapist employed the subject's own self-statements and images wherever possible. As in the treatment of phobic patients, the cognitive processes or "work of worrying" were made explicit in the form of self-statements, thus conveying to the subject a sense of control over his own thoughts and feelings.

As indicated before, the stress-inoculation strategy of exposing subjects to a host of different coping techniques from which they can select and tailor to their own needs and styles is to be contrasted with most studies of experimentally induced pain. In the stress-inoculation procedure the subject from the outset becomes a collaborator, helping to generate from his own experience and with the advice and support of the trainer, an individually tailored coping package that he can employ on the postassessment.

Table 6. Example of Self-Statements Rehearsal in Stress-Inoculation Training for Controlling Pain (from Turk, 1975)

Preparing for the Painful Stressor
   What is it you have to do?
   You can develop a plan to deal with it.
   Just think about what you have to do.
   Just think about what you can do about it.
   Don't worry; worrying won't help anything.
   You have lots of different strategies you can call upon.

Confronting and Handling the Pain
   You can meet the challenge.
   One step at a time; you can handle the situation.
   Just relax, breathe deeply, and use one of the strategies.
   Don't think about the pain, just what you have to do.
   This tenseness can be an ally, a cue to cope.
   Relax. You're in control; take a slow deep breath. Ah. Good.
   This anxiety is what the trainer said you might feel.
   That's right; it's the reminder to use your coping skills.

Coping with Feelings at Critical Moments
   When pain comes just pause; keep focusing on what you have to do.
   What is it you have to do?
   Don't try to eliminate the pain totally; just keep it under control.
   Just remember, there are different strategies; they'll help you stay in control.
   When the pain mounts you can switch to a different strategy; you're in control.

Reinforcing Self-Statements
   Good, you did it.
   You handled it pretty well.
   You knew you could do it!
   Wait until you tell the trainer about which procedures worked best.

The value of providing subjects with a choice of strategies for reducing pain from which they could individually select was underscored by Chaves and Barber (1974). They found that some subjects in their cognitive strategy training study reported that they would have preferred to use their own strategy rather than the one provided by Chaves and Barber to handle the pain. The present stress-inoculation procedure incorporates an individualized tailoring package into the training procedure.

In summary, the stress-inoculation subjects were given a conceptualization of pain and information, as well as an opportunity to rehearse a variety of behavioral and cognitive coping techniques to be employed as they saw fit during the various phases of the painful experience. This completed the educational and rehearsal phases of stress-inoculation training and the last application phase remained before the postassessment began.

Whereas in the stress-inoculation training with phobics the application phase included exposure to real-life stressors, in the initial pain study the application phase was conducted by means of imagery-rehearsal and role-playing, two widely used behavior therapy procedures (Turk, 1975). In the second Turk study the subjects following imagery and behavioral rehearsal also received exposure to a real-life stressor of having to submerge their nondominant arm in a cold tub (2°C) of circulating ice water (i.e., cold pressor test) (1976).

In order to review and consolidate the training procedures, subjects in Turk's studies were asked to imagine themselves in stressful situations, including the ischemic pain situation. They were to imagine how they would use the variety of coping techniques (e.g., statement of stages, self-statements, relaxation, and other strategies). Initially, the subjects verbalized aloud the sequence of strategies they were imagining, but with the development of proficiency, verbalizations were faded until the imagery process was engaged in without verbalizations.

Such imagery procedures can be viewed as the subject's providing himself with a model of how he should behave in a stressful situation—as indicated by what Sarbin called muted role-taking (1972). Prior research has indicated that one can enhance the therapeutic value of such covert modeling procedures by having the subject imagine himself faltering, experiencing anxiety, and then coping with these inadequacies (Kazdin, 1973, 1974a,b; Meichenbaum, 1971b, 1972). In this way the therapist anticipates the thoughts and feelings his client is likely to experience in the real-life situation, and by including them in the imagery process they later assume a "déjà vu" quality for the client. The client's anxiety, tenseness, negative self-statements, self-doubts, etc., become something the therapist prepared him for: They are the cues, the reminders, to use the coping procedures. Thus, in the imagery procedure, the stress-inoculation subject was encouraged to include any failings, self-doubts or anxiety and to then see himself coping with these.

In order to further consolidate the coping strategies the subject was asked to role-play giving advice to a novice subject on how to cope with stress—specifically with the experience of pain. The trainer in this instance played the role of the novice subject, while the subject readily took on the role of the trainer.

Thus prepared with stress-inoculation training, the volunteer students underwent a postassessment on the ischemic test. On the preassessment the subjects were able to tolerate the pain for a mean of seventeen minutes; on the posttest they tolerated the ischemic pain for a mean of thirty-two minutes, a highly significant difference ($p < 0.002$). This fifteen-minute improvement in tolerance takes on particular significance when one learns that Smith, Chiang, and Regina found that subjects' tolerance for ischemic pain was prolonged by only five to ten minutes following the administration of 10 mg of morphine (1974). Verbal pain intensity reports (Hilgard *et al.*, 1967), which were collected throughout the assessment, indicated that the subjects subjectively perceived the arm pressure as less painful on the postassessment. Subjects who were remaining twice as long in the postassessment offered pain ratings the same as, or lower than, their preassessment ratings. In other words, the pain rating offered by a treated subject at forty minutes on the posttest was the same rating the subject offered at twenty minutes on the preassessment.

The effectiveness of the stress-inoculation training takes on added significance when compared to a "strong" attention-placebo control group who received both the pre- and postassessments as well as exposure to a pseudotraining package. This group controlled for such influences as expectation and placebo factors. The pseudotraining included a general statement that cognitive preparation à la "work of worrying" facilitates the coping process. The major difference between the control group and the stress-inoculation group was the absence of specific coping techniques. The control group demonstrated minimal change in tolerance time from the pre-to-postassessments, namely, from eighteen minutes, pretest, to nineteen minutes, posttest. There were no significant differences in pain ratings on the two occasions for the control group. Turk has recently replicated these findings in a more extensive, carefully controlled study (1976). (See Turk, 1976, for a detailed therapist manual of the stress-inoculation training procedure.)

Clinical Applications

What about pain in nonexperimental settings? What role do cognitive factors play there? In this context, Turk brought the following quote from Arthur Koestler's work *Darkness at Noon* to my attention. In it Koestler describes Rubashov's reaction to the forthcoming interrogation by his prison officials:

> Rubashov had been beaten up repeatedly during his last imprisonment, but of this method he only knew by hearsay. He had learned that every known physical pain was bearable; if only one knew beforehand exactly what was going to happen to one, one stood it as a surgical operation—for instance the extraction of a tooth. Really bad was only the unknown, which gave no choice to foresee one's reactions and no scale to calculate one's capacity of resistance. . . . He called to memory every particular he knew about the subject 'steambath'. He imagined the situation in detail and tried to analyze the physical sensations to be expected, in order to rid them of their uncanniness. The important thing was not to let oneself be caught unprepared. (1940, pp. 55–56)

How about something a little bit less extreme and a bit more clinically relevant? In a recent case study, Levendusky and Pankratz used a cognitive-behavioral approach to treat a sixty-five-year-old male patient who was manifesting symptoms of chronic abdominal pain (1975). The patient was taught to control his pain through a program of relaxation, and a cognitive coping strategy of imaginative transformation of pain (which were specifically tailored to the patient) and cognitive relabeling. As a result of the cognitive-behavioral intervention the patient reduced his report of pain and his dependence on analgesic medication. A number of other studies could be cited to highlight the possibility of using cognitive-behavioral treatment intervention procedures (e.g., Chappell & Stevenson, 1936; Draspa, 1959; Egbert, Battit, Welch, & Bartlett, 1964; Langer *et al.*, 1975; Mulcahy & Janz, 1973; Reeves, 1976). Perhaps the most comprehensive cognitive-behavioral treatment approach to pain comes from Gottlieb, Strite, Keller, and Hockersmith (1975). Gottlieb and his colleagues have noted the important role of cognitive and social factors (e.g., anger, depression, anxiety, fear, feelings of helplessness) that contribute to the etiology and maintenance of chronic low back pain. The patients in Gottlieb *et al.*'s project were treated through a variety of interventions, which included educational lectures, biofeedback training and physical exercises, relaxation, assertion training, and social reinforcement.

Several important comments must be offered with regard to stress-inoculation and the other techniques that have been described. The first comment hearkens back to my comments on self-instructional training. First, the evidence for the efficacy of stress-inoculation is encouraging but not proven. The data on the full usefulness of the procedure have yet to be obtained. The stress-inoculation procedure is not offered as a panacea nor a replacement for other treatment approaches. Rather, it is designed to increase the clinician's armamentarium.

Given the increasing demand for people to deal with stress, the possibility of using stress-inoculation training for prophylactic purposes is exciting (e.g., work by Novaco on training policemen). The notion of providing individuals with a prospective defense against stress is in some respect analogous to immunization against attitude change (McGuire, 1964; Tannenbaum, 1967) and, of course, medical inoculation against biological disease. The general underlying principle in these two analogous situations is that a person's resistance is enhanced by exposure to a stimulus that is strong enough to arouse the defenses without being so powerful as to overcome them. An examination of the way in which this principle is applied by both social psychologists and physicians may suggest methods for refining and improving stress-inoculation. For instance, it may prove helpful to expose a client to a variety of graded stressors (e.g., cold pressor test, stress-inducing films, fear-inducing imagery, deprivation conditions, fatigue). Presumably, the more varied and extensive the application training, the greater the likelihood the client will develop a general learning set, a general way of talking to himself in order to cope. Cognitive coping modeling films can also be used to facilitate learning.

Several investigators have pointed to the potential of preventive intervention approaches, especially with high-risk populations (Henderson, Montgomery, & Williams, 1972; Poser, 1970; Seligman, 1973). The possibility of explicitly teaching even nonclinical populations to cognitively cope by such diverse techniques as information-seeking, anticipatory problem-solving, imagery rehearsal, task organization, altering attributions and self-labels, shifting attention, and using abstraction and relaxation seems to hold much promise. An explicit training program that would teach coping skills and then provide application training in handling a variety of stressors is in marked contrast to the haphazard and chance manner in which people now learn to cope with stress. The research on stress seems to indicate the necessary skills required to cope, and the method of cognitive-behavior modification seems to provide a promising means for teaching such skills.

Cognitive Restructuring
Techniques

Man is disturbed not by things but the views he takes of them.

—E̓PICTETUS[26]

The only feature common to all mental disorders is the loss of common sense (sensus communis) and the compensatory development of a unique private sense (sensus privatus) of reasoning.

—IMMANUEL KANT

If we wish to change the sentiments it is necessary before all to modify the idea which has produced [them], and to recognize either that it is not correct in itself, or that it does not touch our interests.

—PAUL DUBOIS

It is very obvious that we are influenced not by "facts" but by our interpretation of facts.

—ALFRED ADLER

Cognitive restructuring therapy and semantic therapy are generic terms that refer to a variety of therapeutic approaches whose major mode of action is modifying the pa-

[26] Since Epictetus' statement appears in several books by cognitive therapists, as a sort of rallying cry, it may be of interest to note the context in which Epictetus made his infamous remarks. "Men are disturbed not by things which happen,

tient's thinking and the premises, assumptions, and attitudes underlying his cognitions. The focus of therapy is on the ideational content involved in the symptom, namely, the irrational inferences and premises. Thus, the semantic or cognitive therapist attempts to familiarize himself with his patient's thought content, style of thinking, feelings, and behaviors, in order to understand their interrelationships.

For the semantic therapist, mental illness is fundamentally a disorder of thinking—the patient consistently distorts reality in an idiosyncratic manner and/or reaches unreasonable conclusions concerning his ability to cope with his environment. The patient's distorted thought processes adversely affect his view of the world and lead to unpleasant emotions and behavioral difficulties. The cognitive therapist helps the patient to identify specific misconceptions, distortions, and maladaptive attributions and to test their validity and reasonableness.

Ellis noted that several Greek and Roman philosophers (including Epictetus), as well as ancient Buddhist thinkers, perceived the close connection among reason, emotion, and behavior and offered advice for changing behavior by altering thinking patterns (1962). In this century, a number of therapists, including Dubois (1905), Coué (1922), Korzybski (1933), Johnson (1946), Low (1950), Kelley (1955), Phillips (1957), Frank, (1961), Ellis (1962), Blumenthal (1969), Beck (1976), and Lazarus (1972), have emphasized the role of cognitive factors in contributing to mental illness and have focused on altering the client's maladaptive self-verbalizations. Shaffer, for example, defined therapy as a "learning process through which a person acquires an

but by the opinions about the things: for example, death is nothing terrible, for if it were, it would have seemed so to Socrates; for the opinion about death, that it is terrible, is the terrible thing. When then we are impeded or disturbed or grieved, let us never blame others, but ourselves, that is, our opinions. It is the act of an ill-instructed man to blame others for his own bad condition; it is the act of one who has begun to be instructed, to lay the blame on himself; and of one whose instruction is completed, neither to blame another, nor himself" (Epictetus, *The Enchiridion*).

ability to speak to himself in appropriate ways so as to control his own conduct" (1947, p. 463).

Miller further underscored this tradition when he highlighted the potential importance of language in directing behavior:

> My major interest in psychology has been in research on psychological aspects of language and communication. Because our uniquely human capacity for speech is continually in my mind, I can never approach questions of behavior control without remembering that the most precise technique we have for behavior control is human language. This "technique" can cause you to do things you would never think of doing otherwise. It can change your opinions and beliefs. It can be used to deceive you. It can make you happy or sad. It can put new ideas in your head. It can make you want things you do not have. *You can even use it to control yourself.* (Miller, 1970, p. 999, emphasis added)

In a critical examination of cognitive restructuring approaches to therapy, it is well to avoid an error that has commonly been made in therapy outcome research. This pitfall can be illustrated by reference to an important doctoral dissertation entitled *Insight vs. Desensitization in Psychotherapy: An Experiment in Anxiety Reduction* that was conducted by Paul while I was a graduate student at the University of Illinois (1962–1966). Indeed, the dissertation was published as a book (Paul, 1966) and Paul received the award that year for the most creative doctoral dissertation in North America. Many people then considered it a landmark study, which documented the relative superiority of the behavior therapy procedure of desensitization over "insight" therapy. Paul deserved his kudos, for the study provided a prototype for therapy outcome studies. There was only one shortcoming: One of the independent variables, namely, "insight," was not operationally defined to permit ready replication. In describing the treatments in his study, Paul presented an explicit therapist manual of the desensitization treatment; but in describing the insight-oriented psychotherapy he said only,

This treatment consisted of the traditional interview procedures used by the respective therapists [there were five
therapists] in their daily work. With this approach, the
therapist attempts to reduce anxiety by helping the client
gain "insight" into the bases and interrelationships of his
problem. (1966, p. 18)

The only hint of the therapists' techniques was given by
their scores on a self-report Therapist Orientation Sheet.
The explicit treatment techniques used by the therapists to
effect "insight" and their respective definitions of "insight" were not indicated by Paul.

The reason I mention the Paul study is that it falls
victim to what Kieslar calls the "therapist uniformity myth"
(1966). When applied to psychotherapy research, the uniformity myth assumes that findings from most procedures
labeled "insight-oriented therapy" or what I am here calling cognitive restructuring therapy will be equivalent
since the treatment methods are assumed to be equivalent.
However, there are many different ways to conceptualize
"insight" and many ways to conduct insight-oriented
therapy. I will argue that, given the present state of cognitive restructuring *therapies,* we should not subsume them
under one umbrella term or impose a "uniformity" myth.
Let us examine some of the similarities and differences that
characterize semantic or cognitive therapies.

Reconsider the assessment procedure described in the
last chapter on stress-inoculation training, in which the
client was asked to close his eyes and replay in his mind's
eye a movie of his problem situation, reporting the
thoughts and feelings that preceded, accompanied, and followed the maladaptive act. For a moment let's leave the
"head" of the client and shift our focus to what the therapist
may be thinking (in some sense, saying to himself) as he
listens to the client's description. Put yourself in the place
of the therapist. How do you view your client's thoughts
and images? Are they seen as reflections of irrational belief
systems and faulty thinking styles, *or* as instances of

problem-solving ability and coping skills, *or* as instances of behavior *per se*, part of the client's complex response chain? Each of these conceptualizations (and others are possible) gives rise to different treatment interventions. Indeed, the host of different therapy procedures may be distinguished by the therapists' conceptualizations of their clients' cognitions. What a therapist says to himself about his client's thoughts and images, the way he views his client's internal dialogue will influence the questions he will ask the client, the tests he will administer, the nature of the homework assignments he will give, and how he will conduct therapy. We will explore therapists' self-statements concerning the therapy process by examining the different conceptualizations that have guided cognitive restructuring therapies.

Cognitions as Instances of Irrational Belief Systems

The semantic therapy that has received the most attention in recent years is Ellis' rational-emotive therapy (RET). The basic premise of rational-emotive therapy is that much, if not all, emotional suffering is due to the irrational ways people construe the world and to the assumptions they make. The assumptions lead to self-defeating internal dialogue or self-statements that exert an adverse effect on behavior. Thus, the task for the RET therapist is threefold. He must first determine precipitating external events that upset his patient. Then he must determine the specific thought patterns and underlying beliefs that constitute the internal response to these events and give rise to negative emotions. Third, he must assist the client in altering these beliefs and thought patterns. Ellis proposed that a major core of emotional disturbances has to do with the client's preoccupation with what others think of him (1962). Ellis encouraged the clinician to note the themes, the irrational premises, that underlie our patient's self-statements, images, and cognitions. He attempts to have clients examine the ideas, such as the following, that give rise to misperceptions: (1) I must be loved or approved of by practically every significant person in my life, and if I'm not it's awful; (2) I must not make errors or do poorly, and if I do it's terrible; (3) people and events should always be the way I want them to be.

Ideas that are based, as these are, on the belief that a person's self-worth is basically determined by others represent an irrational extrapolation of the consequences of personal actions. The extrapolation is irrational because it does not reflect realistically the events that the client has experienced in the past.

In order to counteract such beliefs, the rational-emotive therapist encourages, goads, challenges, educates by means of a Socratic dialogue, provides information, conducts rational analyses, assigns behavioral homework assignments, and so on, in order to have the client entertain the notion that his maladaptive behavior and emotional disturbance are a reflection of a commitment to irrational beliefs.

As a result of such therapeutic interventions, it is hoped that the client will replace the beliefs described above with the following: (1) It's definitely nice to have people's love and approval, but even without it, I can still accept and enjoy myself; (2) doing things well is satisfying, but it's human to make mistakes; (3) people are going to act the way they want, not the way I want.

It should be stressed that a client, before semantic therapy (including RET), is unlikely to "tell himself" various things consciously or deliberately when he is confronted with real-life situations. Rather, because of the habitual nature of one's expectations or beliefs, it is likely that such thinking processes become automatic and seemingly involuntary, like most overlearned sets. Moreover, the patient's maladaptive cognitions may take a pictorial form instead of or in addition to the verbal form (Beck, 1970). For example, a woman with a fear of walking alone found that her spells of anxiety followed images of her having a heart attack and being left helpless. A college student discovered that her anxiety at leaving the dormitory was triggered by visual fantasies of being attacked. Such idiosyncratic cognitions (whether pictorial or verbal) are usually very rapid and often contain an elaborate idea compressed in a few seconds or less. Beck points out that these cognitions are experienced as though they were automatic and involuntary and that they usually possess the quality of appearing plausible, rather than unrealistic.

The semantic therapist attempts to make his client aware of negative self-statements and images and of the anxiety-engendering, self-defeating, and self-fulfilling-prophecy aspects of such thinking. The first goal of therapy is to have the patient entertain the possibility that his maladaptive behaviors and emotional upset are contributed to by what he says to himself. The therapist, after initially listening to the patient's complaints, may give the patient the assignment of listening to himself over the course of the week and conducting a situational analysis of the times at which he experiences behavioral and affective upsets and engages in negative self-statements. Through careful questioning by the therapist, the patient begins to accept a cognitive conceptualization of his problem, one that is shared by the therapist. When the patient returns with examples of his negative self-statements, the therapist may ask, with some tact and skill, "Are you telling me that these kinds of thoughts are part of your problem? How do they cause you to become upset?" At this point the patient begins to provide evidence that negative self-statements are contributing to his problem. Once the patient entertains the possibility that his maladaptive behaviors result from what he tells himself, then a whole set of therapeutic assignments makes sense to him. *Whether the patient did or did not actually talk to himself prior to therapy is less important than that he is willing to view his behavior as if it were affected by self-statements and modifiable by them.* The semantic therapist usually employs homework assignments to engender the patient's acceptance of this viewpoint. The patient is asked to engage in graduated performance tasks to help him identify the ways in which his cognitions contribute to maladaptive behavior.

Ellis, in a rather forceful manner, has the client adopt the point of view that maladaptive behaviors and feelings derive from his belief system.[27] However, one must clearly distinguish between (a) the intentional use of such a belief-system analysis in RET, which leads to change, and (b) the natural occurrence of such belief systems, which contributes to maladaptive behavior in the first place. We may find that having the client view his behavior from Ellis' perspective leads to change but it does not follow that the existence of such self-negating beliefs is the key characteristic that distinguishes clients from nonclients. Elsewhere, I have argued that it may not be the *incidence* of irrational beliefs that is the distinguishing characteristic

---

[27] As you may recall, Ellis was instrumental in setting forth my journey of cognitive-behavior modification. Dr. Ellis' own therapy style must be distinguished from the rational-emotive therapy (RET) approach. This distinction will be particularly relevant for those readers who have seen Dr. Ellis conduct therapy in person, in films, or heard him on audiotapes. His approach is forcefully didactic—so forceful, that on one occasion I was moved to suggest, rather tongue-in-cheek, that RET as conducted by Ellis would only be successful with New Yorkers. (Ellis practices therapy in New York.) And I went on to suggest that wherever else in the world RET was successfully conducted, it would be with a patient who had moved from New York. In fantasy I began to consider at what point one of Dr. Ellis' patients might terminate therapy: One of Ellis' patients gets into a taxi on Forty-Second Street in New York and says, "You have to hurry, I'm going to be late for my therapy hour." After a slight pause, the taxi-driver turns and says, "Don't rush me, Mister. Why are you so hung-up about what your therapist will think of you if you're late?" etc. When the patient arrives at Dr. Ellis' office, the patient begins to describe his run-in with the taxi-driver, at which point Dr. Ellis says, "Why are you so upset with your concern about what the taxi-driver thinks of you? Your self-worth. . . ." The similarity in the advice offered by Ellis and the taxi-driver dawns on the patient and therapy ends. End of fantasy!

The point of these anecdotes is not to detract from the pioneer contributions of Ellis, for they are immeasurable, but rather to underscore the importance of distinguishing therapist style from therapy content. Perhaps this point could be most simply underscored by having the reader conjure-up the image of Carl Rogers conducting RET.

between normal and abnormal populations, as Ellis suggests (Meichenbaum, 1976b). Nonclinical populations may also hold many of the unreasonable premises that characterize clinical populations. But what the nonclinical subjects say to themselves about the irrational beliefs, the coping mechanisms they employ, may be what distinguishes clinical from nonclinical populations. In other words, it may *not* be the absence of irrational thoughts *per se* but rather the set of management techniques employed to cope with such thoughts and feelings that characterizes the nonpatient population or determines the "recovery" time from emotional upsets. The *nonpatient* may be more capable of "compartmentalizing" such events and be more able to use coping techniques such as humor, rationality, or what I have come to call "creative repression."

Although therapeutic procedures such as Ellis' rational-emotive therapy (RET) have been available and professionally visible for well over a decade, there is a paucity of controlled experimental data bearing on their efficacy. A few encouraging studies of the efficacy of RET have been offered (Baker, 1966; DiLoreto, 1971; Karst & Trexler, 1970; Meichenbaum, Gilmore, & Fedoravicius, 1971; Trexler & Karst, 1972; Wolfe & Fodor, 1975).[28] However, after reviewing the outcome literature for RET and cognitive restructuring therapy in general, Mahoney concludes, and my own assessment of the literature is in full accord, "the clinical efficacy of Ellis' rational-emotive therapy has yet to be adequately demonstrated" (1974, p. 182). However, a similar assessment could be made of other therapies and the studies reviewed in this book are grounds for encouragement.

Cognitions as Instances of Faulty Thinking Styles

Closely akin to Ellis' rational-emotive approach is Beck's analysis of the stylistic qualities of our client's cog-

[28] The interested reader should see a bibliography of outcome RET studies by Murphy and Ellis (1976).

nitions, especially those of depressives (Beck, 1976; Braff & Beck, 1974). Beck attempts to have clients become aware of the distortions in their thought patterns (1970). These distortions include: (1) arbitrary inference—the drawing of a conclusion when evidence is lacking or actually supports the contrary conclusion; (2) magnification—exaggeration of the meaning of an event; (3) cognitive deficiency— disregard for an important aspect of a life situation; (4) dichotomous reasoning—overly simplified and rigid perception of events as good or bad, right or wrong; (5) overgeneralization—taking a single incident such as failure as a sign of total personal incompetence and in this way generating a fallacious rule. Such cognitive distortions result in the client's selectively attending to and inaccurately anticipating consequences. Beck's therapy is directed toward the client's identifying such stylistic qualities so that he can come to understand that his affective experiences and maladaptive behaviors are a result of his particular thinking processes—thinking processes that he is capable of changing and controlling by himself.

Cognitive therapy that derives from Beck's analysis of the client's cognitions involves helping the patient to evaluate both his attributions and performance more realistically by focusing on his negative self-judgments. Asking the client to engage in a set of graded tasks, homework assignments, and maintain activity lists provides the therapist with the behavioral data around which to examine the client's thinking style. Although individual treatment strategies may vary with the severity of the patient's problem and his ability and readiness to conceptualize in a certain manner, the process of the cognitive-behavioral therapy developed by Beck and his colleagues has a common pattern. The patient is taught to recognize and monitor his cognitions as well as to test and validate the relationship between cognition and affect. Both semantic and behavioral techniques are used to question the validity of or basis for the negative cognitions and misconceptions. After the patient recognizes the distortions in his cognitive set, the belief system or "silent assumptions" that support his attitudes and conceptions are then challenged. The therapist demonstrates to the patient that his interpretation of daily experiences is unrealistic. The patient, in a collaborative fashion with the therapist, discovers his cognitive distortions by his own data collection. For instance, a patient's assertion, "I had a terrible week," is examined in the context of his list of undertakings that week that he is asked to record. In this way the patient is made aware of how he assigns peculiar and upsetting meanings to experiences. Beck's use of an activity record allows the patient to review his behavior and to examine it in context and in perspective. In doing so, the client's cognitive distortions become more apparent and alternative interpretations can be brought to bear.

The initial results using this therapy approach have been encouraging but, as yet, not definitive. In a review of the literature Beck found ten studies that compared cognitive therapy, behavior therapy, and the combination of the two in the treatment of depression. "The major conclusion which can be drawn from these studies is that treatment procedures which directly change cognitions and/or behaviors are effective in alleviating depression. Furthermore, they are more efficacious than nondirective and supportive [treatments]" (Beck, 1976, p. 95). The studies Beck cited included Shipley and Fazio (1973), Taylor (1974), Shaw (1975), Schmickley (1975), Hodgson and Urban (1975), Fuchs and Rehm (1975), Rehm, Fuchs, Roth, Kornblith, and Roman (1975), Gioe (1975), and Klein and Seligman (1976). Unfortunately, these studies were predominantly dissertations involving college student populations. A few studies have applied Beck's procedures to psychiatric populations but these are the exception (e.g., Rush, Beck, Kovacs, Khatami, Fitzgibbon, and Wolman, 1975a; Rush, Khatami, and Beck, 1975b). For example, Rush *et al.* compared twice weekly cognitive therapy with chemotherapy

for a period of ten weeks in depressed patients (1975b).[29]
The results indicated an equivalent efficacy of drug therapy
and psychotherapy at an immediate posttest, and at a
three-month follow-up. In addition, a lower drop-out rate
was noted in the cognitive therapy group compared to the
chemotherapy group.

Cognitions as Instances of Problem-Solving Ability and Coping Skills

Whereas the Ellis and Beck cognitive therapy approaches sensitize the therapist to listen for the *presence* of
maladaptive self-statements, assumptions, and beliefs, the
cognitive therapist with a problem-solving and coping-
skills orientation listens for the *absence* of specific, adaptive
cognitive skills and responses. D'Zurilla and Goldfried
(1971) and Goldfried and Goldfried (1975) suggest that our
client's cognitions evidence a deficit in systematic,
problem-solving skills. The problem-solving treatment is
designed to have the client learn how to identify problems,
generate alternative solutions, tentatively select a solution,
and then test and verify the efficacy of that solution. The
clinical potential of such a problem-solving approach is illustrated in the treatment research reviewed by Hanel
(1974), Meichenbaum (1974a), Schneider and Robin
(1975), and Spivack and Shure (1974). Each of these investigators highlighted the therapeutic value of teaching
clients cognitive problem-solving skills. A number of recent studies further illustrates how a problem-solving training approach can be employed with various clinical populations. The applications have included the use of
problem-solving in crisis clinics (McGuire & Sifneos,

---

[29] It is important to recall the discussion of drug treatment with hyperactive children. Medication not only has pharmacological effects but likely also alters the
client's internal dialogue. It would be interesting to take the interview
schedule that Whalen and Henker used for studying changes in attribution with
hyperactive children who were receiving medication and apply it to depressives who receive medication.

1970), with hospitalized psychiatric patients (Coché & Flick, 1975), in assisting adolescents to handle various conflict situations (Kifer, Lewis, Green, & Phillips, 1973), in helping ex-drug addicts to remain drug-free (Copeman, 1973) and various high school and college students to deal with interpersonal anxiety (Christensen, 1974).

Common to each of these problem-solving approaches is an attempt to teach the client to engage in covert problem solving, entailing symbolic stimulus-transformation, cognitive rehearsal, and tests of alternate solutions. The problem-solving training usually includes: (1) cognitive reappraisal, which is based on training in discrimination among observation, inference, and evaluation—the individual learns to reappraise the evaluation that he places on the stimuli; and (2) behavioral experimentation—the individual learns to generate and experiment with a range of alternative behaviors in response to identified interfering social stimuli. The approach is a broad social competence training model, unrestricted in its application to various populations.

Whereas some cognitive restructuring therapists emphasize problem-solving, others are more concerned with coping skills. The problem-solving approach teaches the client to stand back and systematically analyze a problem situation in the absence of any acute stress; the coping-skills approach concentrates on what the client must do when immediately confronted with an acute stressful situation. Indeed, the problem-solving process may include rehearsal of coping skills, as clients imagine dealing with stressful events. The research reviewed in the last chapter on stress-inoculation training illustrates how a coping-skills orientation can be employed in therapy.

Cognitive Restructuring Therapies—Some Differences

Ellis, Beck, D'Zurilla and Goldfried, Meichenbaum—what are the differences? Irrational beliefs,

faulty thinking styles, inadequate problem-solving skills
and coping skills—what difference does it make? They
are all cognitive restructuring therapies.[30] How important are the nuances? Once again, the answer is that we
don't know. However, a logical analysis of the various
therapy approaches may help direct our search for the
answers.

The therapist manuals that have been written by these
various cognitive restructuring therapists vary in several
respects. Most notably, they vary in terms of the relative
emphasis placed on formal logical analysis (i.e., isolation
and evaluation of premises), the directiveness with which
the therapeutic rationale and procedures are presented and
the relative reliance on adjunctive behavior therapy
procedures.

A major distinction among the various cognitive restructuring therapy approaches is the differential emphasis
placed on the rational analysis of the client's belief system.
Ellis, and to a lesser extent Beck, highlights the implicit
assumptions and premises that give rise to negative self-
statements and emotional disturbance. In examining the
client's maladaptive behaviors Ellis has the client "become
aware of" or "entertain the notion" that certain irrational
beliefs guide faulty thinking and contribute to maladaptive

[30] A number of different therapy approaches using various procedures have the
clients become aware of and alter their internal dialogues. For example, in
Moreno's psychodramatic method the therapist encourages the client through
dramatic interplay to make his private fantasies public, to play out his internal
dialogue in a safe setting. By means of role reversal the client can then gain
the viewpoint of significant others. In Gestalt therapy the client becomes aware
of his internal dialogue by identifying with two opposing parts of his conflict in
an exercise called "topdog-bottomdog." The client plays the role of each side of
the conflict, usually locating each side in a separate chair, and then proceeds to
have a dialogue or encounter between them (e.g., "I want to, but I can't," "I
wish I could, but what would people think," "I feel like crying, but I'm holding
back"). In Berne's transactional analysis the client is made aware of his internal
script. Note, that it is not as if clients actually have scripts or conflict polarities
but rather each of these therapy procedures provide a plausible way for the
client to conceptualize their problems—a conceptualization that will lead to
particular therapy interventions.

behavior. The task for the patient is to challenge these faulty beliefs. Ellis states:

> Cognitively, RET teaches clients the A-B-C's of personality formation and disturbance-creation. Thus, it shows people that their emotional Consequences do *not* directly stem from the Activating events in their lives, but from their Belief Systems *about* these Activating events. Their Belief systems, when they feel disturbed, consist of, first, a set of empirically-based, rational Beliefs. For example, when they fail at a job or are rejected by a love partner they rationally convince themselves, "How unfortunate it is for me to fail! I would much rather succeed or be accepted." If they stick rigorously to these rational Beliefs, they feel appropriately sorry, regretful, frustrated, or irritated; but they do *not* feel emotionally upset or destroyed. To make themselves feel inappropriately or neurotically, they add the nonempirically-based, irrational Beliefs "How *awful* it is for me to fail! I *must* succeed. I am a thoroughly *worthless person* for failing or for being rejected!" *Then* they feel anxious, depressed, or worthless. In RET, the therapist or teacher shows people how to vigorously challenge, question, and Dispute their irrational Beliefs. Thus, they are shown how to ask themselves: "*Why* is it awful that I failed? Who says I *must* succeed? Where is the evidence that I am a *worthless person* if I fail or get rejected?" If people persistently and forcefully Dispute their insane ideas, they acquire a new cognitive *Effect*, namely, the Beliefs that: (1) "It is not awful but only very inconvenient if I fail"; (2) "I don't *have* to succeed, though there are several good reasons why I'd *like* to"; (3) "I am never a *worthless person* for failing or being rejected. I am merely a person who has done poorly, for the present, in these areas, but who probably can do better later. And if I never succeed or get accepted, I can *still* enjoy myself in *some* ways and refrain from downing myself. (Ellis, 1971, p. 19)

In Ellis' form of cognitive therapy the client views his behavior as influenced by maladaptive beliefs and the challenging of these beliefs is the central task of therapy.

Beck's focus on irrational beliefs is in the context of a host of cognitive therapeutic tactics such as reality testing, authenticating observations, validating conclusions, and distancing (i.e., regarding thoughts objectively). Patients are systematically taught such skills as self-observation in order to note the relationship between thoughts and emotions and then taught to regard such thoughts as hypotheses rather than facts. Beck's focus is more on the specific self-statements that occur in particular situations (usually graded task assignments) and how the client can test the validity of these self-statements. Finally, the assumptions and beliefs that underlie and generate the client's hypotheses are examined. The rational analysis of the client's belief system follows from the client's own behavioral data.

My own approach is closer to that of Beck than to Ellis, as I attempt to have clients increase their awareness of the negative self-statements and images they emit but without formally doing a rational analysis of the so-called irrational belief system. Instead, the focus is on the client's learning to employ specific problem-solving and coping skills. There is a clear need to compare the importance of using different cognitive interventions.

The present discussion of the variety of different cognitive restructuring therapy techniques presents a dilemma for the cognitive-behavior therapist in choosing among the different therapeutic approaches. This dilemma is magnified when we consider the host of different ways behavior therapy procedures such as modeling and imagery rehearsal and so on can be employed to alter the client's cognitions (as described in Chapter 4). The use of imagery in psychotherapy nicely illustrates this dilemma. Desensitization, emotive imagery, aversive images, implosive images, symbolic modeling, "depth" images, psychosynthesis, guided affective images, etc.—one could go on and on generating over twenty different ways images alone can be employed in psychotherapy. It is almost as if we had asked psychotherapists to take Guilford's creativity test and asked them to answer the item "What are all the unusual uses of . . . imagery in psychotherapy?" When we add to this list the many other ways cognitions can be employed in therapy the list becomes overwhelming. Such a lengthy list of alternative therapy procedures leads to a technical eclecticism, a trial-and-error clinical approach. From a research viewpoint the host of therapy techniques leads to what I have come to call a preoccupation with "engineering" questions. As phrased by Paul:

> What treatment, by whom, is most effective for this individual, with what specific problem, under what set of circumstances? (1969, p. 162).

Engineering questions are not unimportant but the question of "why" and "how does change come about" is often not considered. Instead, we are offered numerous comparative studies all addressed to answering "engineering" questions. Perhaps we can short-circuit some tedious and expensive comparisons by engaging in theory construction. It seems that the field of behavior therapy and for that matter, psychotherapy in general, has adopted an atheoretical stance. Whether it is London (1972) appropriately calling for an "end of ideology" or Lazarus (1972, 1976) counseling us to use "what works" we have become overly concerned with "engineering" questions. The next two chapters are designed to provide a beginning toward filling the vacuum by providing a theory of behavior change and attempting to address the "why" and "how" questions.

The Nature of Internal Dialogue—Foundations of a Theory of Behavior Change

For a good part of their waking life, people monitor their thoughts, wishes, feelings, and actions. Sometimes there is an internal debate as the individual weighs alternatives and courses of action and makes decisions. Plato referred to this phenomenon as an "internal dialogue."

—BECK (1976)

Central to the theory of behavior change proposed in this book is the phenomenon of internal dialogue or inner speech. Before we consider the theory, *per se*, let us first examine the function and structure of internal dialogue.

There is a variety of constructs that normally describe the various aspects of a person's activities that may be affecting his behavior at any given moment. These constructs include physiological responses, affective reactions, cognitions, and interpersonal interactions; and many or all of them may occur at once. How does inner speech affect and how is it affected by these concurrent events?

Perhaps I can phrase the concern in slightly different but analogous terms. Think of the ethological psychologist who is conducting a naturalistic observational study of a mother's interaction with her infant daughter. The psychologist usually proceeds by generating an observational coding scheme for mother-behaviors and infant-behaviors and then records the sequence of behaviors of both. Out of this sequence the psychologist attempts to derive the functional relationships among the various categories of behaviors in the particular dyad. For example, category X behavior in mother is usually followed (in probability terms) by category Y in infant and so on and so forth.

The present concern with the functional role of internal dialogue parallels this example but the behaviors of interest are those of one person. The goal of a cognitive-functional assessment is to describe, in probabilistic terms, the functional significance of engaging in self-statements of a particular sort followed by an individual's particular behavior or emotional state (e.g., mood), or his physiological reactions or his attentional processes, etc. How does the internal dialogue influence and, in turn, is it influenced by other events or behavioral processes?

In order to answer such questions the researcher has to categorize two ongoing streams of behavior and note their interdependencies over time and situations. Few investigators have framed their research questions in terms which include the individual's conscious thought or internal dialogue as one of the streams of behavior. The exceptions come from research on young children's private speech and on adult problem-solving, in which subjects have been asked to talk aloud while they are engaged in a task. But even in these studies the full potential of a sequential functional analysis has not been realized. We have to turn to other research areas for suggestions concerning how internal dialogue may influence other ongoing events. In most of these studies the investigator manipulates the subjects' self-statements at one moment in time and notes the resultant consequences. These studies will provide a beginning for addressing the question: How does changing the client's internal dialogue lead to behavior change?

Function of Internal Dialogue

Three sources have proved helpful in generating suggestions for the functional value of inner speech, namely, (1) the work on interpersonal instructions, usually in the context of problem-solving tasks; (2) the research on cognitive factors in stress responses; and (3) the research on the effects of instructional sets on physiological reactions. Let's examine each research area.

Interpersonal Instructions

Let us consider the way in which *interpersonal instructions* operate, in order to determine whether they are similar to *intrapersonal self-instructions*. Several investigators have speculated about the role of interpersonal instructions in controlling behavior (e.g., Gagné, 1964; Marlatt, 1972; Simkins, 1963; Sutcliffe, 1972). They emphasized both the instigational and directive functions of instructions in controlling behavior. For example, Gagné, working within a problem-solving framework, viewed interpersonal instructions as serving the following functions: (1) motivating the subject by eliciting an achievement set; (2) helping him identify the criterion performance and the salient parts of the stimulus situation; (3) aiding recall of relevant subordinate performance capabilities necessary to the task; and (4) channeling thinking in terms of task-relevant hypotheses while controlling extraneous thoughts and behaviors (1964). In this way, instructions provide the subject with a rule or principle by which he can mediate his behavior.

In describing the role of *self*-verbalizations, or *self*-instructions, in a problem-solving task, McKinney offered the following list of functions: the *self*-instructions (1) increase distinctiveness of the stimulus attributes; (2) direct subject's attention to the relevant dimensions; (3) assist the subject in formulating a series of hypotheses; and (4) maintain information in short-term memory (1973b).

The similarity between the Gagné and McKinney lists of psychological functions for inter- and intrapersonal instructions is noteworthy. This leads to a rather obvious hypothesis, that *self-instructions operate in a similar fashion to interpersonal instructions.* As noted earlier, Vygotsky (1962) and Luria (1961) theorized that developmentally, the child comes to exercise verbal control of his behavior by incorporating adults' instructions:

> Apparently, egocentric speech, besides having a purely expressive function and a function of discharge, besides merely accompanying the child's activity, very readily becomes a means of thinking in its own sense, i.e., it begins to fulfill the function of formulating a plan for the solution of a problem emerging in the course of behavior (Vygotsky, as quoted by Zaporozhets and Elkonin, 1971, p. 124).

Cognitive Factors in Stress

Another source of hypotheses for the role of internal dialogue in affecting behavior change is the social psychological work on coping with stress, although this literature is not specifically concerned with self-statements. Consider the following scene. Two individuals, both of whom possess essentially the *same* speaking skills, are asked on separate occasions to present a public speech. The two individuals differ in their level of speech-anxiety: One has high speech-anxiety, the other, low speech-anxiety. During each speaker's presentation, some members of the audience walk out of the room. This exodus elicits quite different self-statements or appraisals from the high versus the low speech-anxiety individuals. The high speech-anxiety individual is likely to say to himself: "I must be boring. How much longer do I have to speak? I knew I never could give a speech," and so forth. These self-statements both reflect and engender anxiety and in turn become self-fulfilling prophecies. On the other hand, the low speech-anxiety individual is more likely to view the audience's departure as a sign of rudeness or to attribute their leaving to external considerations. In his internal dialogue he is likely to say something like: "They must have a class to catch. Too bad they have to leave; they will likely miss a good talk."

A similar pattern of differential thinking styles is evident for high and low test-anxiety individuals. An exam during which some students hand in their papers early, will, for the high test-anxiety individual, elicit "worrying" statements: "I can't get this problem. I'll never finish. How can that guy be done?", resulting in increased anxiety and further task-irrelevant and self-defeating thoughts. In comparison, the low test-anxiety student readily dismisses the other students' performance by saying to himself: "Those guys who handed in their papers early must know nothing. I hope they score this exam on a curve."

In short, the high test-anxiety individual tends to be self-oriented and to personalize the situations and challenges with which he is confronted. There is considerable evidence that the high test-anxiety individual is strongly self-deprecating and ruminative in evaluative situations (Sarason, 1973).[31] Wine, in a review of the relationship between evaluation and anxiety, concluded, "arousal appears to bear no consistent relationship to performance" (1970). On the other hand, she noted, "self-referential worry is attention-demanding and detracts from attention processes." It was not the arousal *per se*, but rather whether the individual was attending to his arousal (what he was saying to himself about the arousal) that led to performance debilitated by evaluation anxiety.

A related example was offered by Wheelis (1969). He suggested that a student who fails an examination may say to himself, "I would not have failed if the teacher had not asked that question on Cromwell—which, after all, had not come up in class" *or* "I would not have failed if I had

---

[31] Interestingly, Mandler has suggested that anxiety scales are an established, although undiscovered, method of measuring the self-instructional tendencies of our subjects (1975). Anxiety scales may be viewed as self-instruction scales that measure individual differences in the manner in which people instruct themselves about their appraisal and response in stressful situations.

studied harder." Both statements are addressed to the same experience and both claim to answer the question "Why did I fail?" and both may be true. "Truth does not here provide the criterion for selection; the way we understand the past is determined, rather, by the future we desire. If we want to excuse ourselves we elect the former view [i.e., that the failure was caused by external events]; if we want to avoid such failures in the future we elect the latter [i.e., that failure was self-determined]" (Wheelis, 1969, p. 66). The two examples of the many alternative self-statements that the student may emit have different impacts on other behavioral and affective events.

These examples suggest that how one responds to stress in large part is influenced by how one appraises the stressor, to what he attributes the arousal he feels, and how he assesses his ability to cope.[32] A similar analysis was offered by the social psychologist, Janis (1965). Although he did not phrase his arguments in terms of "internal dialogue," but rather used terms such as "appraisal" and "work of worrying," he argued that such appraisal (or what I am calling internal dialogue) enabled individuals to cope more readily with stress because it encouraged the individual (1) to make "plans" for coping with a number of different contingencies; (2) to attempt to reassure himself; (3) to ward off disturbing thoughts; and (4) to note which of his behaviors should become cues for actions. The research that was reviewed in the previous chapters indicated that teaching a client to alter his internal dialogue will have directive effects on (a) what the individual attends to in the environment; (b) how he appraises various stimulus events; (c) to what he attributes his behavior; and (d) his expectations about his own capacities to handle a stressful event.

These observations underscore the argument that one function of internal dialogue in changing affect, thought,

[32] See Lazarus, Averill, and Opton (1970), Meichenbaum (1976a), and Meichenbaum *et al.* (1975) for a review of the role of cognitive factors in stress reactions.

and behavior is to *influence the client's attentional and appraisal processes*.

Instructional Sets and Physiological Effects

Altering the client's internal dialogue not only influences his attention and appraisal but also it will have physiological effects as well. The literature on the effect of instructional sets on autonomic functioning indicates that changing the client's style of self-instructions can have major physiological effects (Barber, 1965; May & Johnson, 1973; Platonov, 1959; Schwartz, 1971; Sternbach, 1964; Zimbardo, 1969). Cognitive activity has even been suggested as a mediational factor (i.e., facilitator or inhibitor) in operant, autonomic conditioning. Katkin and Murray proposed that an internal source of stimulation, rather than the external, experimenter-controlled reinforcers, may control autonomic responses (1968). The subject may be involved in arousing or inhibiting subvocal activity, which produces a previously conditioned autonomic response. An illustration of the role of cognitive set is found in the work on emotion by Schachter, who provides evidence for the important role that the client's restructuring of a situation plays in mediating behavior (1966). In our own research, the clients, following cognitive-behavior modification treatment, came to label their physiological arousal as facilitative rather than debilitative (Meichenbaum, 1972; Wine, 1970). Sweaty palms, increased heart and respiratory rates, muscular tension, now became "allies," cues to use the coping techniques for which they had been trained. The physiological arousal that the client had *previously* labeled as totally debilitating anxiety and fear, the harbinger of further behavior deterioration leading to feelings of helplessness, was now relabeled as eagerness to demonstrate competence, as a desire to get on with a task and as a sign to cope. In other words, the client learned to respond to the same physiological cues when they do arise with different cognitions: Originally he entertained cognitions that mediated further autonomic arousal (e.g., "I'm really nervous; I'm sweating; others will see it; I can't handle this"); after treatment, his cognitions had a coping orientation and moved the focus away from his arousal toward response alternatives. This shift in cognitions in itself may mediate a shift in autonomic functioning. The present theory postulates that it is not the physiological arousal *per se* that is debilitating but rather what the client says to himself about that arousal that determines his eventual reactions.

Many other illustrations could be offered for forging links between physiological events and internal dialogue but perhaps most telling is the work by Graham and his colleagues, who studied the relationship between clients' cognitive sets and psychosomatic conditions. Graham, Lundy, Benjamin, and Kabler interviewed various psychosomatic patients (ulcer patients, asthmatics, patients with hives) and noted what was going on prior to the onset of a flare-up of symptoms (1962). They then related the content and style of the clients' thinking processes with each of the respective psychosomatic disorders. What the client felt about the events in his life and what he wanted to do about them had diagnostic value. Graham, Kabler, and Graham were able to demonstrate that when normal subjects were hypnotized and asked to *feel* the attitudes previously given by psychosomatic patients, the hypnotized normal subjects actually suffered those same symptoms (1962). The production of particular self-statements had major specific physiological effects.

Graham's results are consistent with the studies on cognitive factors in emotion by Goldfried and Sobocinski (1975), Rimm and Litvak (1969), and Strickland and her colleagues (Hale & Strickland, 1976; Strickland, Hale, & Anderson, 1975). Typical of the research on cognitive factors in emotion is the study by Velten, who examined the effect of self-statements on mood states (1968). Velten had subjects read self-referent statements that varied in content. Some of the statements reflected elation ("This is great, I really feel good"); others were depressive in tone ("I have too many bad things in my life"), and still others were neutral ("Utah is the Beehive State"). Using various mood indicators, such as reaction time and writing speed, Velten found a direct influence of statements used and resultant mood state.

A fuller discussion of the complex interrelationship between emotion and cognition is beyond the scope of the present book but a thoughtful document summarizes a viewpoint similar to mine. Averill argues that cognitive appraisal is not simply an ancillary precursor of emotion but is an integral part of what we mean by emotion:

> The term "cognition" is ambiguous. When contrasted with emotion it often denotes rational, deliberate, problem-solving activity. We have no quarrel with the distinction in this sense; phenomenologically, emotions are not conducive to orderly thinking. But "rational" thought (however broadly conceived) is only one aspect of cognitive activity. . . . It is easy to lose sight of the many aspects of cognition related to emotion since, in philosophy and academic psychology alike, the rational processes have been the primary focus of interest. (1974, p. 179)

Part of the problem in understanding the relationship between cognitions and feelings in the behavior change process is the often *mistaken* equation by some therapists of cognitive change with a purely "intellectual" insight (e.g., Berenson & Carkhuff, 1967). The cognitive changes that are described in this book refer to changes that are closely tied to emotional, motivational, and behavioral processes.

Further Characteristics of the Internal Dialogue

Beck has noted several other characteristics of the internal dialogue process that are worth highlighting. Using the term "automatic thoughts" to describe the internal dialogue, because the thoughts seem to emerge automatically and extremely rapidly, Beck describes their characteristics as follows:

> [1] They [automatic thoughts] generally are not vague and unformulated, but are specific and *discrete*. They occur in a kind of shorthand; that is, only the essential words in a sentence seem to occur—as in telegraphic style.
>
> [2] The thoughts do not arise as a result of deliberation, reasoning, or reflection about an event or topic. There is no logical sequence of steps such as in goal-oriented thinking or problem-solving. The thoughts 'just happen'. . . . They just seem to be relatively *autonomous* in that the patient made no effort to initiate them and in more disturbed cases they are difficult to 'turn off'.
>
> [3] The patient tends to regard these automatic thoughts as *plausible* or reasonable, although they may seem far-fetched to somebody else. . . . The content of automatic thoughts, particularly those that are repetitive and seem to be most powerful, are *idiosyncratic*." (Beck, 1976, pp. 36–37)

Beck's observations concerning the characteristics of our client's internal dialogue are provocative hypotheses that need careful confirmation. But the discussion of internal dialogue and automatic thoughts may give the reader the wrong impression, the impression that people are going about always thinking before they act. This is not the case. As Thorngate has argued—and I concur—the role of thought in social interactions has been overstressed (1976). Factors such as time, mental effort, and the redundancy of social interactions cause habit to be a much more common determinant of social behavior than cognition. Thorngate argues persuasively that most social transactions take place on the basis of habit or on the basis of the learned rituals that Berne (1964) and Goffman (1967) have described. Although I agree with Thorngate's analysis that we don't always have to think before we act, I believe that if we are *going to change a behavior then we must think before we act*. Such thinking (i.e., the production of inner speech) "deautomatizes" the maladaptive behavioral act and provides the basis for providing the new adaptive behavior. This view will be developed more fully in the next chapter.

Structure of Internal Dialogue

I have been making the case that inner speech plays an important role in being able to influence the client's behaviors, but this is only half the story. There is a second important function of inner speech, and that is to influence and alter what I call the client's *cognitive structures.*

Let us explore why the construct *cognitive structure* is required in an explanation of behavior change. Consider the following questions and observations. What shapes the content of the client's internal dialogue; that is, why does an individual emit one set of self-statements rather than another? If internal dialogue has meaning, where does this meaning come from? For example, in the prologue I included a quote from Sokolov's book *Inner Speech and Thought*, which illustrated the implicit need for some construct such as cognitive structure. To quote Sokolov once again:

> Inner speech is nothing but speech to oneself, or concealed verbalization, which is instrumental in the logical processing of sensory data, in their realization and comprehension with a *definite system of concepts and judgments.* (1972, emphasis added)

The phrase to be highlighted is "a system of concepts and judgments." The meaning system or "structure" that gives rise to a particular set of self-statements and images must be taken into consideration in the change process.

Consider the example offered earlier of my son David's learning to control his behavior by saying to himself, "Bappy—door—all done." What is the meaning system that gave rise to such self-statements, which come to guide his behavior? A clinical example of the need for the construct cognitive structures comes from Novaco's work with patients who have anger control problems. As one aspect of the stress-inoculation training, the patients learned to emit self-statements such as "Don't get bent out of shape." The patient did not respond to this self-statement literally. Rather, the expression only took on self-controlling influence within a particular meaning system. Another observation, and one which may have puzzled the reader, is that throughout this book I have used the term internal "dialogue" rather than internal "monologue." This suggests that an important element in the behavior change process is not only speaking to oneself but also listening to oneself. It is close to a self-communication system, a dialogue with oneself, that comes to influence behavior. That the process is indeed a *dialogue* was illustrated in the case of a test-anxious client (Meichenbaum, 1972). Following therapy, when the client was taking an examination and was employing the host of behavioral and cognitive coping responses, he became anxious anyway, for there was an accompanying thought that "I must really be anxious if I have to use all these techniques." What the client said to himself about using the coping responses—the meaning he imposed on the use of these procedures—influenced their efficacy. If we wish to explain why people change their behavior we must not only consider the function of the coping, self-engineering procedures (the inner speech) but also how they "fit" within the individual's cognitive structure.

However, the construct of "cognitive structure" is difficult to define. Cognitive structures seem to be the cognitive psychologist's Rorschach card or "Linus-blanket"—he can see anything he wants in it and it gives him a sense of security. Hilgard in 1976 pointed out that the term *cognitive structure* was made familiar by Tolman (1932) and Lewin (1935). Under the banner of "cognitive structure" fall such concepts as Miller, Galanter, and Pribram's (1960) images and plans, Piaget's (1954) schema, Sarbin's roles (Sarbin and Coe, 1972), and Hilgard's (1976) control systems.

By *cognitive structure* I mean to point to that organizing aspect of thinking that seems to monitor and direct the strategy, route, and choice of thoughts. I mean to imply a kind of "executive processor," which "holds the blueprints of thinking" and which determines when to interrupt, change, or continue thought. By cognitive structure I mean to imply that which is *unchanged* by learning a new word but which *is* changed by learning a new word-skill, such as the skill of listening to one's own internal dialogue. The cognitive structure I refer to is, by definition, the source of the scripts from which all such dialogues borrow.[33]

What will be the nature of the reader's internal dialogue after reading this book? How will that inner speech affect the reader's interaction with patients, the way he conducts experiments, in short, his cognitive structures? Neisser, following Piaget's notion of assimilation and accommodation, described the kinds of structural changes that may come about: *absorption*, in which new structures are developed that effectively contain old structures; *displacement*, in which the old and new structures continue to exist side by side; and *integration*, in which new structures at a more comprehensive level still contain parts of the old (1962). Which process will take place will depend upon the history and evaluation of the old structure and the development and value of the new structure. What is the nature of the evidence that is necessary for the reader's cognitive structures to undergo the processes of absorption, displacement, and integration? What is the nature of the data and what is the content of the inner dialogue that is required to change the reader's cognitive structures? For a change in structure will lead to new inner speech and new behaviors and the further strengthening of the structures and so on. A kind of "virtuous" cycle is established.

I can illustrate the way in which the processes of internal dialogue and cognitive structures contribute to the

---

[33] I am particularly grateful to Barney Gilmore for his help with the theory chapter and the section on cognitive structure.

change process in our clients if I use the analogous case of the scientist. If we consider how these processes operate in ourselves, then we will have a better feel for how they may apply to our clients.

Much has been written about the behavior of scientists and the more that is revealed (e.g., Brush, 1974; Hebb, 1975; Mahoney, 1976; Polanyi, 1958), the better the analogue scientists become for the study of our client's behavior. The scientist holds a set of beliefs, some of which are implicit (or what some of our clinical colleagues characterize as "unconscious"), while other beliefs are explicit. The beliefs (or cognitive structures) about the phenomena under investigation give rise to conscious thought of which the scientist is aware (or what I am calling inner speech or internal dialogue). The internal dialogue concerning hunches, hypotheses, etc., guide and influence what the scientist will attend to, how he will appraise phenomena, and all of the other functional aspects of inner speech reviewed above. The internal dialogue contributes to a heightened awareness or a "raised consciousness" which makes the scientist sensitive to new observations. Following from such an internal dialogue the scientist behaves by collecting data which yields results (behavioral outcomes) that are consistent with *or* anomalous with his belief systems (structures), which affects the scientist's internal dialogue and which in turn leads to the acceptance or rejection of the data. Central to the behavior change process is the nature of the scientist's cognitive structures, the accompanying inner speech, and the behavioral outcomes (the results of one's actions). What the scientist says to himself about behavioral outcomes will determine whether he considers the results as evidence which can then alter his beliefs (cognitive structures).

But so few of my clients are scientists. It is time to see how the processes of inner speech, cognitive structures, and behavioral outcomes come into play in the therapy process with our clients.

A Cognitive Theory of
Behavior Change

> *The attempt to describe features common to all forms of psychotherapy requires consideration of a wide variety of patterned personal and social interactions. To keep our bearings in this exploration, a general* conceptual framework *is needed. . . . This is obviously a very big order, and to handle it adequately would require a complete theory of personality development and structure as related to social and cultural influences.*
>
> —JEROME FRANK (1974, p. 24)

The student of psychotherapy is faced with a conundrum. Many therapists, espousing a wide variety of theories and techniques, claim to be therapeutically effective. In some instances their claims are empirically supported. Moreover, behavioral change results from nonprofessional contacts which persons encountered during the course of day-to-day life. The conundrum, then, is attempting to understand and explain the behavioral change process as it occurs in so many different contexts. What are the underlying mechanisms of change that are common to the various procedures and contexts in which change occurs?

The purpose of the present chapter is to begin to deal with this conundrum, to provide the conceptual framework for therapy that Jerome Frank called for. As the reader might suspect by now, central to the theory of behavior change that will be offered are the individual's cognitive processes.

A Clinical Example

In describing the successful treatment of psychoanalysis, Singer explains the change in a client as follows:

> A patient experiences a sudden sense of unrest or annoyance upon entering a room. Under some past conditions he might have hastily left the room or perhaps talked rudely in response to questions raised. His analytic experience now alerts him to the fact that this sudden unease is occasioned by an irrational anticipation or transference in the situation. He replays in his mind the thoughts just previous to entering the room or what he was thinking about immediately prior to this situation. On this mental screen, he "instant replays" the thoughts and perceptions that occurred and suddenly is aware that he had been thinking about some obligation to one of his parents and that on entering the room he noticed across the way an elderly gentleman who rather resembled his father. He now perceives that his distress is a combination of anticipatory image plus the scene occurring in the room and generally is freed of his anxiety and certainly is less likely to engage in an irrational and self-defeating bit of behavior in this new situation. (1974, p. 64)

The Singer quote nicely illustrates several points that I would like to make concerning the change process. First, in order to bring about change, the client must recognize some "behavior" in which he engages (be it a set of thoughts, images, physiological *or* behavioral responses) *or* in some instances the interpersonal responses of someone else. Thus, Singer's patient became "aware of," "sensitive to" his sudden sense of unease and his preceding thoughts. The client's "recognition" is a necessary but not sufficient condition to bring about change. This recognition or self-awareness acts as a cue for producing a certain internal dialogue. The content of the client's internal dialogue and indeed what the client will attend to is guided by the orientation of the therapist and the nature of the conceptualization that evolves between the client and the therapist. The client's internal dialogue may be in terms of psychoanalytic interpretations as in the Singer example, or learned response habits à la Wolpe, or faulty belief systems à la Ellis, etc. Indeed our clients seem to have sufficient life experiences to provide data consistent with any one of these therapy conceptualizations and they can maintain the employment of a host of therapists of widely different persuasions.

Prior to therapy when a client notices some maladaptive behavior, some symptom, this is usually the occasion for him to produce an internal dialogue comprised of negative self-statements and images, which likely have deleterious effects. The recognition of anxiety-engendering thoughts, feelings, physiological reactions, interpersonal behaviors triggers inner speech that fosters a sense of "helplessness" and "hopelessness," a fear of "losing one's mind," a sense of demoralization, all of which have been described by Frank (1974), Raimy (1975), and Strupp (1970). For example, upon entry into therapy, an obsessive-compulsive patient may claim that he is a "victim" of his feelings and thoughts; an anxious or phobic patient may believe that external events are causing his malady. Rarely does the client consider the role of his own thinking processes and/or the interpersonal meaning of his behavior as sources of disturbance.

However, as a result of therapy a *translation* process takes place, one which we will discuss more fully below. The translation is from the internal dialogue the client engages in prior to therapy to a new language system that emerges over the course of treatment. Whereas, prior to therapy the obsessive-compulsive patient may view his compulsion to wash as a sign of "losing his wits," during therapy he may come to view his washing in terms of a "communication" problem, or as a manifestation of a

deep-seated conflict about guilt, or as a behavioral repertoire that is maintained by secondary gains. Which reconceptualization predominates will be influenced by whom
the client sees in therapy.

The translation process is the result of what occurs
both in and outside of therapy. In therapy, the therapist
uses a host of clinical tools, such as reflection, explanation,
interpretation, information-giving, and cognitive modeling,
to provide the conditions whereby the client will change
what he says to himself. Outside of therapy, the client engages in coping behaviors that have been discussed and
rehearsed in therapy. The coping behaviors lead to new
behavioral outcomes and different reactions from significant others in the client's life. These behavioral outcomes
and reactions elicit an internal dialogue in the client that
affects both his cognitive structures (e.g., belief about himself, about his ability to cope, etc.), as well as his ongoing
behaviors.

The scenario is thus set for explaining the behavior
change process. The three basic processes of change have
been introduced in the form of (1) the client's behaviors
and the reactions they elicit in the environment; (2) the
client's internal dialogue or what he says to himself before,
accompanying, and following his behavior; and (3) the
client's cognitive structures that give rise to the specific
internal dialogue. In short, I am proposing that behavior
change occurs through a sequence of mediating process
involving the interaction of inner speech, cognitive structures, and behavior and their resultant outcomes. If an individual (whether a client, or scientist, or whatever) is
going to change his pattern of responding, he must introduce an intentional mediational process. The mediational
process involves the recognition of maladaptive behavior
(either external or internal) and this recognition must come
to elicit inner speech that is different in content from that
engaged in prior to therapy. The altered private speech
must then trigger coping behaviors. Some clients require
explicit teaching of such coping responses and this is

where the technology of behavior therapy is of particular value.

Let us examine this change process more microscopically by viewing it as consisting of three phases. These phases should not be seen as a lock-step progression. Rather, they form a flexible sequence, during which cognitive structures, inner speech, and behaviors, with their resultant outcomes, interweave in contributing to behavior change. As each phase is described, we can consider how therapy can efficiently make use of the processes that are examined in our analysis.

Phase 1: Self-Observation

The first step in the change process is the client's becoming an observer of his own behavior. Through heightened awareness and deliberate attention, the client monitors, with increased sensitivity, his thoughts, feelings, physiological reactions, and/or interpersonal behaviors. As a result of the translation process that occurs in therapy, the client develops new cognitive structures (concepts) which permit him to view his symptoms differently. Attending to one's maladaptive behaviors takes on a different meaning—a meaning that contributes to a heightened vigilance or "raised consciousness." This is important because one of the things that already characterizes some clients prior to therapy is a heightened awareness, a self-preoccupation. Prior to therapy the client's internal dialogue about his maladaptive behaviors is likely to be delimited, repetitive, and unproductive, contributing to a sense of helplessness and despair. A good illustration of this maladaptive thinking style was offered by Beck, Rush, and Kovacs in the case of the depressed client who, over time and in response to his fatigue, came to say the following to himself:

1. I am a depressed patient who can't do much because I get fatigued easily. . . .
2. I'm a person who can't do much. . . .

3. I can't do anything. . . .
4. I can't now, never could and never will do anything of value. . . .
5. A person who can't do anything is a loser. . . .
6. A person who is a loser is unlovable, unwanted and a burden to others. (1976, p. 30)

In order to change his behavior the depressed client must come to produce thoughts and behaviors incompatible with these maladaptive ones. As a result of therapy, the client must come to view his thoughts and behavior differently. The depressed client must come to see that he is no longer a "victim" of such thoughts and feelings, but an active contributor to his own experience. The recognition of the prodromal signs of the maladaptive behaviors must trigger a different internal dialogue. An internal dialogue that notes the opportunities for engaging in adaptive behaviors, behaviors that will be discussed and rehearsed in therapy. As mentioned before, the process of self-observation is necessary but not a sufficient condition for change.

The exact behaviors upon which the client will focus depends upon the conceptualization process that evolves during therapy. The important role of this conceptualization process in therapy needs to be further underscored. Whereas the client usually enters therapy with some conceptualization of his problems (as well as expectations concerning therapy and the role of the therapist), the client's conceptualization of his problems must undergo change, if he is to alter his behavior. One goal of the (re)conceptualization process is for the client to redefine his problems in terms that will give him a sense of understanding and with it the feelings of control and hope which are necessary for acts of change. One of the by-products of the increased self-awareness and the translation process is that the client gains a sense of control of his emotional state, thoughts, and behaviors. In short, the client is changing what he is saying to himself about his maladaptive behaviors.

Many observers of the therapy process, such as Frank (1972) and Marmor (1975), have also pointed to the importance of this *translation* process in the therapy enterprise. This has been most explicitly stated by Lewis:

> A look at various schools of psychotherapy reveals that many of the operations involved consist of translations, supplying new verbal categories for old ones. Therapists speak of "differentiating fine shades of feeling from one another," and "improving communication." A patient's initial statement, "I'm afraid of heights," may become translated in the course of therapy into various other statements depending upon which conceptual framework the therapist holds and transmits to the patient. If the therapist is a psychoanalyst, the patient might say much later, "I'm not really afraid of physical heights—I know this now—it is rather that as a child I feared another type of physical fall—that is, sexual surrender. I was afraid of a symbol—being on a cliff no longer seems so scary." If the therapist is a behaviorist, the translation proceeds along a different path: The patient may say, "I now realize that I am lumping all heights together, and that I can train myself to relax in a situation of slight elevation, so that I am finding that I feel more and more relaxed in higher and yet higher ones." An existential translation might be "I realize that I have been deceiving myself with this symptom—that I never before could tolerate the idea of nothingness—of nonexistence. But, sharing this basic fear with my therapist has diminished my misguided fear of heights." (1972, p. 81)

It is unlikely that clients engage in the formal internal dialogue that Lewis has described. Rather, the thoughts more likely approximate the automatic thoughts described by Beck. However, the Lewis quote does underscore the translation process that contributes to change. A similar observation has been offered by two psychoanalysts, Ezekiel and Mendel. Ezekiel suggested that the essence of the psychoanalytic method is that it gives meaning to an apparently meaningless sequence of thoughts and actions and thus provides a rational explanation for apparently irrational behavior (1965). Mendel suggested that the assignment of meaning is part of every therapist-patient interaction, a process that is independent of the theories or techniques of the therapist (1968). Mendel states, "All schools [of psychotherapy] help their patients to assign meaning to behavior, thoughts, fantasies, dreams, delusions, and hallucinations." I would suggest that a similar claim could be made of the behavior therapies.

A number of observations are important concerning this initial self-observation phase and about the translation process. First, I am *not* suggesting that each and every therapy conceptualization will prove to be equally effective in facilitating change. But, one of the more essential variables that determines therapy outcome is the degree to which a given conceptualization leads to specific behavioral changes that can be transferred to the real-life situation.

Secondly, we must be concerned with how the therapist prepares the client to accept (implicitly) a particular conceptualization or therapy rationale with its accompanying treatment intervention. Some therapists are very directive and didactic and seem to force upon the client a particular conceptualization by power of their personalities, jargon, or positions. In some cases such a "hard sell" approach clearly does prove successful. But the therapist must be concerned not only with the client's self-statements and attributions concerning his presenting problems but also with those concerning the therapy process and dependence on the therapist. An alternative way to proceed is to have the client and therapist evolve a common conceptualization so that the client feels he is an active participant and contributor.

The manner in which the therapist queries the client about his presenting problem, the type of assessment procedures the therapist employs, the kinds of homework assignments he gives, the type of therapy rationale he offers, all influence the conceptualization process. Thus, the therapist tries to understand the client's description and definition of his problem but does not merely accept uncritically the client's view. Instead the therapist and client attempt to redefine the problem in terms that are meaningful to both of them. Note that a client's acceptance of a particular conceptualization of his problem is not usually a formal, explicit agreement, but rather an implicit byproduct of the interaction between client and therapist. With skill, the therapist has the client come to view his problem from a different perspective, to fabricate a new meaning or explanation for the etiology and maintenance of his maladaptive behavior.

The initial phase of the cognitive theory of behavior change is concerned with the increased awareness that evolves from the translation process; but more must occur if change is to take place.

Phase 2: Incompatible Thoughts and Behaviors

I have argued that intrinsic to all therapies is the client's reconceptualization of his problem and that the initial stages of therapist-client interactions fosters this "translation" process. Furthermore, the premise that is implicit or explicit in the first contacts of therapy is that the client must attend to his maladaptive behaviors and begin to notice opportunities for adaptive behavioral alternatives if he is to produce behavioral-cognitive-affective changes.

As the client's self-observations become attuned to incipient low-intensity aspects of his maladaptive behavior, the client learns to initiate cognitions and behaviors that interfere with the maladaptive ones. The self-observation signals the opportunity for producing the adaptive thoughts and behaviors. This point was illustrated before, with the quote from Singer's book. The recognition of the maladaptive behavior triggered an internal dialogue. The content of what the client learns to say to himself will vary with the conceptualization that emerged in therapy. However, if the client's behavior is to change, then what he says to himself and/or imagines, must initiate a new behavioral chain, one that is incompatible with his maladaptive behaviors.

The new internal dialogue or inner speech will serve all of the functions which were described in the last chapter (namely, affecting attentional and appraisal systems, physiological responses, and instigating new behaviors). Thus, when I speak of the recognition of maladaptive behaviors triggering internal dialogues, this should be interpreted as involving all of the functional properties that inner speech can serve.

With the self-recognition of the maladaptive acts, feelings, thoughts, come accompanying thoughts (inner speech), the content of which is guided by the translation that has evolved in therapy. Not only does the inner speech have functional properties with regard to other ongoing streams of behavior but it also has an impact on the client's cognitive structures. The client learns that he can organize his experiences around the new conceptualization and can do so in a way that enables him to cope more effectively. This "reinforcement" of the therapist's conceptualization helps to consolidate the client's newly emerging cognitive structures.

In summary, the refocusing of the client's attention, the alteration in appraisal, and physiological reactions will help change the internal dialogue that the client brought into therapy. In turn, the internal dialogue comes to guide new behavior, the results of which have an impact on the individual's cognitive structures. This leads us to the third phase of the change process, which has to do with the client's emitting coping behaviors *in vivo*, and what he says to himself about the outcomes of these "personal experiments."

Phase 3: Cognitions Concerning Change

Recall that in our discussion of the basic processes for the present theory we not only spoke about cognitive structures and internal dialogue but we also made reference to the client's behaviors and the impact they have on significant others. Whether the client views these outcomes and reactions as consistent with or discrepant with his cognitive structures (e.g., beliefs) will influence the nature of the change. How the client views the reactions or nonreactions of significant others will influence what he says to himself, which in turn will influence the behavioral acts, and so on.

The third phase of the cognitive theory of behavior change is concerned with the process of the client's producing new behaviors in his everyday world and how he assesses (or what he says to himself about) the behavioral outcomes.

One of the major contributions of behavior therapy has been to highlight the particular needs of some patients in learning the behavioral skills required to emit new adaptive acts. But just focusing on such skills training is not sufficient to explain the change process. For what the client says to himself about his newly acquired behaviors and their resultant consequences will influence whether the behavioral change process will be maintained and will generalize. As the client attempts to behave differently, he will often elicit different reactions from significant others. What the client says to himself and imagines about these reactions and his own behavior change influences the stability and generalization of treatment. A person can behave in a variety of new ways because these ways pay off and yet he may not be willing to assume that he is a changed person or that he has in any sense gotten anything out of the therapy process. To the extent that the client changes both his behavior and his internal dialogues, to that extent therapy becomes a success. In other words, a person is how he behaves, as well as what he says to himself (including his attributions), which says much more than that a person is only how he behaves.

Another way to consider this question is to ask what will our client be willing to consider as *evidence* to alter his cognitive structures? Like the scientist, our client has a

host of "defensive" rationalizations and cognitive techniques to discount or accept the importance of data derived
from behavioral outcomes. The issue of what constitutes
evidence becomes critical for both the scientist and the
client. Why? Because if the change process is to be lasting
then one must not only teach new behavioral skills, alter
internal dialogue, but also one must influence cognitive
structures.

The reader may now view each of the many therapy
procedures as differentially focusing on any one or more of
the three basic processes, cognitive structures, inner-
speech, and behavioral acts. Some therapies such as Ellis'
rational-emotive therapy primarily focus on cognitive
structures, challenging premises and beliefs. Beck's approach to cognitive therapy focuses more on getting the
client (especially depressed clients) to engage in new behavioral acts so they can examine the inner speech which
follows from behavioral outcomes. Once the client's inner
speech is examined the implications this has for the underlying cognitive structures is examined during therapy. In
my stress inoculation approach, I focused on altering
clients' inner speech, which encouraged the production of
new behaviors and an examination of the resultant behavioral outcomes which permitted an exploration of the
clients' cognitive structures. The behavior therapy approaches usually limit their focus to the acquisition of new
behaviors and insure that the resultant behavioral outcomes will be favorable by means of manipulating
graded task assignments and environmental consequences
(reinforcements).

If what I have boldly asserted in the present cognitive
theory of behavior change is "valid" and heuristically useful, then as therapists we should be concerned with all
three basic processes, cognitive structures, inner speech,
and behaviors and the interpretation of their impact. Focusing on only one will likely prove insufficient.

Where should we begin? Should we focus most on

cognitive structures *or* try to alter inner speech *or* teach new behaviors and manipulate environmental consequences? These are important research questions. Beck's depressives might require us to focus on behavioral events and work toward inner speech and cognitive structures. Ellis' neurotics may be responsive to "frontal" attacks on the cognitive structures. My phobic and anxious clients may need cognitive-skills training that focuses on inner speech. Although each therapy approach focuses mainly on only one of the three mechanisms, it is suggested that the other two processes are also involved in change. We have to develop measures to assess the nature of the client's cognitions as related to each of these three processes. We have to begin to rethink how we go about understanding our client's deficits. It is to these concerns that we now turn our attention in the next chapter on assessment.

A Cognitive-Behavior Modification Approach to Assessment

> Psychiatric patients suffer from a variety of disorders of affect, cognition, and volition. A large number, if not the majority, of papers published by psychologists do not deal with these phenomena. Instead, they report upon the performance, by psychiatric patients, of a variety of tasks which might be described, without much loss of accuracy, as puzzles and indoor games. Examples are such tests as the pursuit rotor, the mirror drawing test, the block design test, the Rorschach test and the Thematic Apperception Test.
>
> —SHAPIRO AND RAVENETTE, 1959

Although one may disagree with Shapiro and Ravenette's evaluation of the various tests cited, their quote does sensitize us to the need to develop more explicit ways of assessing our client's *affects, cognitions*, and *volitions*. The present chapter conveys some preliminary attempts at developing this assessment armamentarium, which follow from a cognitive-behavioral treatment approach. Specifically, the present chapter has two purposes. The first is to examine various assessment strategies that have been employed to study psychological deficits. This analysis indicates some shortcomings and an alternative, namely a

cognitive-functional analysis approach. The second purpose of the chapter is to describe specific techniques that
can be employed to assess more directly the client's cognitions. Let's begin with an examination of the current assessment and research strategies.

To introduce the different strategies, let me share with
you a coping device that I have occasionally employed at
various conferences. Recently, for example, I was asked to
review the literature on the cognitive deficits of children
with learning disabilities and then to present a theoretical
statement. After reviewing the literature, I concluded that
the data base was sufficiently equivocal that it would be
premature to make theoretical statements.

"What shall I do ? I'm scheduled to present for thirty
minutes at the conference."

My method of coping, and the sort that I am becoming
more and more disposed to employ in such situations,
involved writing a paper about the cognitive style of investigators who study children with learning disabilities. Writing such papers has led me to the discovery that psychologists, although studying quite different populations, seem
to redo the same studies, go through the same arguments,
and confront similar methodological problems in studying
different psychological deficits. The rules of the game seem
to apply across populations; only the terminology and the
players change. Without a program you can't tell if you're at
a conference on learning disabilities, schizophrenia, or
high-risk populations. Indeed, one of my other coping
techniques at such conferences is to generate a score card.
On one side I list the issues that will arise in the form of the
participants' likely statements, such as, "I think we have to
define our populations more carefully," *or* "I found a difference between population X and a control population," *or*
"I wonder what this deficit means; is it a can't or won't
problem?" *or* "Has anyone observed this child in real
life?" and so on, usually ending the list with "What have
we been talking about for three days?" In a second list I

place the participants' names. One can then check off who says what, when.

What accounts for the apparent consistency across conferences, the apparent consistency in how we approach the study of psychological deficits? I suggest that two implicit general research strategies lead to this consistency. The two research strategies are called the comparative populations approach and the specific deficit approach.

The Comparative Groups Approach

The comparison of a target population (e.g., schizophrenics, learning-disabled children, high-risk groups) with matched, nonindexed control groups is deeply steeped in the tradition of psychopathological *search-for-the-deficit* research (e.g., Hunt & Cofer, 1944). Thus, one finds research-clinicians giving their subjects (or clients) a comprehensive battery of tests and noting performance relative to some normative population. As a result, not infrequently the clinician's report or study looks like a brochure for a *Mental Measurement Yearbook*. Illustrative of this approach is a study I reviewed for my learning disability paper by Myklebust, Bannochie, and Killen, who compared learning-disabled children with normal controls on a comprehensive psychoeducational battery (1971). The children were tested on the WISC, the Leiter International Performance Scale, the Healy Picture Completion Test I, Goodenough-Harris Drawing Test, and eight subtests from the Detroit Tests of Learning Aptitude. The results of these tests were related to a host of academic achievement measures. One must admire the children's endurance.

Is such a comparative groups approach, with its comprehensive battery of tests useful in elucidating the precise nature of an individual's deficit? Whether one is working with learning-disabled children, schizophrenics, or some other population manifesting a behavioral or performance deficit, it is doubtful that a comparative groups assessment

approach will yield data of much scientific or clinical significance. What we do learn from a battery of tests is that
the target population as a group performs more poorly on
assessment devices than do their normal counterparts—a
rather underwhelming and noninformative finding. Usually, these comparative studies, through a discriminant-
function analysis also indicate which tests were the most
sensitive markers of group differences. The intercorrela-
tional matrix of the test performances for the respective
groups led Myklebust *et al.* to draw the conclusion:

> A learning disability affects the organization of the intellect:
> hence, cognition itself is modified. The mental abilities of
> learning disability children are structured differently. (1971,
> p. 227)

But such "conclusions" from comparative group
studies are of little assistance in revealing the nature of the
learning process and how the learning-disabled child is
affected. Rather, such an approach tends to lead only to a
circularity in which the learning disability is attributed to
an inadequate performance on a specific test or set of tests,
still leaving us with the problem of what it means to be
unable to achieve a certain standard on this measure, what
underlies, causes this inability, what can affect a change
from incompetence to competence.

A deficient performance can arise for a variety of different reasons and a given level of performance may arise in
many different ways. Kinsbourne commented on the performance of schizophrenics:

> Subjects fail to focus attention on a task or situation if they
> lack interest in it, if they have emotional resistance toward
> participating, if they find that it makes excessive demands on
> their abilities, or if they are otherwise preoccupied. In the
> mere demonstration of a failure in selective attention, there is
> no discrimination between primary physiological causation
> and distractibility secondary to other causes, any or all of
> which might be applicable to a schizophrenic subject . . .
> rather than on independent manifestation of disturbed
> neuronal activity. (1971, p. 309)

Kinsbourne's comments highlight the fact that our client's manifestation of a particular performance deficit, especially on the highly demanding cognitive tasks employed in a comparative assessment battery, does not help us diagnose the psychological subprocesses contributing to the performance deficit.

The limitations of the comparative approach, which depends on summary group data, were stated most starkly by the eminent physiologist Bernard:

> If we collect a man's urine during twenty-four hours and mix all this urine to analyze the average, we get an analysis of a urine which simply does not exist; for urine, when fasting, is different from urine during digestion. A startling instance of this kind was invented by a physiologist who took urine from a railroad station urinal where people of all nations passed, and who believed he could thus present an analysis of *average* European urine! (Bernard, 1957, p. 134–135)

The Specific Deficits Approach

The comparative groups or "shot-gun" test battery is just one approach used by clinicians. A second assessment strategy employed is a specific deficits assessment approach. In this instance the clinician hypothesizes that a particular type of deficit forms the basis of the client's deficient performance and the clinician then attempts to assess that specific, hypothesized deficit through a battery of tests. This approach also typically involves the comparison of the client with a normative control group but the focus is on a test battery designed to assess a specific deficit rather than on a more global assessment battery.

The clinician thus proposes that a single deficiency underlies the client's problem and performance deficit. These specific deficits are usually labeled as problems in attention, memory, and so on. The clinician then selects a battery of tests to assess the specific deficit. For example, Kleuver hypothesized that a memory deficit contributed to children's poor reading ability (1971). He then administered sixteen memory tests, based on Guilford's (1967) structure of intellect model, to good and poor readers. He found that "normal" readers were superior to poor readers on several aspects of memory. However, Meachem suggested that we conceptualize memory as an epiphenomenon consisting of various cognitive activities such as classifying, rehearsing, labeling, visual imagery, and sentence elaboration (1972). Kleuver's results, then, tell us that learning-disabled children who are poor readers have a "memory" deficit relative to a control group but in the light of Meachem's analysis of memory, this is not really a further specification of the nature of the psychological deficit. It simply amounts to a new label, rather than an explanation or definition of the problem. Salkind and Poggio reached a similar conclusion in a discussion of activity level in hyperactive children (1975), as did Kopfstein and Neale in an examination of attention deficits in schizophrenics (1972). In each case, the authors called for an explication of the number of different psychological subprocesses involved in fostering motoric or attentional controls. Memory, activity level, attention, and such processes should not be viewed as single or homogenous phenomena. Rather, they are "chapter headings," which summarize psychological subprocesses.

Hypothetical speculation. Following a comparative groups and/or specific deficit assessment approach leads to the psychologist's tendency to engage in premature model-building and "neurologizing." To illustrate these dangers let's take an example from the work on deficits with schizophrenics. The literature is replete with constructs to explain the schizophrenic's performance deficit. A major source of such theorizing has been Broadbent's model of the human mind as an information channel of limited capacity (1958). This model has led various investigators to attribute the schizophrenic performance deficit to (1) a deficient attentional filter (Chapman & McGhie, 1962); (2) an input dysfunction (Venables, 1964); (3) a deterioration in channel capacity (Pishkin, Smith, & Leibowitz, 1962); (4) a failure in scanning processes (Silverman, 1964); (5) a slowness in processing data in the primary channel (Yates, 1966); (6) defective programs (Callaway, 1970). The schizophrenic deficit has also been conceptualized in terms of neurological models. Thus, for instance, schizophrenia has been hypothetically explained in terms of (1) a primary deficit in central nervous system organization (Belmont, Birch, Klein, & Pollack, 1964); (2) a deficit in the cortical regulatory system (Venables, 1963); (3) a defect in excitatory modulation (Claridge, 1967). One sees a similar trend to build models and "neurologize" the deficit with other clinical populations, such as learning-disabled children.

Elsewhere I have argued that such hypothetical speculation, whether derived from an information-communication model or a neurological model, seems premature and essentially nonproductive (Meichenbaum, 1976c; Meichenbaum and Cameron, 1973).[34] I suggested that at present, empirical investigation and theorizing may be more productively directed at a cognitive-functional approach to deficit analysis.

A Cognitive-Functional Approach

The tradition of a *functional* analysis of behavior emphasizes a careful examination of environmental antecedents and consequents, as related to a given response repertoire. A functional analyst carefully defines the specific response class, notes its naturally occurring topography and frequency within various situational settings, and then systematically manipulates environmental events in order to describe a causal relationship.

[34] These comments do not deny the fact that neurological deficits may contribute to a variety of behavioral problems, including schizophrenia and learning disabilities, but rather they highlight the fact that diagnostic evidence for brain dysfunction is often very difficult to obtain, and frequently the evidence that is offered is "presumptive."

A *cognitive-functional* approach to psychological deficits is in the same tradition but includes and emphasizes the role of the client's cognitions (i.e., self-statements and images) in the behavioral repertoire. In short, a functional analysis of the client's thinking processes and a careful inventory of his cognitive strategies are conducted in order to determine which cognitions (or the failure to produce which key cognitions), under what circumstances, are contributing to or interfering with adequate performance.

In detail, the cognitive-functional approach analyzes *sequential psychological processes.* Since most tasks, especially those employed in comparative groups studies, are complex, the cognitive-functional assessor must be concerned with the psychological demands of a particular task and with the sequentially organized set of cognitive processes that are required for adequate performance. The assessor asks the question, "In what psychological processes must the successfully achieving individual engage and in which of these is my client failing?"

In order to speculate about what leads to poor performance, the clinician can himself take the task or test on which his client manifested a performance deficit. Upon completion of the test, he can introspect about the thoughts, images, and behaviors he employed in order to perform adequately on the task. The clinician may wish to take the task once again, focusing on the cognitive and behavioral strategies he is employing. He may have other individuals examine their strategies following performance on the task. During each performance he is carefully watching for cues that may indicate the use of particular strategies. The clinician's concern is with the "process" variables, the "why" and "how," rather than merely the performance outcome.

Perhaps, for example, our client's inadequate performance on the task results from his failure to spontaneously and appropriately engage in task-relevant cognitive and behavioral strategies and/or from a number of client-generated task interruptions and distractions and the way in which the client notices and copes with these interruptions. In short, a failure in the internal dialogue of the client, what he says or fails to say to himself prior to, accompanying, and following his performance on a task, becomes the concern of analysis. An analysis of such cognitive strategies will help elucidate the nature of the psychological deficit.

A Cognitive-Functional Sampler

Some examples of such a cognitive-functional task analysis will help elucidate the value of this approach.

Schizophrenia. Price examined the nature of schizophrenics' deficit in a concept identification task (1968). Price noted that his task not only measured a subject's ability to form or identify a particular concept but also required the following: (1) experimentally demonstrable understanding of the task instructions; (2) discrimination of the dimensional properties of concept stimuli; (3) the ability to use symbolic information relevant to the concept; and (4) the retention of information relevant to the concept. As Price indicated, a failure of the subject to meet any one of these task requirements would result in a performance deficit. Price therefore assessed how each process contributed to inadequate performance by conducting functional manipulations and noting alterations of performance when each support was introduced and removed. Using an analysis of task requirements, Price systematically (1) determined that the schizophrenics understood the task instructions by means of pretraining on sample concept identification tasks; (2) controlled the amount of information given subjects about the concept by providing all relevant concept information on a cue-card preceding each test trial; (3) measured the subjects' ability to discriminate and manipulate the concept symbols by presenting the concept dimensions separately and combined; (4) assessed the amount of performance deficit due to inability to retain the relevant concept information by simultaneous and successive presentation of cue and test stimuli. Thus, by breaking the concept identification task into its components, Price could specify the particular reasons for a schizophrenic's inadequate performance. Our concern here is not in his particular conclusions concerning schizophrenics (which are somewhat complex), but in his paradigm as one means of carrying out a cognitive-functional assessment.

Similarly, Gholson and McConville, in studying children's concept identification performance, were able to identify specific deficits involving several factors: stimulus differentiation, verbal coding, visual imagery, memory storage and retrieval, and forms of logical deduction or inference (1974).

Cognitive style. Recently in our laboratory, Cameron examined the problem-solving performance of cognitively impulsive and reflective children (1976). In an initial study he confirmed a finding in the literature (reviewed in Chapter 1) that cognitively impulsive children performed less efficiently than their reflective counterparts. This much of Cameron's data is consistent with a comparative groups approach. The cognitive-functional analyst, or sleuth, is after the reason why. What is the nature of the process that accounts for the poor performance? Is it the same for all the inefficient children? Does the reason for poor performance change developmentally?

There are a number of ways to conduct our detective search. (Are you ready, Watson?) What Cameron did was to give all the children—both impulsives and reflectives—the problem-solving task on a second occasion, providing a reliability check as well as permitting a task analysis. He identified three essential components of the task: (1) comprehension and recall of the task instructions, (2) the formulation of a decision rule or solution strategy, and (3) implementation of the decision rule, or the child's behaving consistently with his own decision rule. Thus an impulsive child who does poorly on the problem-solving task (in this case a Neimark and Lewis, 1967, pattern-matching task) could do poorly if he falters at any one of the three demands of his task. The data indicate that of the 154 children included in the study, 18 showed a deficit at locus (1)—comprehension and recall of strategy, 36 children showed deficits at locus (2)—the development of the strategy, and, interestingly, 17 children manifested poor performance at locus (3), indicating that an effective solution strategy was within their repertoire but that it did not consistently guide or influence their performance. (See Cameron, 1976, for details concerning how he differentially assessed the components.) Research is surely needed to assess the importance of these differential deficits on other tasks, settings, and so on, and in fact this is being done. The point to be emphasized is that the task analysis goes beyond merely indicating that a deficit is present—it specifies the "why." Such analyses, as we will see, lead naturally into a consideration of remediation proposals. Assessment and treatment become indistinguishable.

Attentional vigilance. One final example will illustrate in particular how one assesses the cognitive component of the cognitive-functional analysis.

For the last few years in our research with hyperactive children and schizophrenics we have been employing an attentional vigilance task developed by Rosvold (1965). The Continuous Performance Task (CPT), as it is called, requires the subject to watch letters that appear one at a time on a memory drum or similar presentation device. The subject is to press a key when he sees an *X* that immediately follows an *A* and not to press the key for any other letters or sequence. Orzack and Kornetsky (1966) and Sykes, Douglas, and Morganstern (1973) have, respectively, reported that schizophrenics and hyperactive children have difficulty in maintaining attention on this vigilance task over a prolonged period of time, such as fifteen minutes. The reason that I describe this task is *not* to suggest any relationship between hyperactive children and schizophrenia but, instead, to have the reader consider a cognitive-functional analysis of this reliable deficit pattern. One could allow himself to be seduced into building psychological models or neurologizing about why these groups exhibit this particular deficit—in fact, this is what repeatedly happens at those conferences I was describing. But let us instead sharpen our "sleuthing" skills and begin with the task itself.

Imagine yourself taking the CPT task. What are you saying to yourself? "What am I supposed to do? Every time the letter *X* follows the letter *A*—press, good!" First you likely will repeat the task instructions. Subjects who do well on the CPT report that they attempt to monitor their performance and note when attention is waning. This recognition of wandering attention triggers a variety of cognitive and behavioral strategies, such as trying to visualize the *A-X*, setting more stringent response standards, and self-instructing, or producing motor responses such as shaking themselves, in order to remain vigilant. As you imagined yourself taking the task, did you employ any of these strategies?

In this manner, the clinician performs an analysis of not only the behaviors but also the thinking that is necessary to perform the task adequately. Thus, inadequate performance on the CPT may result (1) from the subject's failure to spontaneously and appropriately engage in task-relevant, cognitive and behavioral responses and strategies and/or (2) from a number of subject-generated task interruptions and distractions and the way in which the subject notices and deals with these interruptions. In short, a failure in the internal dialogue of the subject, what he says to himself prior to, accompanying, and following his performance on a task, is central to analysis. The analysis of such cognitions should help elucidate the nature of the psychological deficit.

In summary, the "cognitive" portion of this hyphenated cognitive-functional assessment approach comprises describing the nature of cognitive strategies required to perform a task. By means of a logical analysis of the task demands, by taking the task oneself and introspecting about one's cognitive strategies, by observing and interviewing others who take the task, and, finally, by systematically manipulating the task demands, one can better appreciate the sequential psychological processes required. This latter approach of manipulating the task demands leads us into our discussion of the functional aspects of the recommended diagnostic approach.

The manipulation. Just as the operant conditioner studying psychological deficits conducts a functional analysis by systematically manipulating environmental consequences, the cognitive-functional analyst notes the behavioral and performance changes that result from environmental manipulations. From such alterations in performance, the clinician can readily infer the presence or absence of particular cognitive strategies. Three types of manipulations may be employed in a cognitive-functional approach. First, one may directly modify the task, thus affecting the psychological demands. These manipulations may be in the form of speeded performance requirements; increasing the rate of stimulus presentation, thus not permitting rehearsal processes to occur; presenting the task through another modality in order to infer at what particular phase of operation the deficit occurs; or making important cues in the stimulus more salient, in an attempt to elicit the solution strategy on a simpler task, then gradually returning to the more difficult tasks to see whether the client generalizes the solution strategy. Through this approach one can assess the client's capabilities and his deficits, under which task parameters he is able to demonstrate competence, and under which conditions the client's performance begins to deteriorate. By systematically manipulating the task demands one can pinpoint the aspect of the client's response repertoire that is deficient. By having the client perform the same task over a number of trials, the clinician can note the changes in strategies with the development of proficiency at the task.

A second type of manipulation that can aid in investigating cognitive strategies is *altering nontask, environmental variables.* Assessment can be carried out in a room with few distracting stimuli present, or interpersonal factors may be arranged so as to reduce anxiety, and so on. Through such means the clinician can learn whether the client is able to emit adequate cognitions "spontaneously" under ideal environmental conditions and then he can proceed to determine what aspects of the situation cause a reinstatement of the deficit. Another source of such information is the client himself. Soliciting from the client his perception of the task, his description of his strategy, his appraisal of his performance, and his assessment of his own situation are key elements of a cognitive-functional analysis. Not infrequently, the client may offer a post-hoc strategy, which, if followed, would have led to adequate performance. That is, the client demonstrates that the correct strategy is within his repertoire yet he fails to spontaneously and appropriately employ it. Flavell *et al.* characterized such a deficit as a "production deficiency" (1966). As emphasized before, our clients have something to tell us if we would only ask and then listen.

The third manipulation employed by the cognitive-functional analyst is *providing the client with supports* in the form of (1) direct task aids, such as memory prompts, descriptions of the task demands by breaking the stimuli into components, explicit feedback, opportunities for note-taking; (2) instructional aids given to the client to help him appraise the task, focus attention, self-evaluate performance, and so on. How a client's performance varies in response to such supports will help clarify the nature of the deficits.

Vygotsky suggested that a most useful way to assess capabilities, especially in children, is to have the client perform a task and then note the degree and kind of improvement that derives from the administration of instructions (1962). For Vygotsky, the individual's ability to employ and benefit from instructions was the best reflection of intellectual capabilities. Vygotsky's use of the child's response to adult instructions is consistent with his view that what the child is able to do only with such help will eventually be incorporated into his own action; eventually the child will internalize the organizational principles that are inherent in the assistance he receives from others. As Luria quotes Vygotsky, "The function which is today divided between two persons will be interiorized and become the independent mental function of the child himself" (1961, p. 6).

Wozniak, in a fine review of the Soviet position, indicates that Vygotsky's principle of the social origins of cognitive development can be applied to psychological assessment (1976). From this orientation comes Vygotsky's notion of "zone of potential development," which is the difference in the child's performance pre- and posttest the experience of having received the help of an adult. This difference reflects the child's ability to benefit from adult-provided organizational cues. Wozniak offers many examples of how the "zone of potential development" has been used in the Soviet Union to study learning disabilities, an approach consistent with the presently proposed cognitive-functional approach.

In a cognitive-functional assessment approach each candidate for assessment becomes the subject of an experimental investigation. Each case is a separate experiment. Let us explore some of the implications of adopting such an approach.

Consequences of adopting a cognitive-functional assessment approach. The first impact that the adoption of a cognitive-functional assessment approach would have would be on the way we write our diagnostic reports. At present, reading a case folder is usually a tedious task:

> Test A was given; the scores indicated. . . . This is consistent
> with Test B. . . . and the teacher's report . . . [etc., etc.].

Such reports usually include a list of tests and a "cook-book" interpretation of each. Imagine instead a report in which the clinician shared with the reader his thinking processes, hypotheses, and attempts to test each of them, that is, the detective work. For example:

> The child was referred for this reason. . . . After an examina-
> tion of school records, interview with teacher, parent, and
> child, the following tests were administered because. . . .
> The performance level and profile were surprising in that the
> child demonstrated. . . . In order to assess the robustness of
> these findings another test . . . which seems to assess the
> same psychological processes was administered under
> highly supportive conditions in order to assess the child's full
> capabilities. These supportive conditions included. . . . The
> performance deficit was still evident and seemed reliable,
> especially in light of the referral comments. . . . In order to
> determine why the child did poorly on this task, the follow-
> ing functional operations were conducted sequentially. . . .
> The logic and rationale for each of these is offered and the
> changes in the child performance in response to each is
> described. . . .

Within such an assessment, the administration of any psychological test such as the Wechsler intelligence scales would represent the beginning not the end-product of our inquiry. The client's profile on the WAIS, for example, may serve as a clue for beginning the experimental work, the exciting detective investigation, in order to pinpoint the nature of deficit.

It is appropriate to juxtapose the fun and excitement of conducting such case study experiments as evidenced in the Soviet approach to assessment with a Western concern for consideration of issues of psychometrics and rival hypotheses. Are there rival hypotheses in the Campbell and Stanley sense (1966) that can explain the child's vari-able performance? Factors such as regression effects, prac-tice effects, intercurrent life events, and so on. A somewhat overlooked rival hypothesis highlighted by Chapman and Chapman provides an important *caveat* for the cognitive-functional assessor as he compares his clients' performance on two occasions or compares it with a normal control group on the same task under different conditions (1973). The following example illustrates the possible rival hypothesis. Consider, for example, the situation in which clients are assessed on an attentional task under neutral and distracting conditions. The client group is found to be inferior to the matched normal control group under the distraction condition but not under the neutral condition. Such a differential deficit may be due to an ability characteristic of the client *or* (here is the rub) it may be attributable to the psychometric properties of the measurement instruments employed. Chapman and Chapman pointed out that the magnitude of the performance deficit obtained by any generally less able group (clients) in comparison to another group (normals) is a direct function of the discriminating power of the test employed. A more discriminating test will reveal a larger discrepancy. Discriminating power is primarily a function of test reliability and mean and variance of item difficulty. Oltmanns and Neale indicated that differential deficits obtained may reflect statistical artifacts of the measurement procedures rather than a specific deficit characteristic of the client group (1974).

The caveat for the cognitive-functional analyst is to be as concerned with the characteristics of his instruments as with the nature of the psychological deficit of the client. With this in mind he can conduct a cognitive-functional assessment, focusing on the intellective activity, the nature of our client's cognitive strategies, and the content of his internal dialogue rather than merely the intellectual product or test score.

In perspective. Putting the present cognitive-functional assessment approach in historical perspective may be helpful. A number of investigators have similarly commented on the need for an experimental (functional)

approach to assessment. For example, Werner (1937) called
for a functional analysis of process and achievement and
Scheerer (1945) stated, "Success or failure are only the *end
products* of performing. As such they do not disclose the
how of succeeding or the *why* of failing" (p. 656). Instead,
Scheerer argued, we need a psychological analysis of the
task. "This demands a 'phenomenological' and experimental identification of those processes which are *requi-
site* to the solution" (p. 658). Both Werner and Scheerer
called for the use of aids or "crutches" to help patients
perform on tasks and then confronting the client with the
original task with the aids removed. Such an approach is
consistent with Vygotsky's concept of the "zone of potential
development" and the general assessment approach of
"testing the limits."

The present cognitive-functional assessment approach
is also in the tradition of Shapiro (1951) who has received
little attention, except for the efforts of Inglis (1966) and
Yates (1970). In contrast to a test battery approach, Shapiro
offered an experimentally oriented assessment in which the
client's problems were formulated and specified into certain hypotheses. The clinician was encouraged to ask himself what effect the confirmation of each of his hypotheses
would have on the treatment and disposal of the client. As
Shapiro indicated, if any of these hypotheses is not likely to
have an effect on treatment, the clinician should be disin-
clined to test it. The task for the clinician is to formulate
and sequentially test various hypotheses. The client becomes the object of an experimental investigation, often
acting as his own control. In such a cognitive-functional
experimental assessment approach, the distinction between
assessment and treatment becomes obscure. A systematic
experimental approach to a particular deficit will permit
the clinician to make specific suggestions for remediation.
Assessment of deficiencies and capabilities go hand-in-
hand with remediation.

Consistent with Shapiro's experimental case approach
is Kinsbourne's approach to neuropsychological disorders

(1971). Once the patient demonstrates a reliable incapacity or deficit, for instance on an aphasia test, Kinsbourne "pounces": he does a systematic sensitive analysis of the client's capabilities by presenting the test items in a different format or a different modality. For example, is the deficit central or does it involve specifiable subprocesses? Thus, by systematically manipulating the modality and form in which the test is administered, Kinsbourne can infer the nature of the psychological deficit and the neurological involvement.

A somewhat different approach, of converging operations, offered by Garner, Hake, and Eriksen, also provides a model for the cognitive-functional approach (1956). Although the concept of converging operations was offered in the context of a debate about perception, the logic of the approach is applicable to any experimental investigation that is designed to elucidate the nature of psychological processes. By converging operations, Garner *et al.* meant any set of two or more independent experimental procedures that could explain or allow the selection or elimination of alternative hypotheses or concepts (i.e., establish a concept by ruling out alternative interpretations). The value of a set of operations depends less on the nature of the operations themselves than on the quality of the alternative hypotheses that are being considered.

Recently, Estes, in examining the construct of intelligence, argued cogently for a similar process analysis (1974). Estes claimed that we should focus on intellective activity rather than intellectual products, on the constituent processes and the manner of their organization, on what brings about specific kinds of competence and incompetence. We need to develop techniques to localize the sources of deficits in performance revealed by test scores. Estes illustrated his point by describing why a child may do poorly on a vocabulary item on an intelligence test:

> Inability to explain or define a word on request may occur because the necessary memory structure has never been established, because of a lack of retrieval cues for an intact

memory structure, because words required to express the
definition are at low availability owing to disuse, or because
the individual lacks a general conception of the required
solution to this type of problem and thus gives an answer
which is meaningful within his own frame of reference but
not within that of the examiner. (1974, p. 747)

To determine *why* the child fails on the vocabulary test
will require that we remodel the test from an instrument
for prediction of performance to one more useful in the
diagnosis of processes. The adoption of a cognitive-
functional assessment approach will encourage us to aug-
ment our present assessment measures. We don't have to
replace or revise the tests per se but, rather, experiment in
ways to localize the sources of the deficits.

I cannot conclude a section which pays homage to
others who have called for a similar approach without mentioning the superb cognitive-functional analyst, Sherlock
Holmes. " 'Come, Watson. Come!' he cried. 'The game is
afoot.' "

If we learned to play the "game," conferences would
be exciting places to visit and journals would be exciting to
read. I have even had the notion of suggesting that journal
editors should not publish any article where the author
merely reports a difference that follows from a comparative
group or specific deficits approach unless the accompanying detective work is included.

Clinical Applications of a Cognitive-Behavior Assessment Approach

The discussion of research, conferences, and journals is
interesting but exactly how shall I implement a cognitive-
behavioral assessment approach with one of my clients?
The purpose of the following section is to answer this
question.

As mentioned before, the cognitive-behavior therapist
attempts to discern the style and incidence of the client's

cognitions (i.e., internal dialogue and images) and their relationship to the client's behavior and feelings. Two underlying questions influence the assessment procedure. First,
what is the client failing to say to himself, which, if present,
would help lead to adequate performance and adaptive behavior? Second, what is the content of the cognitions that
interfere with adaptive behavior?

The clinical interview. In order to answer these questions the cognitive-behavior therapist uses a host of assessment procedures. Perhaps the most useful tool available is
the clinical interview. The initial assessment session begins
with an exploration of the extent and duration of the client's
presenting problem and of his expectations concerning
therapy. The therapist performs a situational analysis of the
client's behavior. Table 7, taken from Peterson (1968), describes such an interview. In addition to the questions included in the Peterson interview, the cognitive-behavior
therapist is interested in having the client share the feelings and thoughts he has preceding, accompanying, and
following a typical example of his problem behavior. As
briefly mentioned before, the client can be asked to close
his eyes and imagine a recent situation when the anxiety,
depression, anger, pain, or whatever (the client's
symptoms) were particularly severe. The client is encouraged to imagine the scene, to "run a movie through his
head" of a recent incident involving his problem(s). The
client reports the sequence of thoughts, images, and behaviors. What are the thoughts that the client has when he first
notices the problem (e.g., becoming depressed)? What are
the thoughts as the client tries to cope with the depression?
The client can be asked if he recognizes a common theme
or link that runs through these thoughts.

When the client closes his eyes and uses imagery, he is
more likely to attend to aspects and details of the situation
that might be overlooked and deemphasized in a direct
interview. The set given to the client is to attend to the
"nitty-gritty," the particular thoughts, images, fantasies,

Table 7. Clinical Interview (from Peterson, 1968)

A. Definition of problem behavior
   1. Nature of the problem as defined by client
      "As I understand it, you came here because. . . ." (Discuss reasons for con-
      tact as stated by referral agency or other source of information.) "I would
      like you to tell me more about this. What is the problem as you see it?"
      (Probe as needed to determine client's view of his own problem behavior,
      i.e., what he is doing, or failing to do, which he or somebody else defines as
      a problem.)
   2. Severity of the problem
      (a) "How serious a problem is this as far as you are concerned?" (Probe to
      determine client's view of his own problem behavior, i.e., what he is doing,
      or failing to do, which he or somebody else defines as a problem.)
      (b) "How often do you . . . ?" (Exhibit problem behavior if a disorder of
      commission, or have occasion to exhibit desired behavior if a problem of
      omission. The goal is to obtain information regarding frequency of
      response.)
   3. Generality of the problem
      (a) Duration "How long has this been going on?"
      (b) Extent "Where does the problem usually come up?"(Probe to determine
      situations in which problem behavior occurs, e.g., "Do you feel that way at
      work? How about at home?")
B. Determinants of problem behavior
   1. Conditions which intensify problem behavior
      "Now I want you to think about the times when (the problem) is worst.
      What sorts of things are going on then?"
   2. Conditions which alleviate problem behavior
      "What about the times when (the problem) gets better? What sorts of things
      are going on then?"
   3. Perceived origins—"What do you think is causing (the problem)?"
   4. Specific antecedents
      "Think back to the last time (the problem) occurred. What was going on at
      that time?"
      As needed:
      (a) Social influences—"Were any other people around? Who? What were
      they doing?"
      (b) Personal influences—"What were you thinking about at the time? How
      did you feel?"
   5. Specific consequences
      "What happened after (the problem occurred)?"
      As needed:
      (a) Social consequences—"What did (significant others identified above)
      do?"
      (b) Personal consequences—"How did that make you feel?"
   6. Suggested changes
      "You have thought a lot about (the problem). What do you think might be
      done to improve the situation?"
   7. Suggested leads for further inquiry
      "What else do you think I should find out about to help you with this
      problem?"

---

and feelings that he may have experienced in a given situation.

Following the description of the incident and after the imagery or "movie" reporting is over, the therapist can ask the client if he has similar thoughts and feelings in other situations. A number of options are available to the therapist. He can ask the client if he had such thoughts and feelings as a child and thus conduct a developmental history. The client can consider the question, "How long have I been saying or thinking these things about myself?" The therapist can focus on the "here and now" and wonder if the client had similar thoughts, images, and feelings during a behavioral assessment which may have been conducted or during the interview. Moreover, the therapist can suggest that the client conduct a homework assignment of listening to himself with a "third ear," noting whether he experiences similar thoughts, images, and feelings over the course of the week. Such questions, homework assignments, and so on, are all raised in the context of the therapist's curiosity, puzzlement concerning the effect of such thoughts on the client's behavior.

However, the assessment is not only an appraisal of the client's internal dialogue but also in itself acts as a stimulus for the client to *change* his internal dialogue concerning his problem.

As a result of the cognitive-functional assessment the client will come to entertain the notion that part of his problem results from what he says to himself. Implicit in assessment is the idea that the client can control his thoughts and that he is not a victim of such thoughts and feelings nor is he helpless in controlling what he says to himself. Indeed, the therapist can wonder aloud why the client *chooses* to have such thoughts and feelings? That is, by the language and tenor of the interview and assessment the client is given the impression that something can be done to exercise self-control. As a result of the assessment, the client comes to see how he is an active contributor to his presenting problem.

Once again it is appropriate to remind ourselves that it

is unlikely that clients are actively going around talking to themselves prior to assessment. But due to the habitual nature of one's expectations and beliefs, it is likely that such thinking processes and images become automatic and seemingly involuntary, like most overlearned acts. However, the assessment process helps to make the client aware of such thinking processes and it increases the likelihood that the awareness will be the trigger to produce incompatible adaptive thoughts and behaviors.

A variety of different techniques can be used in the assessment of cognitions, including the use of behavioral assessments, videotaping, projective devices (e.g., TAT-type pictures), group assessment, as well as homework assignments, each of which topics is briefly discussed below.

Behavioral tests. A useful way of making the client aware of how his thinking style contributes to his behavior and distress is by having him engage in behavioral tests, either laboratory-based or *in situ.* For example, if the client is interpersonally anxious he can be asked to make a speech before a group, or, if phobic, to confront the phobic situation, or, if depressed, engage in graded task assignments.

Following such a behavioral assessment the client can be encouraged to discuss his problem in terms of the specific assessment situation that he experienced. The client can explore in some detail his thoughts and feelings during the assessment situation. The clinician may try to have him ascertain what were the particular aspects of the environment that triggered specific self-statements and images. At what point did the client begin to feel anxious? When was anxiety greatest? What were the self-statements and images that the client emitted at different points in the assessment? Having the client vicariously relive the behavioral assessment situation by means of the imagery procedure described above will "pull" for his internal dialogue and he can begin to explore the effects of such thought processes on his behaviors.

Another way to tap the client's cognitions is to videotape him while he undergoes the behavioral assessment or role-playing and is displaying the maladaptive behavior. Immediately after the taping, both client and therapist view the tape while the client tries to *reconstruct* the thoughts and feelings he was experiencing on the tape. In this way, the therapist can use the client's videotape like a TAT card. Such reconstructions cannot be equated with what the client actually did during the behavioral assessment; however, the reconstructions can provide a very useful beginning point for assessment and treatment, and from a research viewpoint, they can provide a provocative source of hypotheses.

The value of post hoc description was illustrated in our laboratory when we wanted to understand the nature of the cognitive processes which contribute to pain tolerance. We were interested in how experimental subjects tolerate the pain of holding their arm in a tub of cold water (2°C) for up to five minutes (the cold pressor task). To tap cognitions we videotaped each subject while he engaged in the cold pressor task. The subject's task was to keep his arm in the water as long as possible, although he could remove his arm at any time. At various points during the tolerance period a pain intensity rating was requested by the experimenter. Following the cold pressor assessment the subject was asked to watch himself on the videotape, reporting aloud the feelings and thoughts he had experienced at each point. A small segment of the tape would be played, then stopped by the subject as he reconstructed his thoughts and feelings during that portion. For most subjects, the videotape facilitated their recall of what they had been thinking as well as the sequence of their thoughts. Subjects, although variable in verbal facility, were generally quite capable of providing detailed accounts. Whereas we began the videotape study of pain tolerance with the goal of providing a descriptive prototypic picture of how subjects cope, the subject's reconstructions indicated that we were asking the wrong question. Almost all of our males and 60% of our female college students went the full five minutes, using many different strategies to tolerate the pain. For example, one subject reported that she merely told herself for the full five minutes, "I can do it, I can do it," while others used different imagery and relaxation techniques as described in Chapter 5. However, where the reconstructions proved most fascinating was in permitting us to generate a prototypic description of the 40% of the females who failed— those who stayed less than five minutes, most of whom stayed a minute or less. Briefly the picture that emerged is the following. The first reaction of *all* subjects, both those who stayed the full five minutes as well as those who dropped out, was "Oh, that's cold!"—almost a disbelief that cold water could produce such intense noxious sensations. This was followed by both groups questioning their ability to keep their hands in the water. At this point the two groups seemed to differentiate themselves. The 40% who dropped out at this point start to catastrophize, e.g., "Can I get frostbite? I had a picture of my fingers falling off? It was horrible!" and so on. The subjects who dropped out saw themselves as being overwhelmed, as having little ability to do anything to tolerate the pain, and, unlike the 60% who stayed, they failed to see the task as a challenge, as a problem to be solved. For example, the 60% of the female population who stayed the full five minutes reported having such thoughts as, "I knew other people would be in the task; I wanted to stay in as long as them"; "I thought of how I could use relaxation to stay"; "I managed to get hold of myself; I tried to image myself reaching in a bucket for a beer."

The reason I have gone into such detail about the pain experiment is that it highlights how we can tap the flow of our subject's and client's cognitions and the predictive and explanatory value those statements may have. The videotape pain study led us to develop objective instruments, interview schedules and experimental studies to further assess and manipulate our client's cognitions in pain studies. Naturally, caution is advised in interpreting such self-report data: Did the 40% of subjects who dropped out

give post hoc rationales to justify their previous performance or did they indeed have such thoughts during the
cold pressor test? In order to answer this question we can
employ the procedure of asking our subjects and our
clients to think aloud while engaging in a task. Such an
introspective reporting approach has a time-honored history with its own particular problems, as described by Natsoulas (1970). The main limitation is that we must recognize that when we ask someone to verbalize his thoughts
while doing a task we may in fact be changing both his
thoughts and what he is doing. If we are mindful of this
limitation we can learn a great deal about an individual's
thinking style and then relate it to task performance. The
promise of such a "think-aloud" approach has been illustrated in the work of Bloom and Broder (1950) and DeGroot
(1965).[35]

A TAT-like Approach

Still another possible way to tap the client's internal
dialogue, especially with children, is to employ TAT-like
pictures related to the target behaviors. The pictures employed are *not* the standard Thematic Apperception Test
pictures but rather a set of pictures or slides that have been
selected for the target population. For example, a set of
slides of socially isolated children was used with withdrawn children (Meijers, personal communication). The
withdrawn child was asked not only to report what is happening in the picture, the outcome, etc., but also to tell
what the child in the picture was thinking and feeling, and
what he could do to handle the situation. That is, an at-

---

[35] I would suggest that the various procedures available to assess our clients' and
subjects' internal dialogues, self-statements, and images—in short, their intrapersonal communication systems, can be subsumed under the term *cognitive
ethology*. Like the behavioral ethologist who follows the flight of birds, noting
releasing stimuli, fixed action patterns, etc., I feel we must develop a similar
technology for studying thinking.

tempt was made to tap, by means of a projective device, the content of the client's internal dialogue.

Other Psychometric Tests

A number of other tests can be employed to tap the client's cognitions. For example, the instrument developed by Schwartz and Gottman (1974), which was described in Chapter 4, assessed the client's thinking processes following a role-playing situation. In our own laboratory Henshaw (1977) has applied the Schwartz and Gottman approach to the study of creativity.[36] Following a set of creativity tests, subjects were asked to fill out a questionnaire that asked them about the thoughts they had while taking the tests. For example, they were asked on a one- to five-point scale (going from one = hardly ever had the thought to five = very often had the thought) to answer fifteen questions that tapped negative self-statements such as, "I was worried what others would think of my ideas"; "I was thinking that other people must be doing better than me"; and fifteen positive, creativity-engendering self-statements, such as, "I was letting my ideas play and be a surprise"; "I was confident that my ideas were creative." Interestingly, the scores on the self-report scale of thinking style correlated quite well with creative performance, were reliable over time, and related to an external criteria of creative performance. Perhaps we can begin to tap the psychological "stuckness" Pirsig referred to while fixing his motorcycle (in the quote from *Zen and the Art of Motorcycle Maintenance* in Chapter 2).

But once again, it is pertinent to ask, what exactly are such postperformance scales measuring? Are they merely a reflection of the subject's postperformance rationalization? Perhaps the subject felt he did poorly on the test and indi-

---

[36] Spielberger (1976) and Sarason (1976) have recently developed scales similar in format to Schwartz and Gottman's and Henshaw's which are designed to assess the thought processes of high test-anxious subjects.

cates this on the questionnaire. Or does the reported thinking style actually reflect the thinking process that subjects
engaged in while doing the creativity tasks? Once again the
think-aloud research technique may help us answer these
questions (e.g., see Goor & Sommerfeld, 1975). For the
moment, it is important to indicate that we can develop
instruments to tap our client's cognitions that meet the
psychometric requirements of reliability and validity.

Other tests have been developed by D'Zurilla and
Goldfried (1971) and Spivack and Shure (1974) designed to
assess the client's problem-solving ability, that is, his ability to identify problems and formulate solutions. Such tests
may prove a useful adjunct in assessing cognitions, especially if the tests are employed within a cognitive-
functional framework. Not only must we learn that there is
a deficit in problem-solving, but why. Recall the Schwartz
and Gottman task analysis of low assertive individuals,
which was described earlier. The low assertives knew what
to do and could do it under certain circumstances but their
internal dialogues interfered with execution. Similarly,
with poor problem-solvers we have to conduct a task
analysis. Do they have the knowledge—can I test limits?
What factors interfere with the implementation of the
knowledge? Within such an assessment framework
psychometric tests will prove valuable.

The Role of the Group in Assessing Cognitions

The focus of the description of a cognitive-functional
assessment thus far has been on the individual client and
the format of the assessment has been a one-to-one basis.
There are several advantages in conducting the assessment
on a group basis. Besides the obvious saving in the clinician's time, perhaps the greatest benefit accrues if the
group of clients has a similar referral problem. If all clients
individually have to go through the same behavioral as-

sessment, such as giving a speech or performing similar graded task assignments, then they can subsequently examine as a group their common experiences. The therapist can explore the common behaviors, thoughts, and feelings. A shared exploration of the common set of self-statements and images is invaluable in having the clients come to appreciate the role thoughts play in the behavioral repertoire. The recognition that other individuals have similar thoughts and feelings, similar internal dialogues, provides an additional impetus for self-examination and self-disclosure. The groups can examine the variety of situations in which they have similar self-statements and images.

Another useful function of the group assessment is that the therapist can use the client's behavior in the group setting as an opportunity to analyze the client's internal dialogue. If a client is particularly quiet in the group the clinician can have the client examine his thinking processes about participating in the group. The clinician can have the clients explore the content of their internal dialogues as they experienced them in the behavioral assessment, in the group setting, and in other situations. Such a situational analysis of thinking processes provides fertile ground for assessment. One can also employ homework assignments as a further way to have the client become aware of the role of his cognitions in contributing to his maladaptive behavior.[37]

In *summary*, the clinician has a host of tools available, including interview and imagery procedures, behavioral assessments, videotaping, TAT-like tests, homework assignments, and group assessments in order to conduct a careful analysis of the client's self-statements and images. The purpose of the assessment is to record and analyze, as

[37] In my research on group versus individually administered cognitive-behavior modification, I have found that the group treatment was as effective as the individual treatment and, in general, the group approach greatly facilitated the treatment (Meichenbaum, 1972; Meichenbaum *et al.*, 1971).

well as change, the client's internal dialogue about his presenting problem. In other words, it is strongly suggested that each time we subject a client to particular assessment devices we are also changing the way he views his problem. Assessment and change are interdependent!

Epilogue

In the prologue to this book I spoke of my hope to build a bridge connecting two ostensibly different therapy approaches, behavior therapy, and cognitive-semantic therapy. I trust that I have succeeded in constructing some sort of bridge, although for some readers perhaps it appears more like a rope bridge over "troubled waters" than like the Golden Gate.

As one surveys the current state of psychotherapy a great confluence of interests seems to be taking place. Therapists of various persuasions are coming to appreciate the role the client's cognitions play in the behavioral change process. This recognition is contributing to a new dialogue between the different schools of therapy. What were once regarded as substantially different therapy approaches are now being examined for areas of overlap and mutual exchange; for example, see papers by Frank (1974), Marmor (1975), Szasz (1974), Wexler (1974). Perhaps we are entering a period of "psychological" detente. I hope the present book will contribute to this integration.

References

Anderson, W., & Carter, B. Central nervous system mediation in athletic performance. Unpublished manuscript, Boston University, 1976.

Asarnow, J. Mediational training and serial recall in kindergartens. Unpublished masters thesis, University of Waterloo, 1976.

Ashem, B., & Donner, L. Covert sensitization with alcoholics: A controlled replication. *Behaviour Research and Therapy*, 1968, 6, 7–12.

Ault, R. Problem solving strategies of reflective, impulsive, fast accurate and slow inaccurate children. *Child Development*, 1973, 44, 259–266.

Ault, R., Crawford, D., & Jeffrey, T. Visual scanning strategies of reflective, impulsive, fast-accurate, and slow-inaccurate children on the Matching Familiar Figures Test. *Child Development*, 1972, 43, 1412–1417.

Averill, J. An analysis of psychophysiological symbolism and its influence on theories of emotion. *Journal of the Theory of Social Behavior*, 1974, 4, 147–190.

Averill, J., & Opton, E. Psychophysiological assessment: Rationale and problems. In P. McReynolds (ed.), *Advances in psychological assessment*, Volume 1. Palo Alto, California: Science and Behavior Books, 1968.

Ayllon, T., Layman, D., & Kandel, H. A behavioral-educational alternative to drug control of hyperactive children. *Journal of Applied Behavior Analysis*, 1975, 8, 137–146.

Baker, J. Reason versus reinforcement in behavior modification. Unpublished doctoral dissertation, University of Illinois, 1966.

Bandura, A. Vicarious processes: A case of no-trial learning. In L. Berkowitz (Ed.), *Advances in experimental social psychology*, Volume 2. New York: Academic Press, 1965.

Bandura, A. Modeling approaches to the modification of phobic disorders. In R. Porter (Ed.), *The role of learning in psychotherapy*. London: Churchill, 1968.

Bandura, A. *Principles of behavior modification*. New York: Holt, Rinehart & Winston, 1969.

Bandura, A. *Aggression: A social learning analysis.* Englewood Cliffs, N.J.: Prentice-Hall, 1973.

Bandura, A. Behavior theory and models of man. *American Psychologist*, 1974, *29*, 859–869.

Bandura, A., & Barab, P. Processes governing disinhibitory effects through symbolic modeling. *Journal of Abnormal Psychology*, 1973, *82*, 1–9.

Bandura, A., Blanchard, E., & Ritter, B. The relative efficacy of desensitization and modeling treatment approaches for inducing affective, behavioral, and attitudinal changes. *Journal of Personality and Social Psychology*, 1969, *13*, 173–199.

Barber, T. Physiological effects of "hypnotic suggestions": A critical review of recent literature (1960–1964). *Psychological Bulletin*, 1965, *63*, 201–222.

Barber, R., & Hahn, K. Physiological and subjective responses to pain producing stimulation under hypnotically suggested and waking-imagined "analgesia." *Journal of Abnormal and Social Psychology*, 1962, *65*, 411–418.

Barron, F. *Creative person and creative process.* New York: Holt, Rinehart & Winston, 1969.

Bash, M., & Camp, B. *Think aloud program: Group manual.* Unpublished manuscript, University of Colorado Medical School, 1975.

Bates, H., & Katz, M. Development of verbal regulation of behavior. *Proceedings of the 78th Annual American Psychological Association Convention*, 1970, 5 (Part I), 299–300.

Baudouin, C. *Suggestion and autosuggestion.* London: Allen & Unwin, 1920.

Beck, A. Cognitive therapy: Nature and relation to behavior therapy. *Behavior Therapy*, 1970, 1, 184–200.

Beck, A. *Cognitive therapy and emotional disorders.* New York: International Universities Press, 1976.

Beck, A., Rush, J., & Kovacs, M. *Individual treatment manual for cognitive/behavioral psychotherapy of depression.* Unpublished manuscript, University of Pennsylvania, 1976.

Beecher, H. *Measurement of subjective responses.* New York: Oxford University Press, 1959.

Beecher, H. Pain: One mystery solved. *Science*, 1966, *151*, 840–841.

Bellack, A., Hersen, M., & Turner, S. Generalization effects of social skills training in chronic schizophrenics: An experimental analysis. Unpublished manuscript, University of Pittsburgh, 1976.

Belmont, I., Birch, H., Klein, D., & Pollack, M. Perceptual evidence of CNS dysfunction in schizophrenia. *Archives of General Psychiatry*, 1964, *10*, 395–408.

Bem, S. Verbal self-control: The establishment of effective self-instruction. *Journal of Experimental Psychology*, 1967, 74, 485–491.

Bem, S. The role of comprehension in children's problem solving. *Developmental Psychology*, 1971, 2, 351–359.

Bender, N. Self-verbalization versus tutor verbalization in modifying impulsivity. *Journal of Educational Psychology*, 1976, 68, 347–354.

Berenson, B., & Carkhuff, R. *Sources of gain in counseling and psychotherapy*. New York: Holt, Rinehart & Winston, 1967.

Berger, S. Conditioning through vicarious instigation. *Psychological Review*, 1962, 69, 450–466.

Bergin, A. A self-regulation technique for impulse control disorders. *Psychotherapy: Theory, Research and Practice*, 1967, 6, 113–118.

Bernard, C. *An introduction to the study of experimental medicine* (Trans. H. C. Green). New York: Dover, 1957.

Berne, E. *Games people play*. New York: Grove, 1964.

Bernheim, H. *Hypnosis and suggestion*. New Hyde Park, New Jersey: University Books, 1964.

Birk, L. Biofeedback: Behavioral medicine. *Seminars in Psychiatry*, 1974, 4, 361–567.

Blackwood, R. The operant conditioning of verbally mediated self-control in the classroom. *Journal of School Psychology*, 1970, 8, 257–258.

Blackwood, R. *Mediated self-control: An operant model of rational behavior*. Akron, Ohio: Exordium Press, 1972.

Blank, M. Eliciting verbalization from young children in experimental tasks: A methodological note. *Child Development*, 1975, 46, 254–257.

Blank, M., & Solomon, F. A tutorial program to develop abstract thinking in socially disadvantaged preschool children. *Child Development*, 1968, 39, 379–389.

Blank, M., & Solomon, F. How should the disadvantaged child be taught? *Child Development*, 1969, 40, 47–61.

Blitz, B., & Dinnerstein, A. Effects of different types of instructions on pain parameters. *Journal of Abnormal Psychology*, 1968, 73, 276–280.

Blitz, B., & Dinnerstein, A. Role of attentional focus in pain perception: Manipulation of response to noxious stimulation by instructions. *Journal of Abnormal Psychology*, 1971, 77, 42–45.

Bloom, B., & Broder, L. *The problem solving processes of college students*. Chicago: University of Chicago Press, 1950.

Blumenthal, A. The base of objectivist psychotherapy. *The Objectivist*, June, 1969, 3–11.

Bobey, M., & Davidson, P. Psychological factors affecting pain tolerance. *Journal of Psychosomatic Research*, 1970, 14, 371–376.

Bolles, P. Learning motivation and cognition. In W. Estes (Ed.), *Handbook of learning and cognitive processes*. New York: Halsted, 1975.

Bommarito, J., & Meichenbaum, D. Enhancing reading comprehension by means of self-instructional training. Unpublished manuscript, University of Waterloo, Ontario, 1976.

Bornstein, P., & Quevillon, R. The effects of a self-instructional package on overactive preschool boys. *Journal of Applied Behavior Analysis*, 1976, *9*, 179–188.

Braff, D., & Beck, A. Thinking disorder in depression. *Archives of General Psychiatry*, 1974, *31*, 456–462.

Breger, L., & McGaugh, J. Critique and reformulation of "learning theory": Approaches to psychotherapy and neurosis. *Psychological Bulletin*, 1965, *63*, 338–358.

Brewer, W. There is no convincing evidence for operant or classical conditioning in adult humans. In W. Weimer and D. Palermo (Eds.), *Cognition and the symbolic processes*. New York: Halsted Press, 1974.

Broadbent, D. *Perception and communication*. Oxford: Pergamon Press, 1958.

Brook, C. *The practice of autosuggestion*. London: Allen & Unwin, 1922.

Brown, B. Cognitive aspects of Wolpe's behavior therapy. *American Journal of Psychiatry*, 1967, *124*, 854–859.

Bruch, M. Influence of model characteristics on psychiatric inpatients' interview anxiety. *Journal of Abnormal Psychology*, 1975, *84*, 290–294.

Bruner, J. From communication to language: A psychological perspective. *Cognition*, 1975, *3*, 255–287.

Brush, S. Should the history of science be rated X? *Science*, 1974, *183*, 1164–1172.

Bugenthal, D., Whalen, C., & Henker, B. Causal attributions of hyperactive children and motivational assumptions of two behavior change approaches: Evidence for an interactionist position. Unpublished manuscript, University of California at Santa Barbara, 1975.

Burns, B. The effect of self-directed verbal comments on arithmetic performance and activity level of urban hyperactive children. Unpublished doctoral dissertation, Boston College, 1972.

Bush, E., & Dweck, C. Reflections on conceptual tempo: Relationship between cognitive style and performance as a function of task characteristics. *Developmental Psychology*, 1975, *11*, 567–574.

Butter, E. Visual haptic training and cross model transfer of a reflective cognitive strategy. Unpublished doctoral dissertation, University of Massachusetts, 1971.

Callaway, E. Schizophrenia and interference: An analogy with a malfunctioning computer. *Archives of General Psychiatry*, 1970, *22*, 193–208.

Cameron, R. Conceptual tempo and children's problem solving behavior: A developmental task analysis. Unpublished doctoral dissertation, University of Waterloo, 1976.

Camp, B. Verbal mediation in young aggressive boys. Unpublished manuscript, University of Colorado School of Medicine, 1975.

Camp, B., Blom, G., Herbert, F., & Van Doorwick, W. "Think aloud": A program for developing self-control in young aggressive boys. Unpublished manuscript, University of Colorado School of Medicine, 1976.

Campbell, D., & Stanley, J. *Experimental and quasi-experimental designs for research.* Chicago: Rand McNally, 1966.

Campbell, S. Cognitive styles in reflective, impulsive, and hyperactive boys and their mothers. *Perceptual Motor Skills*, 1973, *36*, 747–752.

Campbell, S. Hyperactivity: Course and treatment. In A. Davids (Ed.), *Child Personality and Psychopathology*, Volume 3. New York: Wiley, 1977.

Carlin, A., & Armstrong, H. Aversive conditioning: Learning or dissonance reduction? *Journal of Consulting and Clinical Psychology*, 1968, *32*, 674–678.

Castaneda, C. *A separate reality: Further conversations with Don Juan.* New York: Pocket Books, 1972.

Cautela, J. A behavior therapy approach to pervasive anxiety. *Behaviour Research and Therapy*, 1966, *4*, 99–111.

Cautela, J. Covert processes and behavior modification. *Journal of Nervous and Mental Disease*, 1973, *157*, 27–35.

Chapman, J., & McGhie, A. A comparative study of disordered attention in schizophrenia. *Journal of Mental Science*, 1962, *108*, 487–500.

Chapman, L., & Chapman, J. Problems in the measurement of cognitive deficits. *Psychological Bulletin*, 1973, *79*, 380–385.

Chappell, M., & Stevenson, T. Group psychological training in some organic conditions. *Mental Hygiene*, 1936, *20*, 588–597.

Chaves, J., & Barber, T. Acupuncture analgesia: A six-factor theory. *Human Behavior*, 1973, *2*, 19–24.

Chaves, J., & Barber, T. Cognitive strategies, experimenter modeling, and expectation in the attention of pain. *Journal of Abnormal Psychology*, 1974, *83*, 356–363.

Christensen, C. *Development and field testing of an interpersonal coping skills program.* Toronto: Ontario Institute for Studies in Education, 1974.

Claridge, G. *Personality and arousal: A psychophysiological study of psychiatric disorder.* New York: Macmillan (Pergamon), 1967.

Coché, E., & Flick, A. Problem solving training groups for hospitalized psychiatric patients. *Journal of Psychology*, 1975, *91*, 19–29.

Conners, C. Pharmacotherapy of psychopathology in children. In H. Quay and J. Werry (Eds.), *Psychopathological disorders of children.* New York: Wiley, 1972.

Constantini, A., Corsini, D., & Davis, J. Conceptual tempo, inhibition of movement, and acceleration of movement in 4-, 7-, and 9-year-old children. *Perceptual Motor Skills*, 1973, *37*, 779–784.

Copeman, C. Aversive counterconditioning and social retraining: A learning theory approach to drug rehabilitation. Unpublished doctoral dissertation, State University of New York at Stony Brook, 1973.

Corbin, C. Mental practice. In W. Morgan (Ed.), *Ergogenic aids and muscular performance*. New York: Academic Press, 1972.

Coué, E. *The practice of autosuggestion*. New York: Doubleday, 1922.

Davison, G. Systematic desensitization as a counterconditioning process. *Journal of Abnormal Psychology*, 1968, *73*, 91–99.

Davison, G., & Wilson, G. Processes of fear-reduction in systematic desensitization: Cognitive and social reinforcement factors in humans. *Behavior Therapy*, 1973, *4*, 1–21.

Deane, G. Human heart rate responses during experimentally induced anxiety: A follow-up with controlled respiration. *Journal of Experimental Psychology*, 1964, *67*, 193–195.

Deane, G. Cardiac rate as a function of changes in respiration. *Psychological Reports*, 1965, *16*, 41–42.

Debus, R. Effects of brief observation of model behavior on conceptual tempo impulsive children. *Developmental Psychology*, 1970, *2*, 202–214.

DeGroot, A. *Thought and choice in chess*. The Hague: Mouton, 1965.

Dember, W. Motivation and the cognitive revolution. *American Psychologist*, 1974, *29*, 161–168.

Denney, D. Reflection and impulsivity as determinants of conceptual strategy. *Child Development*, 1973, *44*, 614–623.

Denney, D. The effects of exemplary and cognitive models and self-rehearsal on children's interrogative strategies. *Journal of Experimental Child Psychology*, 1975, *19*, 476–488.

Dickie, J. Private speech: The effect of presence of others, task and intrapersonal variables. Unpublished doctoral dissertation, Michigan State University, 1973.

Dick-Read, G. *Child birth without fear*. New York: Harper and Row, 1959.

DiLoreto, A. *Comparative psychotherapy: An experimental analysis*. Chicago: Aldine-Atherton, 1971.

Dollard, J., & Miller, N. *Personality and psychotherapy*. New York: McGraw-Hill, 1950.

Dornbush, S. Popular psychology: A content analysis of contemporary inspirational non-religious books. In S. Klausner (Ed.), *The quest for self-control*. New York: Free Press, 1965.

Douglas, V. Stop, look and listen: The problem of sustained attention and impulse control in hyperactive and normal children. *Canadian Journal of Behavioral Science*, 1972, *4*, 259–276.

Douglas, V. Are drugs enough? To treat or to train the hyperactive child. *International Journal of Mental Health*, 1975, *4*, 199–212.

Drake, D. Perceptual correlates of impulsive and reflective behavior. *Developmental Psychology*, 1970, *2*, 202–214.

Draspa, L. Psychological factors in muscular pain. *British Journal of Medical Psychology*, 1959, *32*, 106–116.

Drummond, D. Self-instructional training: An approach to disruptive classroom behavior. Unpublished doctoral dissertation, University of Oregon, 1974.

Dubois, P. *The psychic treatment of nervous disorders: The psychoneuroses and their moral treatment.* New York: Funk & Wagnalls, 1905.

Dweck, C. The role of expectations and attributions in the alleviation of learned helplessness. *Journal of Personality and Social Psychology*, 1975, *31*, 674–685.

Dweck, C., & Reppucci, N. Learned helplessness and reinforcement responsibility in children. *Journal of Personality and Social Psychology*, 1973, *25*, 109–116.

Dykman, R., Ackerman, R., Clements, S., & Peters, J. Specific learning disabilities: An attentional deficit syndrome. In H. Myklebust (Ed.), *Progress in learning disabilities*, Volume II. New York: Grune & Stratton, 1971.

D'Zurilla, T., & Goldfried, M. Problem solving and behavior modification. *Journal of Abnormal Psychology*, 1971, *78*, 107–126.

Egbert, L., Battit, G., Welch, C., & Bartlett, M. Reduction of postoperative pain by encouragement and instruction. *New England Journal of Medicine*, 1964, *270*, 825–827.

Elliott, R. Effects of uncertainty about the nature and advent of a noxious stimuli (shock) upon heart rate. *Journal of Personality and Social Psychology*, 1966, *3*, 343–356.

Ellis, A. *Reason and emotion in psychotherapy.* New York: Lyle Stuart Press, 1962.

Ellis, A. Emotional education in the classroom: The living school. *Journal of Clinical Child Psychology*, 1971, *1*, 19–22.

Epstein, S. Toward a unified theory of anxiety. In B. Maher (Ed.), *Progress in experimental personality*, Volume 4. New York: Academic Press, 1967.

Epstein, S. Natural healing processes of the mind. In H. Lowenheim (Ed.), *Meanings of madness.* New York: Behavioral Publications, 1976.

Estes, W. Learning theory and intelligence. *American Psychologist*, 1974, *29*, 740–749.

Evans, M., & Paul, G. Effects of hypnotically suggested analgesia on physiological and subjective responses to cold stress. *Journal of Consulting and Clinical Psychology*, 1970, *35*, 362–371.

Ezkiel, H. Experimentation within the psychoanalytic session. *British Journal of Philosophy and Science*, 1965, 7, 25.

Farber, I. The things people say to themselves. *American Psychologist*, 1963, *18*, 185–197.

Feather, B., & Rhoads, J. Psychodynamic behavior therapy: Theory and rationale. *Archives of General Psychiatry*, 1972, *26*, 496–502.

Fiedler, P., & Windheuser, H. Modifikation kreativen Verhaltens durch Lernen am Modell. *Zeitschrift für Entwicklungspsychologie und Pedagogische Psychologie*, 1974, 6, 262–280.

Finch, A., Wilkinson, M., Nelson, W., & Montgomery, L. Modification of an impulsive cognitive tempo in emotionally disturbed boys. *Journal of Abnormal Child Psychology*, 1975, *3*, 45–52.

Firestone, P. The effects of reinforcement contingencies and caffeine on hyperactive children. Unpublished doctoral dissertation, McGill University, Montreal, 1974.

Flavell, J., Beach, D., & Chinsky, J. Spontaneous verbal rehearsal in a memory task as a function of age. *Child Development*, 1966, *37*, 283–299.

Frank, J. *Persuasion and healing*. Baltimore: Johns Hopkins Press, 1961.

Frank, J. The bewildering world of psychotherapy. *Journal of Social Issues*, 1972, *28*, 27–43.

Frank, J. *Persuasion and healing: A comparative study of psychotherapy*, Revised edition. New York: Schocken Books, 1974.

Freyberg, J. Increasing the imaginative play of urban disadvantaged kindergarten children through systematic training. In J. Singer (Ed.), *The child's world of make believe*. New York: Academic Press, 1973.

Fuchs, C., & Rehm, L. A self-control behavior therapy program for depression. Unpublished manuscript, University of Pennsylvania, 1975.

Fulop-Miller, R. *Triumph over pain*. New York: The Literary Guild of America, 1938.

Furth, H. *Thinking without language*. New York: The Free Press, 1966.

Gagné, R. Problem solving. In A. Melton (Ed.), *Categories of human learning*. New York: Academic Press, 1964.

Gagné, R. Elementary science: A new scheme of instruction. *Science*, 1966, *151*, 49–53.

Gagné, R., & Briggs, L. *Principles of instructional design*. New York: Holt, Rinehart & Winston, 1974.

Gagné, R., & Smith, E. A study of the effects of verbalization in problem solving. *Journal of Experimental Psychology*, 1962, *63*, 12–18.

Gallwey, T. *The inner game of tennis*. New York: Random House, 1974.

Gal'perin, P. Stages in the development of mental acts. In M. Cole and I.

Maltzman (Eds.), *A handbook of contemporary Soviet psychology*. New York: Basic Books, 1969.

Garner, W., Hake, H., & Eriksen, C. Operationism and the concept of perception. *Psychological Review*, 1956, *63*, 149–159.

Garrity, L. An electromyographical study of subvocal speech and recall in preschool children. *Developmental Psychology*, 1975, *11*, 274–281.

Gaupp, L., Stern, R., & Ratliff, R. The use of aversion-relief procedures in the treatment of a case of voyeurism. *Behavior Therapy*, 1971, *2*, 585–588.

Geer, J., & Turtletaub, A. Fear reduction following observation of a model. *Journal of Personality and Social Psychology*, 1967, *6*, 327–331.

Gendlin, E. *Focusing psychotherapy: Theory, research and practice*, 1969, *6*, 4–15.

Ghiselin, B. *The creative process.* New York: Mentor, 1952.

Gholson, B., & McConville, K. Effects of stimulus differentiation training upon hypotheses, strategies, and stereotypes in discrimination learning among kindergarten children. *Journal of Experimental Child Psychology*, 1974, *18*, 81–97.

Giebink, J., Stover, D., & Fahl, M. Teaching adaptive responses to frustration to emotionally disturbed boys. *Journal of Consulting and Clinical Psychology*, 1968, *32*, 366–368.

Gioe, U. Cognitive modification and positive group experience as a treatment of depression. Unpublished doctoral dissertation, Temple University, 1975.

Glasgow, R., & Arkowitz, H. The behavioral assessment of male and female social competence in dyadic heterosexual interactions. *Behavior Therapy*, 1975, *6*, 488–498.

Glass, C. Response acquisition and cognitive self-statement modification approaches to dating behavior training. Unpublished doctoral dissertation, Indiana University, 1974.

Glass, D., & Singer, J. Stress and adaptation: Experimental studies of behavioral affects of exposure to aversive events. New York: Academic Press, 1972.

Goffman, E. *Interaction ritual: Essays on face-to-face behavior.* Garden City, New York: Doubleday, 1967.

Goldfried, M. Systematic desensitization as training in self-control. *Journal of Consulting and Clinical Psychology*, 1971, *37*, 228–234.

Goldfried, M. Reduction of generalized anxiety through a variant of systematic desensitization. In M. Goldfried & M. Merbaum (Eds.), *Behavior change through self-control.* New York: Holt, Rinehart & Winston, 1973.

Goldfried, M., & Davison, G. *Clinical behavior therapy.* New York: Holt, Rinehart and Winston, 1976.

Goldfried, M., Decenteceo, E., & Weinberg, L. Systematic rational restructuring as a self-control technique. *Behavior Therapy*, 1974, *5*,
247–254.

Goldfried, M., & Goldfried, A. Cognitive change methods. In F. Kanfer
and A. Goldstein (Eds.), *Helping people change*. New York: Pergamon
Press, 1975.

Goldfried, M., & Sobocinski, D. Effect of irrational beliefs on emotional
arousal. *Journal of Consulting and Clinical Psychology*, 1975, *43*,
504–510.

Goldfried, M., & Trier, C. Effectiveness of relaxation as an active coping
skill. *Journal of Abnormal Psychology*, 1974, *83*, 348–355.

Goldsmith, J., & McFall, R. Development and evaluation of an interpersonal skill-training program for psychiatric patients. *Journal of Abnormal Psychology*, 1975, *84*, 51–58.

Goldstein, A., Spraflin, R., & Gershaw, N. *Skill training for community
living: Applying structured learning therapy*. New York: Pergamon
Press, 1976.

Goodman, J. Impulsive and reflective behavior: A developmental
analysis of attentional and cognitive strategies. Unpublished doctoral
dissertation, University of Waterloo, 1973.

Goor, A., & Sommerfeld, R. A comparison of problem-solving processes
of creative students and non-creative students. *Journal of Educational
Psychology*, 1975, *67*, 495–505.

Gottlieb, H.. Strite, L., Kellar, R., & Hockersmith, V. A cognitive-social
learning model as applied to the rehabilitation of the chronic low back-
pain patient. Paper presented at meeting of American Psychological
Association, 1975.

Gottman, J., Gonso, J., & Rasmussen, B. Social interaction, social competence and friendship in children. Unpublished manuscript, Indiana
University, 1974.

Graham, D., Kabler, J., & Graham, F. Physiological responses to the
suggestion of attitudes specific for hives and hypertension.
Psychosomatic Medicine, 1962, *24*, 159–169.

Graham, D., Lundy, R., Benjamin, L., & Kabler, F. Some specific attitudes in initial research interviews with patients having different
"psychosomatic" diseases. *Psychosomatic Medicine*, 1962, *24*, 257–
266.

Gratch, G. The use of private speech by headstart and middle class
preschoolers. Paper presented at the meeting of the Southwestern
Psychological Association, Arlington, Texas, 1966.

Grinspoon, L., & Singer, S. Amphetamines in the treatment of hyperkinetic children. *Harvard Educational Review*, 1973, *43*, 515–565.

Guilford, J. Some theoretical views of creativity. In H. Helson and W.

Bevan (Eds.), *Contemporary approaches to psychology.* New York: Von Nostrand, 1967.

Haggard, E. Psychological causes and results of stress. In D. Lindsley (Ed.), *Human factors in undersea warfare.* Washington, D. C.: National Research Council Press, 1949.

Hale, W., & Strickland, B. Induction of mood states and their effects on cognitive and social behaviors. *Journal of Consulting and Clinical Psychology,* 1976, *44,* 155.

Haley, J. *Strategies of psychotherapy.* New York: Grune & Stratton, 1963.

Hanel, J. Der Einfluss eines Motivänderungsprogramms auf Schulleistung schwach misserfolgsmotivierter Grundschüler der 4 Klasse. Psychol. Institut der Ruhr Universität: Unpublished Dissertation, 1974.

Harrison, A., & Nadelman, L. Conceptual tempo and inhibition of movement in black preschool children. *Child Development,* 1972, *43,* 657–668.

Hartig, M., & Kanfer, F. The role of verbal self-instructions in children's resistance to temptation. *Journal of Personality and Social Psychology,* 1973, *25,* 259–267.

Hebb, D. *The organization of behavior.* New York: Wiley, 1949.

Hebb, D. Science and the world of imagination. *Canadian Psychological Review,* 1975, *16,* 4–12.

Heckhausen, H. Fear of failure as a self-reinforcing motive system. In I. Sarason and C. Spielberger (Eds.), *Stress and anxiety,* Volume II. Washington, D. C.: Hemisphere, 1975.

Heider, E. R. Information processing and the modification of an "impulsive conceptual tempo." *Child Development,* 1971, *42,* 1276–1281.

Henderson, A., Montgomery, I., & Williams, C. Psychological immunization: A proposal for preventive psychiatry. *Lancet,* 1972, May, 1111–1112.

Henshaw, D. Cognitive mediators in creative problem solving. Unpublished doctoral dissertation, University of Waterloo, 1977.

Hersen, M., & Bellack, A. A multiple baseline analysis of social skills training in chronic schizophrenics. *Journal of Applied Behavior Analysis,* 1976, *18,* 180–190.

Hilgard, E. Neodissociation theory of multiple cognitive control systems. In G. Schwartz and D. Shapiro (Eds.), *Consciousness and self-regulation,* Volume I. New York: Plenum Press, 1976.

Hilgard, E., Cooper, L., Lennox, J., Morgan, A., & Voevodsky, J. The use of a pain-state report in the study of hypnotic analgesia to the pain of ice water. *Journal of Nervous and Mental Diseases,* 1967, *114,* 501–513.

Hodgson, J., & Urban, H. A comparison of interpersonal training programs in the treatment of depressive states. Pennsylvania State University, 1975.

Hoffman, M. Moral development. In Paul Mussen (Ed.), *Carmichael's
manual of child development*. New York: Wiley, 1970.

Hokanson, J., DeGood, D., Forrest, M., & Brittain, T. Availability of
avoidance behaviors in modulating vascular-stress responses. *Journal
of Personality and Social Psychology*, 1971, *19*, 60–68.

Homme, L. Perspectives in psychology: Control of coverants, the operants of the mind. *Psychological Record*, 1965, *15*, 501–511.

Horan, J., & Dellinger, J. "In vivo" emotive imagery: A preliminary test.
Perceptual and Motor Skills, 1974, *39*, 359–362.

Hunt, J. McV., & Cofer, C. Psychological deficit. In J. McV. Hunt (Ed.),
Personality and the behavior disorders, Volume 2. New York: Ronald
Press, 1944.

Iggo, A. Critical remarks on the gate-control theory. In J. Payne and R.
Burt (Eds.), *Pain*. London: J. Churchill, 1972.

Inglis, J. *The scientific study of abnormal behavior*. Chicago: Aldine,
1966.

Inhelder, B., Sinclair, H., & Bovet, M. *Learning and the development of
cognition*. Cambridge, Mass.: Harvard University Press, 1974.

Israel, A., & O'Leary, D. Developing correspondence between children's words and deeds. *Child Development*, 1973, *44*, 575–581.

Jabichuk, Z., & Smeriglio, U. The influence of symbolic modeling on the
social behavior of preschool children with low levels of social responsiveness. *Child Development*, 1976, *47*, 838–841.

Janis, I. *Psychological stress*. New York: John Wiley & Sons, 1958.

Janis, I. Psychodynamic aspects of stress tolerance. In S. Klausner (Ed.),
The quest for self-control. New York: Free Press, 1965.

Jensen, A. Verbal mediation and educational potential. *Psychology in the
Schools*, 1966, *3*, 99–109.

Jensen, A. The role of verbal mediation in mental development. *Journal
of Genetic Psychology*, 1971, *118*, 39–70.

Johnson, S., & Sechrest, C. Comparison of desensitization and progressive relaxation in treating test anxiety. *Journal of Consulting and Clinical Psychology*, 1968, *32*, 280–286.

Johnson, W. *People in quandaries*. New York: Harper, 1946.

Kagan, J. Reflection-impulsivity: The generality and dynamics of conceptual tempo. *Journal of Abnormal Psychology*, 1966, *71*, 17–24.

Kagan, J., Moss, H., & Sigel, I. Psychological significance of styles of
conceptualization. In J. Wright and J. Kagan (Eds.), *Basic cognitive
processes in children. Monograph for Society of Research in Child
Development*, 1963, *28*, 73–124.

Kagan, J., & Kogan, N. Individuality and cognitive performance. In P. Mussen (Ed.), *Carmichael's manual of child psychology*, Volume I. New York: Wiley, 1970.

Kahn, M., Baker, B., & Weiss, J. Treatment of insomnia by relaxation training. *Journal of Abnormal Psychology*, 1968, *73*, 556–558.

Kanfer, F., & Goldfoot, D. Self-control and tolerance of noxious stimulation. *Psychological Reports*, 1966, *18*, 79–85.

Kanfer, F., Karoly, P., & Newman, A. Reduction of children's fear of the dark by competence related and situational threat related verbal cues. *Journal of Consulting and Clinical Psychology*, 1975, *43*, 251–258.

Kanfer, F., & Phillips, J. *Learning foundations of behavior therapy.* New York: John Wiley, 1970.

Kanfer, F., & Seider, M. Self-control factors enhancing tolerance of noxious stimulation. *Journal of Personality and Social Psychology*, 1973, *25*, 381–389.

Kanfer, F., & Zich, J. Self-control training: The effects of external control on children's resistance to temptation. *Developmental Psychology*, 1974, *10*, 108–115.

Karnes, M., Teska, J., & Hodgins, A. The effects of four programs of classroom intervention on the intellectual and language development of 4-year-old disadvantaged children. *American Journal of Orthopsychiatry*, 1970, *40*, 58–76.

Karoly, P., & Dirks, M. Developing self-control in preschool children through correspondence training. *Behavior Therapy* (in press).

Karst, T., & Trexler, L. Initial study using fixed-role and rational-emotive therapy in treating public-speaking anxiety. *Journal of Consulting and Clinical Psychology*, 1970, *34*, 360–366.

Katkin, E., & Murray, E. Instrumental conditioning of autonomically mediated behavior: Theoretical and methodological issues. *Psychological Bulletin*, 1968, *70*, 52–68.

Kazdin, A. Covert modeling and the reduction of avoidance behavior. *Journal of Abnormal Psychology*, 1973, *81*, 87–95.

Kazdin, A. Covert modeling, model similarity, and reduction of avoidance behavior. *Behavior Therapy*, 1974, *5*, 325–340 (a).

Kazdin, A. The effect of model identity and fear relevant similarity on covert modeling. *Behavior Therapy*, 1974, *5*, 624–636 (b).

Kelley, G. *The psychology of personal constructs*, Volumes I and II. New York: Norton, 1955.

Kendler, T. Learning development and thinking. In E. Harms (Ed.), *Fundamentals of psychology: The psychology of thinking. Annals of New York Academy of Sciences*, 1960, *19*, 52–65.

Kendler, T., Kendler, H., & Carrick, M. Verbal labels and inferential problem solution of children. *Child Development*, 1966, *37*, 749–763.

Kieslar, D. Some myths of psychotherapy research and the search for a paradigm. *Psychological Record*, 1966, *65*, 110–136.

Kifer, R., Lewis, M., Green, D., & Phillips, E. The S.O.C.S. model: Training pre-delinquent youths and their parents in negotiation responses to conflict situations. Paper presented at the meeting of the American Psychological Association, 1973.

Kimble, G., & Perlmutter, L. The problem of volition. *Psychological Review*, 1970, *77*, 361–384.

Kinsbourne, M. Cognitive deficit: Experimental analysis. In J. McGaugh (Ed.), *Psychobiology*. New York: Academic Press, 1971.

Kleiman, A. The use of private speech in young children and its relation to social speech. Unpublished doctoral dissertation, University of Chicago, 1974.

Klein, D., & Seligman, M. Reversal of performance deficits and perceptual deficits in learned helplessness and depression. *Journal of Abnormal Psychology*, 1976, *85*, 11–26.

Klein, M., Dittmann, A., Parloff, M., & Gill, M. Behavior therapy: Observations and reflections. *Journal of Consulting and Clinical Psychology*, 1969, *33*, 259–266.

Klein, W. An investigation of the spontaneous speech of children. Unpublished doctoral dissertation, University of Rochester, 1963.

Klepac, R. Successful treatment of avoidance of dentistry by desensitization or by increasing pain tolerance. *Journal of Behavior Therapy and Experimental Psychiatry*, 1975, *6*, 307–310.

Kleuver, R. Mental abilities and disorders of learning. In H. Myklebust (Ed.), *Progress in learning disabilities*, Volume 2. New York: Grune & Stratton, 1971.

Knox, J. Cognitive strategies for coping with pain: Ignoring vs. acknowledging. Unpublished Ph.D. dissertation, University of Waterloo, 1972.

Koestler, A. *Darkness at noon*. London: Jonathan Cape, 1940.

Kohlberg, L., Yaeger, J., & Hjertholm, E. Private speech: Four studies and a review of theories. *Child Development*, 1968, *39*, 691–736.

Kopel, S., & Arkowitz, H. The role of attribution and self-perception in behavior change: Implications for behavior therapy. *Genetic Psychology Monographs*, 1975, *92*, 175–212.

Kopfstein, J., & Neale, J. A multivariate study of attention dysfunction in schizophrenia. *Journal of Abnormal Psychology*, 1972, *80*, 294–298.

Kornhaber, R., & Schroeder, H. Importance of model similarity on extinction of avoidance behavior in children. *Journal of Consulting and Clinical Psychology*, 1975, *43*, 601–607.

Korzybski, A. *Science and society*. New York: Lancaster Press, 1933.

Kris, E. Psychoanalytic explorations in art. London: Allen & Unwin, 1953.

Labouvie-Vief, G., & Gonda, J. Cognitive strategy training and intellectual performance in the elderly. *Journal of Gerontology*, 1976, *31*, 327–332.

Lang, P. Fear reduction and fear behavior: Problems in treating a construct. In J. Shlien (Ed.), *Research in psychotherapy*, Volume 3. Washington, D. C.: APA, 1968.

Lang, P. The mechanics of desensitization and the laboratory study of human fear. In C. Franks (Ed.), *Assessment and status of the behavior therapies*. New York: McGraw-Hill, 1969.

Lang, P., & Lazovik, A. Experimental desensitization of a phobia. *Journal of Abnormal Psychology*, 1963, *66*, 519–525.

Lang, P., Lazovik, A., & Reynolds, D. Desensitization, suggestibility, and pseudotherapy. *Journal of Abnormal Psychology*, 1965, *70*, 395–402.

Langer, E., Janis, I., & Wolper, J. Reduction of psychological stress in surgical patients. *Journal of Experimental Social Psychology*, 1975, *11*, 155–165.

Lazarus, A. *Behavior therapy and beyond*. New York: McGraw-Hill, 1972.

Lazarus, A. *Multi-modal behavior therapy*. New York: Springer Publishing Co., 1976.

Lazarus, R. *Psychological stress and the coping process*. New York: McGraw-Hill, 1966.

Lazarus, R., & Alfert, E. Short-circuiting of threat by experimentally altering cognitive appraisal. *Journal of Abnormal and Social Psychology*, 1964, *69*, 195–205.

Lazarus, R., Averill, J., & Opton, E. Towards a cognitive theory of emotion. In M. Arnold (Ed.), *Feelings and emotions*. New York: Academic Press, 1970.

Levendusky, P., & Pankratz, L. Self-control techniques as an alternative to pain medication. *Journal of Abnormal Psychology*, 1975, *84*, 165–169.

Lewin, K. *A dynamic theory of personality*. New York: McGraw-Hill, 1935.

Lewis, W. *Why people change: The psychology of influence*. New York: Holt, Rinehart & Winston, 1972.

Locke, E. Is "behavior therapy" behavioristic? (An analysis of Wolpe's psychotherapeutic methods). *Psychological Bulletin*, 1971, *76*, 318–327.

London, P. The end of ideology in behavior modification. *American Psychologist*, 1972, *27*, 913–920.

Lovaas, O. Interaction between verbal and nonverbal behavior. *Child Development*, 1961, *32*, 329–336.

Lovaas, O. Cue properties of words: The control of operant responding by rate and content of verbal operants. *Child Development,* 1964, *35,* 245–256.

Low, A. *Mental health through will training.* Boston: Christopher Publishing, 1950.

Lund, M. Inner skier: A new way of learning. *Ski,* November, 1975, 74–77.

Luria, A. The directive function of speech in development. *Word,* 1959, *18,* 341–352.

Luria, A. *The role of speech in the regulation of normal and abnormal behaviors.* New York: Liveright, 1961.

Luria, A. Speech and formation of mental processes. In M. Cole and I. Maltzman (Eds.), *A handbook of contemporary Soviet psychology.* New York: Basic Books, 1969.

Maccoby, E. The development of moral values and behavior in childhood. In J. Clausen (Ed.), *Socialization and society.* New York: Little Brown, 1968.

Maccoby, E., Dowley, E., Hogan, J., & Degerman, R. Activity level and intellectual functioning in normal school children. *Child Development,* 1965, *36,* 761–770.

Mackay, C. *Extraordinary popular delusions.* London: George Harrap and Co., 1841.

MacPherson, E., Candee, B., & Hohman, R. A comparison of three methods for elementary disruptive lunchroom behavior. *Journal of Applied Behavior Analysis,* 1974, *7,* 287–297.

Mahoney, M. *Cognition and behavior modification.* Cambridge, Mass.: Ballinger Publishing Co., 1974.

Mahoney, M. *The scientist: Anatomy of the truth merchant.* Cambridge, Mass.: Ballinger, 1976.

Mahoney, M., & Mahoney, K. *Permanent weight control.* New York: W. W. Norton, 1976.

Mandler, G. Comments on Dr. Sarason's paper. In C. Spielberger (Ed.), *Anxiety: Current trends in theory and research,* Volume II. New York: Academic Press, 1972.

Mandler, G. *Mind and emotion.* New York: John Wiley & Sons, 1975.

Marks, I. New approaches to the treatment of obsessive compulsive disorders. *Journal of Nervous Mental Disease,* 1973, *156,* 420–426.

Marks, I., Boulougouris, J., & Marset, P. Flooding versus desensitization in the treatment of phobic patients. *British Journal of Psychiatry,* 1971, *119,* 353–375.

Marlatt, G. Task structure and the experimental modification of verbal behavior. *Psychological Bulletin,* 1972, *78,* 335–350.

Marmor, J. The psychodynamics of realistic worry. *Psychoanalysis and Social Science,* 1958, *5,* 155–163.

Marmor, J. The nature of the psychotherapeutic process revisited. *Canadian Psychiatric Association Journal*, 1975, *20*, 557–565.

May, J., & Johnson, H. Physiological activity to internally elicited arousal and inhibitory thoughts. *Journal of Abnormal Psychology*, 1973, *82*, 239–245.

McConaghy, N., & Barr, R. Classical avoidance and backward conditioning treatments of homosexuality. *British Journal of Psychiatry*, 1973, *122*, 151–162.

McFall, R., & Lillesand, D. Behavior rehearsal with modeling and coaching in assertion training. *Journal of Abnormal Psychology*, 1971, *77*, 313–323.

McGuire, M., & Sifneos, P. Problem solving in psychotherapy. *Psychiatric Quarterly*, 1970, *44*, 667–673.

McGuire, W. Inducing resistance to persuasion: Some contemporary approaches. In L. Berkowitz (Ed.), *Advances in social psychology*, Volume 1. New York: Academic Press, 1964.

McKeachie, W. The decline and fall of the laws of learning. *Educational Researcher*, 1974, *3*, 7–11.

McKinney, J. Problem solving strategies in impulsive and reflective second graders. *Developmental Psychology*, 1973, *8*, 145 (a).

McKinney, J. A developmental study of the effects of hypothesis verbalizations and memory load on concept attainment. Unpublished manuscript, University of North Carolina, Chapel Hill, 1973 (b).

McKinney, J. Problem solving strategies in reflective and impulsive children. Unpublished research report, University of North Carolina at Chapel Hill, 1975.

Meachem, J. The development of memory abilities in the individual and society. *Human Development*, 1972, *15*, 205–228.

Meichenbaum, D. The effects of instructions and reinforcement on thinking and language behaviors of schizophrenics. *Behavior Research and Therapy*, 1969, *7*, 101–114.

Meichenbaum, D. The nature and modification of impulsive children. Paper presented at meeting of the Society for Research in Child Development, Minneapolis, 1971 (a).

Meichenbaum, D. Examination of model characteristics in reducing avoidance behavior. *Journal of Personality and Social Psychology*, 1971, *17*, 298–307 (b).

Meichenbaum, D. Cognitive modification of test anxious college students. *Journal of Consulting and Clinical Psychology*, 1972, *39*, 370–380.

Meichenbaum, D. Therapist manual for cognitive behavior modification. Unpublished manuscript, University of Waterloo, 1973.

Meichenbaum, D. *Cognitive behavior modification*. Morristown, N. J.: General Learning Press, 1974 (a).

Meichenbaum, D. Self-instructional training: A cognitive prosthesis for the aged. *Human Development*, 1974, *17*, 273–280 (b).

Meichenbaum, D. Theoretical and treatment implications of developmental research on verbal control of behavior. *Canadian Psychological Review*, 1975, *16*, 22–27 (a).

Meichenbaum, D. Enhancing creativity by modifying what subjects say to themselves. *American Educational Research Journal*, 1975, *12*, 129–145 (b).

Meichenbaum, D. A self-instructional approach to stress management: A proposal for stress inoculation training. In C. Spielberger and I. Sarason (Eds.), *Stress and anxiety in modern life*. New York: Winston and Sons, 1976 (a).

Meichenbaum, D. Toward a cognitive theory of self-control. In G. Schwartz and D. Shapiro (Eds.), *Consciousness and self regulation*, Volume 1. New York: Plenum Press, 1976 (b).

Meichenbaum, D. Cognitive factors as determinants of learning disabilities: A cognitive-functional approach. In R. Knights and D. Bakker (Eds.), *The neuropsychology of learning disorders: Theoretical approaches*. Baltimore, Md.: University Park Press, 1976 (c).

Meichenbaum, D., & Cameron, R. An examination of cognitive and contingency variables in anxiety relief procedures. Unpublished manuscript, University of Waterloo, 1972 (a).

Meichenbaum, D., & Cameron, R. Stress inoculation: A skills training approach to anxiety management. Unpublished manuscript, University of Waterloo, 1972 (b).

Meichenbaum, D., & Cameron, R. Training schizophrenics to talk to themselves: A means of developing attentional controls. *Behavior Therapy*, 1973, *4*, 515–534.

Meichenbaum, D., & Cameron, R. The clinical potential of modifying what clients say to themselves. *Psychotherapy: Theory, Research, and Practice*, 1974, *11*, 103–117.

Meichenbaum, D., Gilmore, B., & Fedoravicius, A. Group insight *vs.* group desensitization in treating speech anxiety. *Journal of Consulting and Clinical Psychology*, 1971, *36*, 410–421.

Meichenbaum, D., & Goodman, J. The developmental control of operant motor responding by verbal operants. *Journal of Experimental Child Psychology*, 1969, *7*, 553–565 (a).

Meichenbaum, D., & Goodman, J. Reflection-impulsivity and verbal control of motor behavior. *Child Development*, 1969, *40*, 785–797 (b).

Meichenbaum, D., & Goodman, J. Training impulsive children to talk to themselves: A means of developing self-control. *Journal of Abnormal Psychology*, 1971, *77*, 115–126.

Meichenbaum, D., & Goodman, S. The nature and modification of impulsivity. Paper presented at the first international congress of child neurology, Toronto, Ontario, 1975.

Meichenbaum, D., & Goodman, S. Critical questions and methodological problems in studying private speech. In G. Zivin (Ed.), *Development of self-regulation through speech*. New York: Wiley, 1976.

Meichenbaum, D., & Turk, D. The cognitive-behavioral management of anxiety, anger and pain. In P. Davidson (Ed.), *The behavioral management of anxiety, depression and pain*. New York: Bruner Mazel, 1976.

Meichenbaum, D., Turk, D., & Burstein, S. The nature of coping with stress. In I. Sarason and C. Spielberger (Eds.), *Stress and anxiety*, Volume 2. New York: Wiley, 1975.

Meichenbaum, D., & Turk, L. Implications of research on disadvantaged children and cognitive-training programs for educational television: Ways of improving "Sesame Street." *Journal of Special Education*, 1972, 6, 27–42.

Melamed, B., & Siegel, J. Reduction of anxiety in children facing hospitalization and surgery by use of filmed modeling. *Journal of Consulting and Clinical Psychology*, 1975, 43, 511–521.

Melzack, R. *The puzzle of pain*. Harmondsworth, England: Penguin, 1973.

Melzack, R., & Casey, K. Sensory, motivational and central control determinants of pain: A new conceptual model. In D. Kenshalo (Ed.), *The skin senses*. Springfield, Ill.: Charles C Thomas, 1968.

Melzack, R., & Wall, P. Pain mechanisms: A new theory. *Science*, 1965, 150, 971.

Mendel, W. The non-specifics of psychotherapy. *International Journal of Psychiatry*, 1968, 5, 400–402.

Meyer, V., & Gelder, M. Behavior therapy and phobic disorders. *British Journal of Psychiatry*, 1963, 109, 19–28.

Meyers, A., Mercatoris, M., & Sirota, A. Use of covert self-instruction for the elimination of psychotic speech. *Journal of Consulting and Clinical Psychology*, 1976, 44, 480–483.

Miller, G. Assessment of psychotechnology. *American Psychologist*, 1970, 25, 991–1001.

Miller, G., Galanter, E., & Pribram, K. *Plans and structure of behavior*. New York: Holt, 1960.

Miller, J., & Mumbauer, C. Intellectual functioning, learning performance and cognitive style in advantaged and disadvantaged preschool children. Unpublished manuscript, George Peabody College for Teachers, Nashville, 1967.

Miller, L. School behavior checklist: An inventory of deviant behavior for elementary school children. *Journal of Consulting and Clinical Psychology*, 1972, 38, 134–144.

Miller, N. Applications of learning and biofeedback to psychiatry and medicine. In A. Freedman, H. Kaplan, & B. Sadock (Eds.), *Comprehensive textbook of psychiatry*. Baltimore: Williams & Wilkins, 1974.

Miller, R., Brickman, P., & Bolen, D. Attribution versus persuasion as a means for modifying behavior. *Journal of Personality and Social Psychology*, 1975, *31*, 430–441.

Miller, W. Some negative thinking about Norman Vincent Peale. *The Reporter*, Jan. 13, 1955.

Mischel, W. Cognition in self-imposed delay of gratification. In L. Berkowitz (Ed.), *Advances in social psychology*, Volume I. New York: Academic Press, 1973.

Mischel, W. The self as the person: A cognitive social learning view. In A. Wandersman (Ed.), *Behavioristic and humanistic approaches to personality change*. New York: Pergamon Press, 1975.

Mischel, W., & Baker, N. Cognitive transformations of reward objects through instructions. *Journal of Personality and Social Psychology*, 1975, *31*, 254–261.

Mischel, W., Ebbesen, E., & Zeiss, A. Cognitive and attentional mechanisms in delay of gratification. *Journal of Personality and Social Psychology*, 1972, *21*, 204–218.

Monahan, J., & O'Leary, D. Effects of self-instruction on rule breaking behavior. *Psychological Reports*, 1971, 79, 1059–1066.

Morris, L., & Liebert, R. Relationship of cognitive and emotional components of test anxiety to physiological arousal and academic performance. *Journal of Consulting and Clinical Psychology*, 1970, 35, 332–337.

Mowrer, O., & Viek, P. An experimental analogue of fear from a sense of helplessness. *Journal of Abnormal and Social Psychology*, 1948, *43*, 193–200.

Mulcahy, R., & Janz, N. Effectiveness of raising pain perception threshold in males and females using a psychoprophylactic childbirth technique during induced pain. *Nursing Research*, 1973, *22*, 423–427.

Murphy, L. *The widening world of childhood*. New York: Basic Books, 1962.

Murphy, R., & Ellis, A. Rational-emotive psychotherapy outcome studies: A bibliography. Unpublished manuscript, Institute for Rational Living, New York, 1976.

Murray, E., & Jacobson, L. The nature of learning in traditional psychotherapy. In A. Bergin and S. Garfield (Eds.), *Handbook of psychotherapy and behavior change*. New York: Wiley, 1971.

Murray, H. *Explorations in personality*. New York: Oxford Press, 1938.

Myklebust, M., Bannochie, M., & Killen, J. Learning disabilities and cognitive processes. In H. Myklebust (Ed.), *Progress in learning disabilities*, Volume 2. New York: Grune & Stratton, 1971.

Nash, C. *Coping with exercise.* Unpublished manual, Stanford University, 1975.

Natsoulas, T. Concerning introspective "Knowledge." *Psychological Bulletin*, 1970, 73, 89–111.

Neimark, E., & Lewis, N. The development of logical problem solving strategies. *Child Development*, 1967, 38, 107–117.

Neisser, U. Cultural and cognitive discontinuity. In T. E. Gladwin and W. Sturtevant (Eds.), *Anthropology and human behavior.* Washington, D. C.: Anthropological Society of Washington, 1962.

Nelson, T. The effects of training in attention deployment on observing behavior in reflective and impulsive children. *Dissertation Abstracts*, 1969, 29, 2659.

Neufeld, R., & Davidson, P. The effects of vicarious and cognitive rehearsal on pain tolerance. *Journal of Psychosomatic Research*, 1971, 15, 319–325.

Neussle, W. Reflectivity as an influence on focusing behavior of children. *Journal of Experimental Child Psychology*, 1972, 14, 265–276.

Nisbett, R., & Schachter, W. Cognitive manipulation of pain. *Journal of Experimental Social Psychology*, 1966, 2, 227–236.

Novaco, R. *Anger control: The development and evaluation of an experimental treatment.* Lexington, Mass.: Heath & Co., 1975 (a).

Novaco, R. Stress inoculation: A cognitive therapy for anger and its application to depression. Unpublished manuscript, University of California at Irvine, 1975 (b).

Novaco, R. A stress-inoculation approach to anger management in the training of law enforcement officers. *American Journal of Community Psychology* (in press).

O'Leary, D. The effects of self-instruction on immoral behavior. *Journal of Experimental Child Psychology*, 1968, 6, 297–301.

O'Leary, D., Pelham, W., Rosenbaum, A., & Price, G. Behavioral treatment of hyperkinetic children: An experimental evaluation of its usefulness. *Clinical Pediatrics* (in press).

Oltmanns, T., & Neale, J. Schizophrenic performance when distractions are present: Attentional deficit on differential task difficulty. Unpublished manuscript, State University of New York at Stony Brook, 1974.

O'Malley, J., & Eisenberg, L. The hyperkinetic syndrome, *Seminars in Psychiatry*, 1973, 5, 95–103.

Orne, M. Psychological factors maximizing resistance to stress with special reference to hypnosis. In S. Klausner (Ed.), *The quest for self-control.* New York: Free Press, 1965.

Orzack, H., & Kornetsky, C. Attention dysfunction in chronic schizophrenia. *Archives of General Psychiatry*, 1966, 14, 327–336.

Palkes, H., Stewart, M., & Freedman, J. Improvement in maze performance on hyperactive boys as a function of verbal training procedures. *Journal of Special Education*, 1972, 5, 337–342.

Palkes, H., Stewart, M., & Kahana, B. Porteus maze performance after training in self-directed verbal commands. *Child Development*, 1968, *39*, 817–826.

Parnes, S., & Brunelle, E. The literature of creativity, Part I. *Journal of Creative Behavior*, 1967, *1*, 52–109.

Parry, P. The effect of reward on the peformance of hyperactive children. Unpublished doctoral dissertation, McGill University, Montreal, 1973.

Patrick, C. Creative thought in poets. *Archives of Psychology*, 1935, *178*, 74.

Patrick, C. Creative thought in artists. *Journal of Psychology*, 1937, *4*, 35–73.

Patterson, C., & Mischel, W. Effects of temptation-inhibiting and task facilitating plans on self-control. *Journal of Personality and Social Psychology*, 1976, *33*, 209–217.

Patterson, G., Jones, R., Whittier, J., & Wright, M. A behavior modification technique for hyperactive children. *Behaviour Research and Therapy*, 1965, *2*, 217–226.

Paul, G. *Insight vs. desensitization in psychotherapy: An experiment in anxiety reduction*. Stanford: Stanford University Press, 1966.

Paul, G. Outcome of systematic desensitization II: Controlled investigations of individual treatments, techniques, variations, and current status. In C. Franks (Ed.), *Behavior therapy: Appraisal and status*. New York: McGraw-Hill, 1969.

Paivio, A. *Imagery and verbal processes*. New York: Holt, Rinehart and Winston, 1971.

Paivio, A. Neomentalism. *Canadian Journal of Psychology*, 1975, *29*, 263–291.

Pechacek, T. *Coping with stress without cigarettes: A self-study manual*. Unpublished manual, Palo Alto UA Hospital, Calif., 1976.

Pervin, L. The need to predict and control under conditions of threat. *Journal of Personality*, 1963, *31*, 570–585.

Peterson, D. *The clinical study of social behavior*. New York: Appleton-Century-Crofts, 1968.

Phillips, E. *Psychotherapy: A modern theory and practice*. New York: Prentice-Hall, 1957.

Piaget, J. *Construction of reality in the child* (Trans. M. Cook). New York: Basic Books, 1954.

Piaget, J. *The language and thought of the child*. New York: New American Library, 1955.

Pirsig, R. *Zen and the art of motorcycle maintenance*. New York: William Morrow, 1974.

Pishkin, V., Smith, T., & Leibowitz, H. The influence of symbolic stimulus value on perceived size in chronic schizophrenia. *Journal of Consulting Psychology*, 1962, *26*, 323–330.

Platonov, K. *The word as a physiological and therapeutic factor.* Moscow: Foreign Languages Publishing House, 1959.

Plutchik, R., and Ax, A. A critique of "Determinants of emotional states" by Schachter and Singer (1962). *Psychophysiology*, 1967, *4*, 79–82.

Polanyi, M. *Personal knowledge: Towards a post-critical philosophy.* Chicago: University of Chicago Press, 1958.

Polya, G. *How to solve it.* Princeton, N. J.: Princeton University Press, 1945.

Poser, E. Toward a theory of "behavioral prophylaxis." *Journal of Behaviour Therapy and Experimental Psychiatry*, 1970, *1*, 39–43.

Premack, D. Mechanisms of self-control. In W. Hunt (Ed.), *Learning and mechanisms of self-control in smoking.* Chicago: Aldine, 1970.

Price, R. Analysis of task requirements in schizophrenic concept identification performance. *Journal of Abnormal Psychology*, 1968, *73*, 285–294.

Rachman, S. Systematic desensitization. *Psychological Bulletin*, 1967, *67*, 93–103.

Radford, J. Verbalization effects in a non-verbal intelligence test. *British Journal of Educational Psychology*, 1966, *36*, 33–38.

Raimy, V. *Misunderstanding of the self: Cognitive psychotherapy and the misconception hypothesis.* San Francisco: Josey Bass, 1975.

Reese, H. Verbal mediation as a function of age. *Psychological Bulletin*, 1962, *59*, 502–509.

Reeves, J. EMG-biofeedback reduction of tension headache: A cognitive skills-training approach. *Biofeedback and Self-Regulation*, 1976, *1*, 217–225.

Rehm, L., Fuchs, C., Roth, D., Kornblith, S., & Roman, J. Self-control and social skills training in the modification of depression. Unpublished manuscript, University of Pennsylvania, 1975.

Rheingold, K., & Shapiro, J. Children's verbal rehearsal in a free-recall task. *Developmental Psychology*, 1976, *12*, 169–170.

Richardson, A. Mental practice: A review and discussion. Part I. *Research Quarterly*, 1967, *38*, 95–107 (a).

Richardson, A. Mental practice: A review and discussion. Part II. *Research Quarterly*, 1967, *38*, 263–273 (b).

Richardson, F. Coping with test anxiety: A guide. Unpublished manual, University of Texas at Austin, 1973.

Richter, C. The phenomenon of unexplained sudden death in animals and man. In H. Fiefel (Ed.), *The meaning of death.* New York: McGraw-Hill, 1959.

Ridberg, E., Parke, R., & Hetherington, E. Modification of impulsive and reflective cognitive styles through observation of film mediated models. *Developmental Psychology*, 1971, *5*, 369–377.

Rimm, D., & Litvak, S. Self-verbalization and emotional arousal. *Journal of Abnormal Psychology*, 1969, *74*, 181–187.

Risley, T., & Hart, B. Developing correspondence between the non-verbal and verbal behavior of preschool children. *Journal of Applied Behavior Analysis*, 1968, *1*, 267–281.

Robertson, D., & Keeley, S. Evaluation of a mediational training program for impulsive children by a multiple case study design. Paper presented at the meeting of the American Psychological Association, 1974.

Robin, A., Armel, S., & O'Leary, D. The effects of self-instruction on writing deficiencies. *Behavior Therapy*, 1975, *6*, 178–187.

Robin, A., Schneider, M., & Dolnick, M. The turtle technique: An extended case study of self-control in the classroom. *Psychology in the Schools*, 1976, *12*, 120–128.

Rohwer, W. Images and pictures in children's learning: Research results and instructional implications. In H. Reese (Chm.), Imagery in children's learning: A symposium. *Psychological Bulletin*, 1970, *73*, 393–403.

Rosenbaum, A., O'Leary, D., & Jacob, R. Behavioral intervention with hyperactive children: Group consequences as a supplement to individual contingencies. *Behavior Therapy*, 1975, *6*, 315–323.

Ross, L., Rodin, J., & Zimbardo, P. Toward an attribution therapy: The reduction of fear through induced cognitive-emotional misattribution. *Journal of Personality and Social Psychology*, 1969, *12*, 279–288.

Rosvold, H. A continuous performance test of brain damage. *Journal of Consulting Psychology*, 1965, *20*, 343–350.

Rotter, J. Generalized expectancies for internal versus external control of reinforcement. *Psychological Monographs*, 1966, 80.

Rush, A., Beck, A., Kovacs, M., Khatami, M., Fitzgibbons, R., & Wolman, T. Comparison of cognitive and pharmacotherapy in depressed outpatients: A preliminary report. Paper presented at the meeting of the Society for Psychotherapy Research, Boston, Mass., June, 1975. (a)

Rush, A., Khatami, M., & Beck, A. A cognitive and behavior therapy in chronic depression. *Behavior Therapy*, 1975, *6*, 398–404. (b)

Sachs, L., & Ingram, G. Covert sensitization as a treatment for weight control. *Psychological Reports*, 1972, *30*, 971–974.

Salkind, N., & Poggio, J. Hyperactivity: Theoretical and methodological concerns. Unpublished manuscript, Kansas University, 1975.

Saltz, E., Dixon, D., & Johnson, J. Training disadvantaged preschoolers on various fantasy activities: Effects on cognitive functioning and impulse control. Technical report number 8, Center for the study of cognitive processes, Wayne State University, 1976.

Saltz, E., & Johnson, J. Training for thematic-fantasy play in culturally disadvantaged children. *Journal of Educational Psychology*, 1974, *66*, 623–630.

Sanchez-Craig, M. A self-control strategy for drinking tendencies. *Ontario Psychologist*, 1975, *7*, 25–29.

Sanchez-Craig, M. Cognitive and behavioral coping strategies in the reappraisal of stressful social situations. *Journal of Counseling Psychology*, 1976, *23*, 7–12.

Sarason, I. Test anxiety and cognitive modeling. *Journal of Personality and Social Psychology*, 1973, *28*, 58–61.

Sarason, I. An information processing approach to stress and anxiety. Paper presented at NATO Advanced Study Institute, Urbino, Italy, 1976.

Sarbin, T. Imagining as muted role-taking: A historical-linguistic analysis. In P. Sheehan (Ed.), *The function and nature of imagery*. New York: Academic Press, 1972.

Sarbin, T., & Coe, W. *Hypnosis: A social psychological analysis of influence communication*. New York: Holt, Rinehart, and Winston, 1972.

Schachter, S. The interaction of cognitive and physiological determinants of emotional state. In C. Spielberger (Eds.), *Anxiety and behavior*. New York: Academic Press, 1966.

Scheerer, M. Problems of performance analysis in the study of personality. *New York Academy of Sciences*, 1945, *46*, 653–678.

Schmickley, V. The effects of cognitive-behavior modification upon depressed outpatients. Unpublished doctoral dissertation, Michigan State University, 1975.

Schneider, M. Turtle technique in the classroom. *Teaching Exceptional Children*, Fall, 1974, 22–24.

Schneider, M., & Robin, A. The turtle technique: A method for the self-control of impulse behavior. Unpublished manuscript, State University of New York at Stony Brook, 1975.

Schwartz, G. Cardiac responses to self-induced thoughts. *Psychophysiology*, 1971, *8*, 462–467.

Schwartz, R., & Gottman, J. A task analysis approach to clinical problems: A study of assertive behavior. Unpublished manuscript, Indiana University, 1974.

Sears, R., Maccoby, E., & Levin, H. *Patterns of child rearing*. New York: Harper, 1957.

Seligman, M. Fall into helplessness. *Psychology Today*, June, 1973.

Seligman, M., Maier, S., & Solomon, R. Unpredictable and uncontrollable aversive events. In F. Brush (Ed.), *Aversive conditioning and learning*. New York: Academic Press, 1969.

Shaffer, L. The problem of psychotherapy. *American Psychologist*, 1947, *2*, 459–467.

Shapiro, M. An experimental approach to diagnostic psychological testing. *Journal of Mental Science*, 1951, *97*, 748–764.

Shapiro, M., & Ravenette, E. A preliminary experiment on paranoid delusions. *Journal of Mental Science*, 1959, *105*, 295–312.

Shaw, B. A systematic investigation of two treatments of depression. Unpublished doctoral dissertation, University of Western Ontario, 1975.

Shimkunas, A. Demand for intimate self-disclosure and pathological verbalizations in schizophrenia. *Journal of Abnormal Psychology*, 1972, *80*, 197–205.

Shipley, C., & Fazio, A. Pilot study of a treatment for psychological depression. *Journal of Abnormal Psychology*, 1973, *83*, 372–376.

Shmurak, S. Design and evaluation of three dating behavior training programs utilizing response acquisition and cognitive self-statement modification techniques. Unpublished doctoral dissertation, Indiana University, 1974.

Siegal, A., Babich, J., & Kirasic, K. Visual recognition memory in reflective and impulsive children. *Memory and Cognition*, 1974, *2*, 379–384.

Siegal, J., & Spivack, G. A new therapy program for chronic patients. *Behavior Therapy*, 1976, *7*, 129–130.

Siegelman, E. Reflective and impulsive observing behavior. *Child Development*, 1969, *40*, 1213–1222.

Silverman, J. The problem of attention in research and theory in schizophrenia. *Psychological Review*, 1964, *71*, 352–379.

Simkins, L. Instructions as discriminative stimuli in verbal conditioning and awareness. *Journal of Abnormal and Social Psychology*, 1963, *66*, 213–219.

Sinclair-de-Zwart, H. A possible theory of language acquisition within the general framework of Piaget's developmental theory. In D. Elkind and J. Flavell (Eds.), *Studies in cognitive development*. London: Oxford University Press, 1969.

Singer, J. *Imagery and daydream methods in psychotherapy.* New York: Academic Press, 1974.

Skaggs, E. Changes in pulse, breaking and steadiness under conditions of startledness and excited expectancy. *Journal of Comparative and Physiological Psychology*, 1926, *6*, 303–318.

Skinner, B. F. *Science and human behavior.* New York: Macmillan, 1953.

Skinner, B. *The technology of teaching.* New York: Appleton-Century-Crofts, 1968.

Sloan, R., Staples, F., Cristol, A., Yorkston, N., & Whipple, K. *Psychotherapy versus behavior therapy.* Cambridge, Mass.: Harvard University Press, 1975.

Smilansky, S. *The effects of sociodramatic play on disadvantaged preschool children.* New York: Wiley, 1968.

Smith, G., Chiang, H., & Regina, E. Acupuncture and experimental psychology. Paper presented at symposium on pain and acupuncture, in Philadelphia, Pa., April, 1974.

Smith, G., Egbert, L., Markowitz, R., Mosteller, F., & Beecher, H. An experimental pain method sensitive to morphine in man: The submaximum effort tourniquet technique. *Journal of Pharmacology and Experimental Therapeutics*, 1966, *154*, 324–332.

Smith, J. The effect of self-instructional training on children's attending behavior. Unpublished doctoral dissertation, University of Toledo, 1975.

Sokolov, A. N. *Inner speech and thought.* New York: Plenum Press, 1972.

Solyom, L., & Miller, S. Reciprocal inhibition by aversion relief in the treatment of phobias. *Behaviour Research and Therapy*, 1967, *5*, 313–324.

Spanos, N., Horton, C., & Chaves, J. The effect of two cognitive strategies on pain threshold. *Journal of Abnormal Psychology*, 1975, *84*, 677–681.

Spiegler, M., Cooley, E., Marshall, G., Prince, H., Puckett, S., & Slenazy, J. A self-control versus a counterconditioning paradigm for systematic desensitization: An experimental comparison. *Journal of Counseling Psychology*, 1976, *23*, 83–86.

Spielberger, C. Coping with stress and anxiety in the college classroom. Paper presented at NATO Advanced Study Institute, Urbino, Italy, 1976.

Spivack, G., & Shure, M. *Social adjustment of young children: A cognitive approach to solving real-life problems.* San Francisco: Jossey-Bass, 1974.

Staub, E. *The development of prosocial behavior in children.* Morristown, N. J.: General Learning Press, 1975 (a).

Staub, E. To rear a prosocial child: Reasoning, learning by doing, and learning by teaching others. In David DePalma and Jeanne Foley (Ed.), *Moral development: Current theory and research.* New Jersey: Lawrence Erlbaum Assoc., 1975 (b).

Steffy, R., Meichenbaum, D., & Best, A. Aversive and cognitive factors in the modification of smoking behavior. *Behaviour Research and Therapy*, 1970, *8*, 115–125.

Steiner, I. Perceived freedom. In L. Berkowitz (Ed.), *Advances in experimental social psychology.* New York: Academic Press, 1970.

Sternbach, R. The effects of instructional sets on autonomic activity. *Psychophysiology*, 1964, *1*, 67–72.

Stone, G., Hinds, W., & Schmidt, G. Teaching mental health behaviors to elementary school children. *Professional Psychology*, 1975, *6*, 34–40.

Storms, M., & Nisbett, R. Insomnia and the attribution process. *Journal of Personality and Social Psychology*, 1970, *16*, 319–328.

Strickland, B., Hale, W., & Anderson, L. Effect of induced mood states on activity and self-reported affect. *Journal of Consulting and Clinical Psychology*, 1975, *43*, 587.

Strupp, H. Specific vs. nonspecific factors in psychotherapy and the problem of control. *Archives of General Psychiatry*, 1970, *23*, 393–401.

Suinn, R. Rehearsal training for ski racers. *Behavior Therapy*, 1972, *3*, 519–520.

Suinn, R. Anxiety management training for general anxiety. In R. Suinn and R. Weigel (Eds.), *Innovative therapies: Critical and creative contributions*. New York: Harper and Row, 1975.

Suinn, R., & Richardson, F. Anxiety management training: A nonspecific behavior therapy program for anxiety control. *Behavior Therapy*, 1971, *2*, 498–510.

Sutcliffe, J. On the role of "instructions to the subject" in psychological experiments. *American Psychologist*, 1972, 27, 755–758.

Sykes, D., Douglas, U., & Morganstern, G. Sustained attention in hyperactive children. *Journal of Child Psychology and Psychiatry*, 1973, *14*, 213–220.

Szasz, T. Psychoanalytic treatment as education. In H. Greenwald (Ed.), *Active psychotherapy*. New York: Jason Aronson, 1974.

Tannenbaum, P. The congruity principle revisited: Studies in the reduction, induction, and generalization of persuasion. In C. Berkowitz (Ed.), *Advances in experimental social psychology*, Volume 3. New York: Academic Press, 1967.

Tarnopol, L. *Learning disabilities*. Springfield, Illinois: C C Thomas, 1969.

Taylor, F. Cognitive and behavioral approaches to the modification of depression. Unpublished doctoral dissertation, Queen's University, Kingston, Ontario, 1974.

Thorngate, W. Must we always think before we act? *Personality and Social Psychology Bulletin*, 1976, *2*, 31–35.

Thornton, J., & Jacobs, P. Learned helplessness in human subjects. *Journal of Experimental Psychology*, 1971, 87, 367–372.

Thorpe, J., Schmidt, E., Brown, P., & Castell, D. Aversion-relief therapy: A new method for general application. *Behaviour Research and Therapy*, 1964, *2*, 71–82.

Tolman, E. *Purposive behavior in animals and men*. New York: Century, 1932.

Tompkins, S. A theory of memory. In J. Antrobus (Ed.), *Cognition and affect*. Boston: Little Brown, 1970.

Tori, C., & Worrell, L. Reduction of human avoidant behavior: A comparison of counterconditioning, expectancy, and cognitive information approaches. *Journal of Consulting and Clinical Psychology*, 1973, *41*, 269–278.

Torrance, E. *Rewarding creative behavior*. Englewood Cliffs, N. J.: Prentice-Hall, 1965.

Trexler, L., and Karst, T. Rational-emotive therapy, placebo, and no treatment effects on public-speaking anxiety. *Journal of Abnormal Psychology*, 1972, *79*, 60–67.

Trigg, R. *Pain and emotion.* London: Oxford Univ. Press, 1970.

Turk, D. Cognitive control of pain: A skills training approach for the treatment of pain. Unpublished Masters thesis, University of Waterloo, 1975.

Turk, D. An expanded skills training approach for the treatment of experimentally induced pain. Unpublished doctoral dissertation, University of Waterloo, 1976.

Valins, S., & Nisbett, R. Attribution processes in the development and treatment of emotional disorders. In J. Spence, R. Carson, and J. Thibaut (Eds.), *Behavioral approaches to therapy.* Morristown, N. J.: General Learning Press, 1976.

Valins, S., & Ray, A. Effects of cognitive desensitization on avoidance behavior. *Journal of Personality and Social Psychology*, 1967, *7*, 345–350.

Velten, E. A laboratory task for induction on mood states. *Behaviour Research and Therapy*, 1968, *6*, 473–482.

Venables, P. Selectivity of attention, withdrawal, and cortical activation. *Archives of General Psychiatry*, 1963, *9*, 74–78.

Venables, P. Input dysfunction in schizophrenia. In B. Maher (Ed.), *Progress in experimental personality research*, Volume 1. New York: Academic Press, 1964.

Vygotsky, L. *Thought and language.* New York: Wiley, 1962.

Wagner, I. *Aufmerksamkeitstraining mit impulsiven Kindern.* Stuttgart, Germany: Aufbau-Verlag, 1976.

Wallach, M., & Kogan, N. *Modes of thinking in young children.* New York: Holt, Rinehart & Winston, 1965.

Wallach, M., & Wing, C. *The talented student: A validation of the creativity-intelligence distinction.* New York: Holt, Rinehart & Winston, 1969.

Wallas, G. *The art of thought.* New York: Harcourt Brace, 1926.

Weiner, A., & Berzonsky, M. Development of selective attention in reflective and impulsive children. *Child Development*, 1975, *46*, 545–549.

Weiss, G., Kruger, E., Danielson, U., & Elman, M. The effect of long-term treatment of hyperactive children with methylphidate. Paper presented at the Annual Meeting of the American College of Neuropsychopharmacology, Palm Springs, Cal., 1973.

Weitzman, B. Behavior therapy and psychotherapy. *Psychological Review*, 1967, *74*, 300–317.

Werner, H. Process and achievement, a basic problem of education and developmental psychology. *Harvard Educational Review*, 1937, May, 355–368.

Westcott, H., & Huttenlocher, J. Cardiac conditioning: The effects and implications of controlled and uncontrolled respiration. *Journal of Experimental Psychology*, 1961, *61*, 353–359.

Wexler, D. A cognitive theory of experiencing, self-actualization and therapeutic process. In D. Wexler and L. Rice (Eds.), *Innovations in client-centered therapy*. New York: Wiley, 1974.

Whalen, C., & Henker, B. Psychostimulants and children: A review and analysis. *Psychological Bulletin*, 1976, *83*, 1113–1130.

Wheelis, A. How people change. *Commentary*, May 1969, 56–66.

Wilkins, W. Desensitization: Social and cognitive factors underlying the effectiveness of Wolpe's procedure. *Psychological Bulletin*, 1971, *76*, 311–317.

Wine, J. Investigations of attentional interpretation of test anxiety. Unpublished doctoral dissertation, University of Waterloo, 1970.

Wolfe, J., & Fodor, I. A cognitive/behavioral approach to modifying assertive behavior in women. *Counseling Psychologist*, 1975, *5*, 45–52.

Wolff, B., & Horland, A. Effect of suggestion upon experimental pain: A validation study. *Journal of Abnormal Psychology*, 1967, *72*, 402–407.

Wolpe, J. *Psychotherapy by reciprocal inhibition*. Stanford: Stanford University Press, 1958.

Wolpe, J. The systematic desensitization treatment of neuroses. *Journal of Nervous and Mental Disease*, 1961, *132*, 189–203.

Wolpe, J., & Lazarus, A. *Behavior therapy techniques: A guide to the treatment of neuroses*. London: Pergamon Press, 1966.

Wolpin, M., & Raines, J. Visual imagery, expected roles and extinction as possible factors in reducing fear and avoidance behaviour. *Behaviour Research and Therapy*, 1966, *4*, 25–37.

Wood, D., & Obrist, P. Effects of controlled and uncontrolled respiration on the conditioned heart rate in humans. *Journal of Experimental Psychology*, 1964, *69*, 221–229.

Wozniak, R. Verbal regulation of motor behavior: Soviet research and non-Soviet replications. *Human Development*, 1972, *15*, 13–57.

Wozniak, R. Psychology of the learning disabled child in the Soviet Union. In W. Cruikshank and D. Hallahan (Eds.), *Research and theory in minimal cerebral dysfunction and learning disability*. Syracuse: Syracuse University Press, 1976.

Wozniak, R., & Neuchterlein, P. *Reading improvement through verbally self-guided looking and listening* (Summary Report). Minneapolis: University of Minnesota, 1973.

Wright, J. Reflection-impulsivity and information processing from three to nine years of age. Paper presented at meeting of American Psychological Association, 1974.

Yando, R., & Kagan, J. The effect of teacher tempo on the child. *Child Development*, 1968, *39*, 27–34.

Yates, A. Data processing levels and thought disorder in schizophrenia. *Australian Journal of Psychology*, 1966, *18*, 103–117.

Yates, A. *Behavior therapy.* New York: John Wiley, 1970.

Yates, D. Relaxation in psychotherapy. *Journal of General Psychology*, 1946, *34*, 213–238.

Yorkston, N., McHugh, R., Brady, R., Serber, M., & Sergeant, H. Verbal desensitization in bronchial asthma. *Journal of Psychosomatic Research*, 1974, *18*, 371–376.

Zaporozhets, A., & Elkonin, D. *The psychology of preschool children.* Cambridge: M. I. T. Press, 1971.

Zelniker, T., Jeffrey, W., Ault, R., & Parsons, J. Analysis and modification of search strategies of impulsive and reflective children on the Matching Familiar Figures Test. *Child Development*, 1972, *43*, 321–335.

Zelniker, T., & Oppenheimer, L. Modification of information processing of impulsive children. *Child Development*, 1973, *44*, 445–450.

Zimbardo, P. *The cognitive control of motivation.* Glenview, Illinois: Scott, Foresman, 1969.

Zimmerman, B., & Rosenthal, T. Observational learning of rule governed behavior by children. *Psychological Bulletin*, 1974, *81*, 29–42.

Author Index

Subject Index